# The World's End Murders

## The Inside Story

# Tom Wood

Ringwood Publishing

Glasgow

Ringwood Publishing
0/1 314 Meadowside Quay Walk, Glasgow G11 6AY

www.ringwoodpublishing.com
mail@ringwoodpublishing.com

ISBN 978-1-917011-05-1

British Library Cataloguing-in-Publication Data
A catalogue record for this book is available from the British Library

Originally published as *The World's End: A Thirty-Year Quest for Justice*
by Birlinn in 2008 and republished as *The World's End Murders - The
Final Verdict* in 2014.

Ringwood Publishing has acquired the rights to both of these books but
*The World's End Murders -The Inside Story* is much more than an update,
it is essentially a new book with considerable original content.

Printed and bound in the UK
by Lonsdale Direct Solutions

This book is written as a tribute to the young women who were victims of violent crimes in Scotland in the late 1970s, especially Christine Eadie, Helen Scott and their families.

# Contents

# Introduction

It is difficult now, after the passage of so much time, to remember all the things we did not know and could not do in 1977.

Suffice to say that the thirty-seven-year life of the investigation spanned several epochs of advances in criminal investigation and forensic science.

We began the investigation with notebooks and pencils, fingerprints and crime scene photography. We finished with super computers and then sensitive low-copy DNA analysis.

It is a remarkable testimony to the care and precision of the work done in 1977, that the evidence gathered back then was both gathered and retained in such a way that over three decades later it could give up its secrets and deliver justice for two innocent young girls, the families who loved them, and the wider community horrified by their brutal murders.

What became known as "The World's End Murders" defined a time and dominated the police service of myself and many, many others. It was a heavy burden of responsibility that we carried constantly.

I first wrote about these crimes in 2008 following the first disastrous failed trial of Angus Sinclair. I did not want this ground-breaking investigation to be defined by tabloid headlines as a failure in our justice system. The only way to ensure that, was to write the full account myself.

Once the second trial of Sinclair was completed, and justice was at last done, I updated the book to place on record the amazing advances in forensic science and investigation.

Since then, I have participated in numerous television programmes about the murders, all of which were good, but none of which could tell the whole story with all its twists and turns. Now, after so much has been said and done, there is still much to add. Distance lends objectivity, and the passage of time allows more candour.

This is an account of the murder of two young women, Christine Eadie and Helen Scott, who were murdered in October 1977.

It is the story of those crimes but, more, it is the remarkable story of the thirty-seven-year investigation that followed.

This is not a gruesome tale of murder – the families of these young girls have suffered enough. Nor is this an account devoted to the controversy surrounding the ending of the first trial of Angus Sinclair in the autumn of 2007. I do not write to confront the legal profession or lay blame, but only to set the record straight once and for all. This story does, of course, have villains as any tale of murder must, but it concentrates on the heroes, of whom there are many: the families of Helen and Christine who, with quiet dignity, have carried an unimaginable burden down the years; and the police officers, the support staff and the scientists who, over the generations, persisted in their investigations, never gave up and, though they suffered many a setback, never forgot Helen and Christine and never let go. They number so many that it is impossible to name them all but among them are Dr John McGowan, former Detective Superintendent Allan Jones, and Forensic Scientist Lester Knibb. With hundreds of others, these men resolutely pursued the challenges of the longest running continuous murder investigation in Scottish history.

Now the story can be told fully, with previously unpublished information and analysis.

Tom Wood

2024

# 1

# The World's End

The brutal murder of two young friends on a night out in the pubs of Edinburgh's Old Town has always hung heavily on the collective mind of Scotland's capital city. The fact that the girls' killings remained under investigation for nearly thirty-seven years took a terrible toll on their families, as did the collapse of the first trial of the man accused of their killing. The lack of success in the long-running investigation was also the source of great frustration to the police. Over the decades, the force in which I served, Lothian and Borders Police, devoted a huge amount of time and money to trying to solve these awful crimes. There had been many positive leads along the way but all of them petered out sooner or later. The hopes of everyone involved had been raised, only to be dashed again. In policing, though, as in most other walks of life, perseverance pays off. So it was to do in this case. Those who persevered the longest showed the kind of professionalism that bordered on obsession.

For many of the officers and staff involved in the World's End case, the inquiry marked them and, years later, continued to intrigue them. During the final stages of the investigation, I got several calls from long-retired detectives, anxious to know how the case had been concluded and, perhaps more importantly, whether anything they had or hadn't done had been significant.

Police forces generally pride themselves on their murder clear-up rates and we, like the general public, found it unacceptable that these two young women could be abducted from our city, murdered, and no one be brought to justice. It may happen in other places; but not in Edinburgh, not in Scotland. Now, in the 21st century, that may seem a quaint mindset, but back in the 1970s it was a very strong feeling.

On a Saturday night in October 1977, two lovely young seventeen-year-old friends, Helen Scott and Christine Eadie, went for a night out in their hometown of Edinburgh. The day was Saturday, October 15th, and it was to become a date fixed in people's minds for another reason that would help police later, as we asked them to recall the events of that night even long afterwards. It was the day after legendary American entertainer Bing Crosby collapsed and died on a golf course. Events like this can often be used as prompts to nudge their recall. They may not recall one particular night on the town out of many others, but they will remember the night when the radio was playing non-stop Bing Crosby and tributes to the star were being shown on TV.

Helen and Christine were dressed in their best for the night out. Helen was wearing her brand-new Burberry coat. Bought with savings from her first wage, it was her pride and joy. They visited several pubs in the early part of that autumn Saturday night. In some of them they managed to convince the bar staff they were 18 years old and entitled to buy alcohol. In others they were refused. Over the evening they had several drinks and were in high spirits when they reached their final destination about 9:30p.m. They were last seen alive in a bar in the heart of the historic Old Town of Edinburgh. Various friends met up with them during that evening and police were quickly able to establish a detailed picture of events – who they spoke to and what was going on in the lead-up to their disappearance.

Left to Right: Helen Scott and Christine Eadie, on either side of a friend. This picture was taken shortly before their deaths.

The name of the last pub they visited that night has since been inextricably linked with the killings. Even the pub's name, The World's End, has something of a macabre ring to it which seemed to add to the public horror of the events that were about to unfold. The fact the bar stands almost exactly halfway down Edinburgh's historic Royal Mile, between the Castle at the top and the Palace of Holyroodhouse at the bottom, added to the crime's notoriety. It was in the nearby alleyways, known as "closes", that some of Scotland's most chilling crimes were committed.

The pub's name was passed down from the Middle Ages in the aftermath of the Battle of Flodden in 1513 when Edinburgh was a fortified town, and its walls ran close to this spot. To go out of the gates was to leave civilisation and the safety of the town. It was literally the world's end.

The World's End lounge bar, October 1977.

The Old Town provided the backdrop for the crimes of body snatchers Burke and Hare and the notorious Deacon Brodie – figures from history whose foul deeds were recalled day in and day out by the ghost tour operators who took tourists through this ancient district. On that October night, its dark past was brought brutally up to date.

Christine and Helen had gone into the pub with some of their usual group of friends and, by all accounts, fell into the company of two men. After the girls' bodies were found the murder inquiry traced in the region of 150 people who had been in the bar at some time or other during that night. Some of them gave evidence that seemed unimportant or minor at the time but which, thirty years later, would appear significant.

It was clear that slowly the various friends they had been with drifted off, leaving Helen and Christine engrossed in conversation with these

3

men, strangers to the usual company.

They were described as having "country accents" but this clue was not developed at the time. Nowadays, witnesses would be played recordings of various regional accents to narrow it down. This is just one example of how investigation has moved on in almost fifty years.

No one was certain about seeing them leave – there was only one possible sighting. What was beyond doubt was that the men seen talking to the girls were not traced at the time of the original inquiry, despite being the focus of intense police activity and press publicity.

The girls were never seen alive again.

*

When Helen and Christine didn't arrive home that night their families were not unduly concerned. They often stayed at each other's homes if they had been out late in town. Christine's family thought she was staying at Helen's and Helen's family vice versa.

It was only at breakfast time the next morning, Sunday October 16th, that the alarm was raised. Having learned that Helen was not at Christine's home, Helen's Dad, Morain Scott reported the two girls missing to the police. Teenage girls staying out all night was hardly a new phenomenon, but neither Helen nor Christine had done this before. They were very young, little more than children, and such was Morain Scott's urgency that the police took their disappearance seriously from the start.

As the full descriptions of the girls were being taken, the wheels were being set in motion for a vulnerable missing persons inquiry. A detective would be allocated the job to make urgent investigations to trace the girls. This never happened, for as the details of Helen and Christine were being recorded, twenty miles away in East Lothian two dog walkers were making a horrific discovery. The couple were taking their dog for a late morning walk along the narrow beach at Gosford Bay, in East Lothian, just 17 miles east of Edinburgh. It was a beautiful, bright October morning, and it was a walk they often took their dog on before Sunday lunch. As they ambled eastwards, towards the part of the beach that curves sharply as it approaches the small town of Aberlady, they noticed something lying on the tideline.

It was not unusual to see rubbish swept up by the strong tides. The beach was also close to the coastal road which runs parallel to the sea.

They had sometimes seen objects dumped. But as they got closer, their dog ran forward, interested by what appeared to be a tailor's dummy – a mannequin, lying right on the tideline, apparently swept up by the sea.

It was not until they were very close indeed that they saw it was not an innocent piece of flotsam but the naked body of a young dark-haired girl. Before the days of mobile phones, it took time. Running back to their car, the couple went to find the nearest telephone call box to call the police. The nearest police station was at Haddington just five miles away, so it didn't take long for the first police cars to arrive at the scene. What they found was obvious to all as a scene of serious crime – murder. The body of the girl was naked, bound hand and foot with her hands behind her back, and gagged with what appeared to be her underwear. All officers were trained in rudimentary crime scene management and since it was obviously a scene of crime, the detectives of the Criminal Investigations Department (CID) were already on their way.

Every major investigation needs a bit of luck, and it was at this point we got very lucky indeed, for on the call-out rota for scenes of crime that weekend was the young biologist, Lester Knibb. Still in his early twenties, Lester was part of a mixed team of Police Identification Branch officers and scientists from the Police Laboratory that attended Gosford Bay that Sunday afternoon. Throughout his long career, Lester was always fastidious in his duties, and that afternoon in October 1977 was no exception. The meticulous way in which he and his colleagues gathered and retained the tiny specks of forensic evidence would stand the tests of time.

Lester Knibb would go on to play a key role in the long course of the investigation, but this was far in the future, as he did his meticulous work on the beach at Gosford that day.

Lester Knibb in his laboratory.

In the meantime, the wheels that drive a major investigation were getting into gear. By this time, the Force Operations Room at Lothian and Borders Police HQ had taken overall control in coordinating the response to what was now recognised as a major incident. A brief description of the body found on the beach had been quickly matched with that of Christine Eadie, one of the girls reported missing a few hours earlier. Identification would not be confirmed until later, but it was certain enough to beg the question: If the body was that of Christine, where was her friend Helen?

The answer came quickly, and tragically. A few miles away, on the back road between Aberlady and Haddington, a farmer was routinely checking his property when he saw what appeared to be a bag of rubbish dumped in the middle of one of his fields.

Coates Farm grew cereals and by October the harvest was in. The field was covered with barley stubble, so it didn't take long to walk the hundred yards to see what had been dumped. It wasn't a bag of rubbish, but the body of a young blonde woman. She had been partially stripped, her arms were tied with a belt, and ligatures made from her own tights were around her neck. A second ligature made from her own belt was also around her neck. Near her head were a pair of pants that appeared to have been used to gag her but that she had managed somehow to spit out. The body was lying face down on a coat. It was Helen, and the coat was her prized new Burberry, the only large piece of clothing recovered from either of the girls.

As soon as the description of the second body was reported it was pretty certain that the bodies were those of Christine and Helen. The Forensic Team, having completed their examination at Gosford Bay, immediately made their way to Coates Farm.

The crime scenes were very similar. In both cases, except for Helen's coat, most of the clothing belonging to the girls had been removed from the scene. Their own underwear had been used to kill them and they had both been bound and tied in a very precise way. Years later, the singular fashion in which the girls had been killed served as a signpost in the investigation.

After a quick check by a doctor to confirm life was extinct, came the second part of the forensic recovery. The bodies of the girls were taken to the City Mortuary in Edinburgh, where more samples would be taken and the bindings tying the girls carefully removed and preserved. It's at this time that one of the most harrowing jobs in any murder investigation

Near the deposition site of Christine Eadie, October 1977. Primitive crime-scene management by today's standards - no tape or barrier to protect the scene. *SCRAN*

Searches at the deposition site of Helen Scott - haphazard by today's standards - no protective clothing and a lack of a systematic approach makes this a scene from a bygone age. *SCRAN*

must be undertaken – the formal identification of the bodies. There's no escaping it – no matter how often you must take a grieving relative to view their dead family member, it's always the most awful experience. A person may know on one level that their loved one is dead, but it's only when they see their body that it hits home.

The job of taking Helen Scott's Dad to identify her fell to Detective Sergeant Douglas Kerr. A young man with a long and distinguished career ahead of him, he never forgot that day, nor the grief of Morain Scott, Helen's Dad. Both men would be marked by that day, but go on to play significant roles in the investigation as it progressed.

By late afternoon the bodies of Christine and Helen were back at the mortuary and had been formally identified. Back at the deposition sites, officers had been put on guard to protect them during the hours of darkness. The next day, the forensic searches would continue, but for now they were secured as best as was possible.

At the mortuary all items of clothing, the ligatures, the belts and particularly Helen's coat, were carefully bagged and tagged. Once again, Lester Knibb was on hand to carry out his meticulous work. He realised that these soiled items were a treasure trove beyond value, and so it proved.

Back at the Police Headquarters on Fettes Avenue, Edinburgh, a massive criminal investigation was being launched. It was a day I will never forget. I was a young Detective Sergeant just transferred into the CID, and like all new boys I was first posted to the CID Main Office, the 24-hour hub of CID operations, responsible for coordination and logistics. I had come on duty at 2:00p.m. that Sunday October 16th, just as the CID resources were speeding towards the crime scenes or being formed into investigation teams. The early news from the deposition sites was chilling. It was obvious that the girls had been brutally murdered and probably sexually assaulted. But it had been no frenzied attack or crime of passion. The precise nature of the ligatures and bindings, the careful choice of deposition sites, and the fact that no foreign objects had been introduced into the crime scenes all pointed to cool, organised crimes.

Christine and Helen had been executed in a brutal and cold-hearted manner. And it suggested something else, most worrying of all. It was best articulated by an old detective, one of the first back from the mortuary. In a whisper he told one of the senior Detective Inspectors, 'Whoever did this has done it before, and will do it again.' It was a commonly held view.

The newly formed Lothian and Borders Police was to be tested, but no one could have known to what extent.

But the grand strategies of murder investigations were far from my mind that evening as I toiled to requisition cars and office space and call out as many detectives as I could find. By this time the connection with The World's End pub was becoming known and a sizeable squad of uniform and CID officers were dispatched to take control of the pub and interview any witnesses, particularly the bar staff, who had been there the night before.

On Monday October 17th, a conference was convened at Police HQ. The post-mortem examinations of Helen and Christine, now formally identified, had taken place that morning. A "Double Doctor" as prescribed for murder victims, and a whole range of post-mortem samples were taken, including intimate samples that showed that both girls had been raped.

The case was summarised by the first Detective Inspectors on the scene:

The two young Edinburgh girls had been out for the night, and while they had had a drink or two, were not drunk. About 9:30p.m. on the Saturday previous (October 15th), they had met two young men, who were strangers to them and their friends and apparently from out of town. They had left The World's End pub about 10:30p.m. and were seen walking south on nearby St. Mary Street in the company of two young men they had been speaking to in the pub as well as others.

Their bodies were found approximately 14 hours later in East Lothian, some 15 miles east of where they were last seen alive.

They had died from strangulation by ligatures formed from their own tights. They had been sexually assaulted and most of their clothing removed. The approximate time of death established by body cooling indicated that both girls had died late on the Saturday night (October 15th). It appeared from blood alcohol levels that Helen had been killed after Christine. The fact that Christine's belt had been used to strangle Helen supported this theory.

Several assumptions were agreed. First, at least two men were almost certainly involved. The girls had been last seen in the company of two men and it was thought unlikely that one man could subdue two fit and healthy girls.

Second, that a motor vehicle was certainly used, since the deposition sites were only accessible by vehicle.

It was recognised that the orderliness of the crime scenes suggested a cool and organised approach. Most scenes of murder are chaotic; this was not.

It seemed certain that the motive was sexual since both girls had been sexually assaulted around the time of their deaths.

It was apparent that a considerable quantity of the girls' clothing had been removed from the scene. Recovery of the clothing was a top forensic priority.

There was speculation about where the deadly assaults had taken place. The deposition sites had been chosen for their sight lines during the hours of darkness, but it was unlikely that the girls had been killed there. Nearby Gosford Bay was a large beachside car park (the Bents Car Park) which was much favoured by courting couples. It was a likely spot which would have to be forensically examined.

There was also an acceptance that the murders of Helen and Christine were complex crimes, committed by strangers who were aware enough to remove incriminating evidence while leaving no clues as to their identity.

On the first few days after the murders broke, there were few dealings for the new boy in the CID administrative office with the crime that was gripping the whole country, but I still remember the tensions and the huge charge of energy that this crime created in the CID block of the then new force headquarters building at Fettes. There had simply not been a crime like this in our force area. I, of course, had no idea that the World's End case would run the entire length of my police career and that I would have a role to play in the final investigation.

The murders were going to be the first major challenge for the newly formed Lothian and Borders Police, just two years old at this point. It was to be a challenge that would live with the force for many more years to come.

*

As I detail the way this first inquiry developed, it is important to put the events I describe into the context of the times. Certainly, looking back at the newspaper cuttings of the investigation is to peer into another world. The black and white images carried by the *Edinburgh Evening News*, *The Scotsman* and *The Glasgow Herald* seem old-fashioned, almost antique, when viewed today. Police techniques and procedures have probably advanced more in the last thirty years than they had in the previous hundred. This was a major inquiry, conducted in its initial and most crucial stages without the benefit of computers, employing scientific techniques that were limited to say the least, and at a time when DNA was hardly a concept, let alone the major investigatory tool it is today.

Those were the days when senior investigators had no formal training in the investigation and management of major cases. Detectives learned as their service went along. The CID was still mainly a career within a career, with some officers spending most of their time exclusively in the CID with little or no interchange with other branches of the service to build a more rounded experience. The consequence of this was that the quality of CID officers was very varied; Yet, as I look back, it is remarkable how many fine natural detectives there were at all ranks. Putting aside the rose-tinted spectacles, there were some excellent investigators and leaders across the Scottish service, but they were hopelessly handicapped by a lack of technology and the systematic approach now accepted as commonplace in criminal investigations.

Some things, though, change little, like the protocols and procedures for investigations that cross the boundaries of police forces, or even their internal divisional areas. Police procedures then, as they do to this day, give ownership of a murder inquiry to the force or the division where the body was found – where the body lay, not where the person was last seen alive or their place of origin. This, in all truth, gave the World's End inquiry, as it became known, another large hurdle to overcome from the very outset.

Local government in Scotland, and the police service along with it, was undergoing a period of enormous change. A Royal Commission headed by the distinguished Scots Judge, Lord Wheatley, had come up with a plan to replace the country's old burgh councils and county districts with a slimmed-down number of "Super Regional Authorities", each charged with running an area's major services, including the police. So, it was in 1975 that a series of amalgamations were enacted and a massive exercise was going on to try to harmonise working practices and end old rivalries between the newly combined eight forces.

Lothian and Borders Police was formed out of three old forces – Edinburgh City Police, Lothian and Peebles Constabulary, and the

Berwick, Roxburgh and Selkirk Constabulary. Each, of course, felt they had the business of policing down to a fine art and were reluctant to give up their ways for those of another force. In the west of Scotland, the service was facing an even bigger challenge as seven forces worked to become one. Strathclyde Police covered a massive area ranging from the tough inner-city challenges of Glasgow to the remote and beautiful islands of Argyll.

*

Integration is the key word in any merger, be it in the private or public sector. The people at the head of their own little empires are always reluctant, to some greater or lesser extent, to cede power or control to a new and perhaps little-known person. Nonetheless, efforts had been made to mix and match senior officers of the new forces, even though practicalities made this a slow process. These were the tensions lying behind what was going on as the investigation to find the killers of Helen and Christine was being established. The solving of a crime is often dependent on what happens in the first few hours of any major inquiry. The protection of the crime scene and the fast establishment of the basic facts in order to allow the initial inquiries to be channelled in the right direction are vital if a solution is to be reached quickly.

The World's End inquiry was one police operation split into two from the very start. The Edinburgh end was run by a highly regarded city detective chief inspector, Bert Darling, while the East Lothian part, the main part of the inquiry because that was where the bodies had been found, was headed by Detective Chief Inspector Andrew Suddon. He was a man of equal competence, but his background was in the less demanding rural force, which was much smaller in size and without many of the back-up facilities of the larger City Police. Although both men came from solid investigative backgrounds, they were very different in both style and temperament.

Bert Darling was a smooth operator, always beautifully dressed and coiffured, and he had extensive contacts in the press and legal circles in Edinburgh. One of the few detectives still proficient in shorthand writing, he was highly intelligent and just as cunning. He had a fine record in murder investigations, a record he was determined to keep.

Andrew Suddon was a very different character, quiet and understated;

he was a deep thinker with a wealth of experience across the vast and varied landscape of county policing. He would not be rushed, but his judgements were invariably sound.

Acting as officer in overall command was Detective Superintendent George MacPherson. He had the difficult task of bringing the two teams together to act as a single unit. Big Mac, as he was known, long before the hamburger adopted the name, was a tough imposing figure with a long service in the CID. As a young man he had been a singer with a beautiful baritone voice, but the sweetness of his voice had long left him by the time he took charge of the World's End case. He was gruff and no nonsense with a very low tolerance for mistakes made by subordinates. He was both feared and respected as a highly capable detective.

Whilst the county division was nominally in charge of the direction of the inquiry, they were the least involved in the first phase of establishing what had happened in the case of The World's End Murders – the effort in those first days to find witnesses and investigate the backgrounds of the girls. It was quickly established that there were no witnesses to the dumping of the bodies, no hint of the vehicle that had to have been used. The place where Christine's body had been left on the beach was yards from the roadside, on a section of the route between two coastal villages.

On the other hand, a great many people in The World's End pub that night were traced, and a clear picture of the girls' evening was established. Not only were customers of The World's End traced, but hundreds of people who had been drinking in the other pubs visited by the pair that night were also interviewed to see if any of them had an inkling as to who the two men they were seen with may have been. It was confirmed that they appeared to have met the men for the first time that night in The World's End and fallen into conversation with them. Within a short space of time, both men were well described – to the extent that the *Edinburgh Evening News* was able, with help from the police, to print an artist's impression of the scene in the bar that night with the suspects, as they had been described by witnesses, clearly seen talking to Helen and Christine. It was quickly confirmed that these men were not regulars – in fact, no one had a clue who they were. They seemed to be strangers to the Old Town area of Edinburgh, not seen by any of the pub patrons before that night. They had been observed clearly by so many people that a photofit picture of the pair was released by police in the weeks after the killings. Photofits are a risk for detectives. All too often the images created by witnesses in a genuine attempt to assist are so unlike the suspect that they can actually hinder the inquiry by erroneously deflecting attention elsewhere. In this case, though, we would eventually see just how accurate photofit images can be.

A photofit of one of the men seen in the World's End with Helen and Christine. It bears a good resemblance to both Angus Sinclair and Gordon Hamilton.

A reconstruction of the last known movements of Helen and Christine. Police cadets took the role of the girls.

One major issue in a prolonged or high-profile murder investigation is that of public confidence. Murder, particularly multiple murders or the murder of a child, still rightly excites the public imagination. The coverage of crimes such as The World's End Murders get on all branches of the media can stimulate a public panic that can overwhelm and distort the course of an investigation. But this is not always the case. Some killings, like the murder of petty criminals or internecine gang murders, demonstrate that the public can make fine judgements about the worthiness of victims. In one Edinburgh case, where the victim was himself a violent criminal, the overwhelming view that 'he had it coming' led to a poor public response and little information coming forward despite the best police and media efforts.

The very high-profile murder investigation can really be traced back to the original 1880s "Whitechapel Ripper" case. The unique combination of multiple and gruesome crimes with a taunting killer or killers and, crucially, an emerging tabloid press, featuring lithographs and graphic illustrations, combined to give the Ripper case a horror status that still endures today and which, at the time, must have overwhelmed the small amateur group of detectives dealing with it. Today, over a hundred years later, new theories and suspects still emerge with all the racial and class stereotypes intact – the Mad Royal, the Homicidal Foreigner, and the Stranger. It's the nearest thing to the original bogeyman.

Since the "Whitechapel Ripper", there has been a succession of notorious cases – the "Ruxton" case of 1935, the "Moors Murders", the "Black Panther", the "Yorkshire Ripper", "Soham" and, in Scotland, the so-called "Bible John Murders" of the 1960s. All these cases, in their own way, secured a place in the folk memory of the public.

The successful investigation of murder and the murder clear-up rate have always been of special symbolic importance to police forces – it is perceived as an index of proficiency and success. It is ironic when considered objectively because murder is generally not the most difficult crime to solve – most killings are in a domestic situation or where the victim and offender have some degree of relationship, so it is not hard to have a good murder clear-up rate. It's much more difficult to solve offences like housebreaking and robbery – crimes which also have a greater social impact because they affect a far greater number of people.

Murder, however, understandably remains the benchmark, and crimes which catch the public and media imagination place and enormous strain on the investigation team, the police force, and the community.

Two things are essential to maintaining public confidence: the demonstration that police are prioritising the investigation, and signs that the inquiry is making progress. The importance of the investigation is frequently gauged by significant police presence, incident caravans, reconstructions or the more recent and sometimes mawkish practice of parading relatives before the media to make tearful pleas for help. The demonstration of progress and new lines of inquiry is sometimes more problematic, for there is a real media pressure to come up with a new line every day. This can be both dangerous and, in the long term, counterproductive.

A number of investigations I have been involved in were distracted and sometimes misled by red herrings that had been inadvertently originated by the police because they were trying, in good faith, to demonstrate their progress and satisfy an ever-voracious media.

Vehicle inquiries are classics of the type. In every long-running investigation, there is at least one sighting of a white van or a red car and not infrequently complicated and lengthy inquiries are made to trace them. As a senior officer, it's hard to resist the temptation of these leads. It may be crucial but very often it takes the investigation down a very long cul-de-sac. Just as importantly, misleading features associated with the case can also lodge in the mind of the public. This is one reason why police are always reluctant to issue photofit likenesses of suspects. If the photofit is a good likeness, that's fine, but if not, then the public is looking for someone that does not exist and that, by default, excludes everyone else.

*

As the World's End investigation developed, vehicle inquiries, and one vehicle in particular, would be crucial and photofit impressions would also play an important role.

The murders of Helen and Christine were entirely different from the usual domestic killings. From an early stage, it looked as if this crime had resulted from a chance first meeting between two men and two women. It seemed likely that the men had a plan to abduct a victim or victims based simply on the fact that, between the four leaving the bar that night and the bodies being found the next day, there were no sightings of them at all. There could not have been a struggle in a public place so they must have been able to persuade the pair to go with them willingly, probably in a vehicle which they knew would be safe for their evil purpose. In all likelihood, the perpetrators would have had a plan – certainly a rough idea of what they were going to do that night if they got the opportunity. One thing is striking, especially in the light of cases that came after this one. Often men seeking a victim to abduct, abuse and murder have a kit in their possession – rope for bindings and other paraphernalia. The child killer Robert Black had just such a kit in his van when he was eventually arrested. In addition to the bindings and tape for gagging his little victims, there was also a sleeping bag in which to conceal them.

The World's End killers got round the need to carry such items by using their victims' own clothing to suppress them – their tights became bindings, their underwear gags. Whether deliberate or not, this meant that nothing foreign had been introduced into the crime scene, giving few forensic opportunities.

Over the following years we often wondered whether this was part of an organised and deliberate approach or simply a pattern of behaviour. These were questions for later, for there were more urgent matters to consider.

Within hours of the bodies being discovered, there were, in effect, two large-scale inquiries going on. There was the East Lothian-based forensic examination of the discovery sites and searches of the nearby areas to find any clues that may have been left behind, and in Edinburgh, the huge investigation focusing on The World's End pub and the city centre.

In these days of spacious modern incident rooms with air conditioning and the most up-to-date of computer equipment, it's easy to forget that such advances only began in the 1980s.

*

Back in the 1970s, teams investigating murders and major incidents worked out of small offices and all the data was kept on card index systems and in bulky paper files. This worked well enough for a straightforward domestic crime but was seriously inadequate for large or complex investigations. The manual card system dated from the 19th century and, although updated in the subsequent years, it was basically the same, and it depended on the skill and experience of a small administrative team usually made up of an experienced detective sergeant and two detective constable clerks. It was the members of this small team who read the statements of witnesses and created "jobs", the name given to further inquiries arising from them. The senior investigator or his deputy also read the statements and might add further lines of inquiry and that was it. There were no further fail-safes, no automatic review processes, and no high-tech safeguards. It was a rudimentary and very basic system, but it worked amazingly well and was a great testimony to the expertise of the staff who operated it. So crucial was the admin role recognised to be that senior detectives invariably had a favoured sergeant and team to work the admin of his squads – people he knew and trusted and who, above all, had the experience and track record to do the job. This arrangement established a common fund of shared experience, but no unified system. The manual card index system met its nemesis on the "Yorkshire Ripper" inquiry in the 1980s. The sheer size of that investigation swamped the manual index and culminated in several satellite incident rooms being crammed with tens of thousands of cards. The shortcomings were evident, for no matter how able the operators were, it was clear that the scale was beyond human capacity. In the aftermath of the trial and conviction of Peter Sutcliffe and in the knowledge that the killer had been overlooked in the system, the Byford Report recommended a computerised major inquiry system. Thus was born HOLMES, Home Office Large Major Enquiry System; a system which, with regular modernisation, is still used today.

*

Back in 1977, however, two incident rooms were established, and the best teams were picked to run them. In Edinburgh, one of the most experienced admin sergeants, David "Yogi" Brunton, got the call. David, whose nickname arose from his bear-like physique, was a frontline officer with

The early Edinburgh Incident Room. The clutter of paperwork and files seem alien by today's computerised standards. DC Stuart King, nearest the camera, DS David 'Yogi' Brunton and DC Eric Bowman still did a fine job. SCRAN

a tough exterior, but he had also built a reputation for his deft handling of administration work for murder squads. This was to be his greatest test. But years later, when, long after his death, his manual index was computerised, the quality of his team's work shone through.

Armed as I am now with 20/20 hindsight, it is not valid for me to criticise the steps taken in those early days, but everyone in the service will agree that back then standards were very different from the ones in place today. Search techniques, for one, were rough and ready. There is no suggestion that anything was missed by the officers out combing the crime scenes in 1977, but from studying the records of the time and seeing photographs of what went on, it is clear that it would be done differently today. That said, many years later it became clear that the job of gathering forensic evidence and its protection from contamination was done to the highest standard, giving us a treasure trove of evidence that we counted on in later investigations.

In the city, detectives were making frequent appeals through the press for people who had visited The World's End that night to come forward, even if they believed they had not seen anything relevant. Scores of them did and thankfully many of them had seen the girls. Some paid passing attention to the men who had befriended them, but nothing in their behaviour in public that night would have given reason for any concern to bystanders.

Like many teenagers who had been on a night out, the girls were showing some signs that they had been drinking. One part of that initial inquiry was to try to discover exactly how much each of them had drunk during the evening. The significance of this was to give us an estimate of how long after leaving The World's End they had met their deaths. A fairly accurate account of the lapse of time can be given by determining what their blood alcohol level would have been when they left the pub and what the level was in the body when it was found. A straightforward calculation can be made of the time that had elapsed by the reduction in that reading. Far from intoxicated, the girls drank about the same that night, but Helen's blood alcohol level was considerably lower than Christine's, suggesting quite powerfully that she had been alive rather longer than her friend.

One of the first lines of inquiry at the city end of the investigation involved the local beat officers whose patch included The World's End. Today this may sound odd, but in the 70s, the foot-beat system was still the backbone of city policing. Back then, the constables knew their beats and they took pride in their ownership of the particular patch they had responsibility for.

During the night, each night shift officer would only have a very small area to patrol so that they could check the security of property, provide a constant visible street presence and be on hand to supervise the emptying of the pubs and clubs. Because of this, the chances were that when Helen and Christine left The World's End late on October 15th, a police officer would have been near at hand, and this indeed proved to be the case.

Early publicity for the investigation. Detective Constable John Capaldi, a stalwart of the early enquiry, stands to the right. *SCRAN*

Coincidentally, one of the very young policemen working in the vicinity of the High Street that night was Malcolm Dickson. Later, as Deputy Chief Constable and Assistant Inspector of Constabulary, he would become a close colleague and friend of mine. We often discussed that night and, although he saw nothing of significance himself, neither he nor any of the officers on duty that night ever forgot October 15th 1977. In fact, the beat men who were patrolling outside The World's End gave valuable information to the inquiry team, for they had seen two girls like Helen and Christine that night, in the company of two men; it was a small step but an important one. The two men had appeared to be hanging around outside The World's End, but not in a threatening kind of way. Two police officers, casually observing closing time in the High Street, spoke of how it seemed that the men were trying to engage with the girls. Those sightings were probably the last time Helen and Christine were seen alive. It is extraordinarily difficult for the senior officers in charge of a large inquiry like this to keep control of all aspects of the case and monitor with exact precision the various directions in which it is going. It remains difficult to this day but would have been even more so in 1977 when, without computers, there was a huge reliance on the recollections of individual officers and the primitive card index systems to try and ensure that the key threads of the investigation were identified.

There is huge pressure on them, from both within and outside the police service, to come up with results and to do so quickly. The danger always is that, in the absence of any clear leads and direct evidence, it is too easy to be distracted by hunches and suspicions not born of hard evidence, or to be led astray to pursue inquiries that do not justify a priority. A good example was the hunt for the so-called "Washington Sniper", which was predicated on the fact that he drove a white van to the scenes of his shootings. This threw a cloud of suspicion over every white van man in the D.C. area. Of course, it was later discovered that the presence of the van was coincidental, and the sniper drove no such vehicle. Decisions must be taken when weighing up the quality of evidence and which lines of inquiry are to be pursued. It would be possible to start tracing the owners and drivers of all white vans in order to eliminate the innocent. But it's easy to see just how quickly this could engulf the whole inquiry, and ultimately, a sizeable part of the nation's police service.

The World's End had something of a white van lead, only it was slightly more manageable. All the descriptions of the two men given by the various witnesses agreed on the fact that one of them had short, cropped hair – a soldier's haircut in a time when long hair was popular. This man was also said to be of very smart appearance which added to the impression that he could have a military background. Significantly, his clothes were described as smart but not quite of the latest fashion. Again, this pointed to a soldier who spent most of his time in uniform, only donning civvies when out on the town. The Royal Mile was popular with off-duty soldiers from the various barracks in and around Edinburgh. So it was that, early in the investigation, a substantial part of the inquiry team's manpower was devoted to speaking to soldiers based at Dreghorn, Glencorse and the other camps near the capital who had been out that Saturday night. The soldier scenario was an appealing one. It could explain why the pair were strangers in the pub on a Saturday night and, such is the transient nature of life in the army, they could be well out of the area by the time the murder inquiry was underway. Naturally, checking out this possibility was a demanding task. The fact that the events under examination had taken place late on a Saturday evening did not help the recollections of many of the young soldiers being interviewed.

The various leads that came up from the interviews with soldiers, friends of the girls and other witnesses were pursued with vigour but, despite the commitment of the officers directly involved and the huge manpower deployed, the World's End inquiry was soon running out of steam. As well as the many red herrings, there were also the false witnesses, ranging from fantasists to clairvoyants, who tend to be drawn to major police investigations of this kind. This category includes people so fascinated or horrified by events that they imagine themselves to have key roles in the drama.

One case in particular highlights this phenomenon. I was a detective inspector involved in the investigation of the abduction of five-year-old Caroline Hogg from the promenade at Portobello, a seaside area of Edinburgh. Her disappearance, coming as it did just a short time after the abduction and murder of another little girl, Susan Maxwell in the Borders, turned into one of those missing person inquiries that instantly had all the resources of our force thrown at it. I became fascinated by the emergence of several witnesses who, on the face of it, seemed perfectly credible and who had been in the area that day. They had become so overcome with grief and the emotion of the whole case – Caroline was missing for a considerable period before her body was found – that some imagined themselves into positions of importance in the investigation. They amassed substantial knowledge of the events surrounding this little girl's disappearance by avidly reading every newspaper article and soaking up the details of the case. Such was the volume of knowledge that these false witnesses built up that they could appear to be central to events until they had been subjected to time-consuming interviews. Sometimes these people are deluded through mental illness and sometimes they cannot be characterised as liars or fakes because they are well-motivated people who actually believe what they have imagined to be true. Whatever category they fall into, these people are extremely dangerous to an investigation that is desperate for new leads and lines of inquiry. They can be difficult to deal with and can tie up huge amounts of manpower as officers try to get to the bottom of false stories. And, worst of all, they can lead the investigation down a completely wrong track.

But if the traditional inquiry was bogging down, in the Forensic Science Laboratory they had struck gold, which eventually would prove crucial.

Helen Scott's new Burberry coat was the only major item of clothing belonging to either girl that was recovered. The knots of the bindings and ligatures were carefully preserved still tied, but it was the coat that offered most opportunities. It was ideal for forensic examination. It was made of high-quality material, and it was new and clean. Helen's body had been found lying on the lining of the coat, so its potential was evident.

After meticulous examination, Lester Knibb and his colleagues detected a large stain on the lining of the coat where Helen had been lying. Tests carried out on the area proved positive for traces of semen, male ejaculate. Nothing further could be ascertained with the scientific knowledge of the day, but Lester Knibb and his scientist colleagues had a vision. While the stain on Helen's coat could not be further analysed at that time, the scientists believed that one day, as science progressed, the stain would give up its secrets and the man whose semen was on the coat would be identified.

And so it was that Helen's Burberry coat became the central focus for forensic examination in the case. It was like The Rosetta Stone, concealing its secrets in indecipherable hieroglyphics, awaiting the code that would unlock its mysteries. The vision and the unshakable confidence in the future advance of forensic science marked out the scientific staff of Lothian and Borders Police as outstanding.

The confidence in the future value of the coat also ensured that it was protected across the ensuing years. Lester Knibb kept it under his personal control, every examination carefully logged and documented to ensure there was no cross contamination and that a complete audit of the coat was retained.

As the months passed, avenues of inquiry turned into dead ends and information dried up. The teams were slowly wound down as their work came to an end and, within the relatively short time of about seven months, it was decided there was insufficient new material coming in to continue to devote the huge squads of detectives to the investigation. The massive card indexes were tidied up and the inquiry was put on a care and maintenance basis with a smaller squad. But the pressure to solve this case did not let up, for in the west of Scotland there were other similar crimes.

In December 1977, while the hunt for the killers of Christine and Helen was in full flow, a young woman, Agnes Cooney, was abducted and murdered in Glasgow. The similarities were evident, and she was not the only victim in the west of Scotland. Anna Kenny had disappeared in August, and Hilda McAuley had been abducted and murdered just two weeks before the Edinburgh crimes. Then there was Frances Barker, another young Glasgow woman abducted and killed in the same period. Her murder had been solved, but there was still some uneasiness about the case. There were differences in the killings and the profile of the victims was subtly different, but the similarities were certainly strong enough for suspicions to be raised.

While the press were quick to ask whether the killings could be connected, the police were anxious to play down any possibility that the cases were linked. In hindsight, it seems a strange decision for murders with such apparent similarities not to be investigated together, or at least for them to be the subject of enhanced cooperation and liaison between the forces involved. In fact, linking the cases was seriously considered at a secret conference held in Perth Police Station in the summer of 1980. The Heads of CID from Lothian and Borders and Strathclyde, along with the Senior Investigating Officers from all the cases, met to discuss the similarities and decide whether to link or not. To preserve the confidentiality of the conference no formal minutes were taken, but after lengthy discussions it was decided not to link the cases but to monitor each other's progress.

The reasons were logical and made sense at the time. All knew that the card index system used to administer murder investigations was deeply flawed where major investigations were concerned. The "Yorkshire Ripper" case had exposed the flaws but, still, there was no solution. The prospect of trying to link the card systems of five different investigations must have horrified the senior investigating officers who knew that the potential for error grew with attempts to link large manual card systems. But behind that, there was probably also a reluctance by SIOs to give up control of their inquiry. Murder investigations were a matter of professional pride. No one wanted to be sidelined. And there was perhaps another factor: the spectre of "Bible John."

The failed "Bible John" investigation of a decade earlier will be discussed in more detail later but suffice to say, it had made senior detectives wary of declaring that a serial killer was at work, lest they end up playing catch-up to a full-blown media witch-hunt.

Whatever the combination of reasons, it was decided that Lothian and Strathclyde would continue to go it alone.

Meanwhile, Strathclyde Police were facing the same challenges as Lothian and Borders as they struggled to amalgamate seven smaller forces into one cohesive organisation. Officers in the west of Scotland were faring little better with their three cases than we in the east were doing with ours, and soon all the various inquiries had run out of new leads and, one by one, the investigations were slowly being wound down.

But such was the desire within Lothian and Borders to solve The World's End Murders that, whilst the case may have spent long periods of time ticking over, it was never forgotten. A senior officer within the force CID was always responsible for monitoring the investigation and keeping an eye open for new lines of inquiry.

On down the years, The World's End was never a dead case. For close on thirty-seven years, it was truly 'under investigation', for there was always a belief that the breakthrough would come. It was unthinkable that these dreadful crimes would go unsolved. And besides, there was always Helen's coat, our ace card. There was always confidence that the coat would provide the forensic answers when we were smart enough to ask the right questions.

# 2

# Helen and Christine

Victims of crime, and sadly in the case of the World's End their bereaved family and friends, invariably ask themselves one question which goes right to the heart of their emotions: Did they do anything to make themselves vulnerable? In simple terms, the answer always must be no – offending is always the responsibility of the offender. There is no doubt that in some cases, people are more likely to be targeted in certain situations and places and that their behaviour or lack of awareness can increase the likelihood of their victimisation. This is not to justify or to excuse the perpetrator, but ultimately, we all have the responsibility to take reasonable care of ourselves.

In the World's End case, however, this was not a factor. Helen and Christine had enjoyed an evening out. They had been drinking but this probably didn't contribute in any significant way to their fate. They simply had the tragic misfortune to meet one of the most evil and predatory men who has walked the streets of our nation in modern times.

When the perpetrators of these crimes walked into their hunting ground, be it in a pub or a dance hall, from the very moment they crossed the threshold, they would be callously weighing up the potential of all the young women in the room. They would be looking for the girl or girls that would fit their bill. They had probably subconsciously created a target profile in their own minds of who would make an ideal victim. They would quickly dismiss those who presented problems that could stand in the way of their intended control and violent sexual gratification.

Casting an eye round the room, they would instantly exclude the female halves of obvious couples. Out too would be the quiet group of young women who were deep in conversation. The picture would soon become clear. The target would be girls in high spirits, the ones who have had a drink or two which perhaps might mean that their guard was lowered – in fact, the sort of girls you see every night of the week in pubs and clubs in every part of the country. Normally, girls on a night out owe their safe return home at the end of these evenings to the simple fact that they did not have the misfortune to bump into a predatory criminal before their front door closes with them safely on the inside. Helen and Christine were tragically unlucky that Saturday night in October 1977. They were barely more than children, on the very cusp of adulthood.

Helen and Christine - the best of pals and hardly more than girls.

Helen Scott and Christine Eadie had known each other since their first days at secondary school. Helen, the older of the two by a matter of five months, and Christine met up at Edinburgh's Firrhill High School in the Oxgangs area of the city. The 1960s buildings housed a school of about 1,000 pupils. The pair had spent their entire secondary school life there and, even as seventeen-year-olds who had been out in the world of work for some time, many of their regular friends hailed from that area and Firrhill School. The school then, as now, serves a close-knit, largely working-class community.

The area was quite different from the quiet beauty of the Scottish Borders where Helen spent the first part of her life. Her mum Margaret had moved from the Edinburgh area to Coldstream on the banks of the River Tweed in the late 1950s. The epitome of a quiet town, Coldstream is famed as the place where, in 1660, General Monck raised his Regiment of Foot, the Coldstream Guards, and marched them to London. Once in the capital, Monck helped to secure the restoration of the Stuart monarchy. It is also a town that has been touched by tragedy. Just a few miles away is Flodden Field, the scene of the battle in 1513 that saw the flower of Scots nobility cut down by the English. And, a few years after Helen's death, it was the centre of an inquiry into the disappearance of little Susan Maxwell, who was subsequently found to have been murdered by that monster of Scottish criminal history, the child-killing van driver, Robert Black.

Margaret met and married Morain Scott and, a year later, Helen was born. Helen had two older half-sisters, and eventually the family would be completed with the birth of her brother Kevin. By the time Kevin was born, the family had moved to Penicuik, a dormitory town to the south of Scotland's capital. The family's final move was into the suburbs of Edinburgh after Helen's Dad started a new job as a British Telecom engineer.

Helen was part of a close and loving family. At school, she had been quite quiet at first, a little reserved, but eventually her bright personality had come to the fore, and she was a pupil who was well-liked by staff and students alike. She left Firrhill at the age of fifteen and, just like many of her age group, she was mainly interested in fashion, music and going to the cinema. When she left school, her closest friend was a girl called Jacqueline Inglis. She remained friends with Jacquie to the end. Jacquie was with Helen in The World's End the night she disappeared and was therefore one of the last people who knew her to see the teenager alive.

Helen had worked hard since leaving school and was never out of a job. At the time of her murder, she had recently started a new job at a kilt shop on Edinburgh's main shopping thoroughfare, Princes Street. Everything was going well for her. She had a stable group of friends and a determination to improve herself which was evidenced by a recent decision to start night classes with the aim of passing Higher English and Maths. It seemed she saw her job in the kilt shop as a temporary one while she set about getting the qualifications she would need to pursue a career in what seems to have been her chosen occupation of childcare. She had already demonstrated her aptitude for this by becoming the favoured babysitter for her sister's two children.

Like many girls in their mid-teens, Helen's weekend fun centred on her newly found ability to get into Edinburgh pubs and clubs with a group of friends. Although they were underage, they could sometimes convince the bar staff that they were 18. It was the sport of many teenagers in the 1970s.

Helen's last night began in the usual sort of way. She had arranged to meet her close friend Jacquie Inglis at Jenners corner on Princes Street. The landmark store in the heart of the city centre no longer exists, but was often referred to as the Harrods of the North, and was a regular starting point for people meeting up for a night out in Edinburgh. The pair walked through the fading autumn light to the Mount Royal Hotel which overlooks the valley of Princes Street Gardens, lying between Edinburgh's Old and New Towns.

After a drink at the Mount Royal, the girls began to head for their next rendezvous in the High Street, the central part of the famous Royal Mile. Their journey that night took them over Waverley Bridge and, from there, it was a long steep climb up Cockburn Street to the High Street. Helen and Jacquie were heading for the Royal Mile Centre and the Wee Windaes pub where they had arranged to meet Christine Eadie and a newer member of their group, a young woman called Toni Kivlin. She was a bit older than the rest of the girls, but they enjoyed her company, and she fitted in well.

Detailed examination of the statements provided by many of the people present that night showed clearly that, by the time the four met up at about eight o'clock, they had all had only a drink or two.

During the later investigation I re-read in detail the statements given by Christine and Helen's friends at the time of the original inquiry, and it was striking just how ordinary a night out it was for this group of teenage friends. The little dramas played out that evening were just the same as those played out in every town centre across the country every weekend but, in this case, the knowledge of how the night was to end could only add considerable poignancy to these descriptions of innocent, everyday events.

Helen and Christine managed to get another drink at the World's End as they squeezed into a space near the payphone in the crowded bar. Just how busy it was that night was shown to the wider public by a striking artist's impression of the scene, printed in the *Edinburgh Evening News* to help what had become a double murder investigation. There were of course no mobile phones in those days but, then as now, teenagers love to talk on the phone and first Helen and then Toni called pals on the bar payphone. It was clear from the statements given by people in the pub that the group were in a boisterous mood; bickering, then making up as friends do.

The girls managed to get a seat at a table and soon other friends had joined them. They were now a large group who were engaged in animated conversation. Everybody knew one another – they were a regular crowd who met up most weekends. Boys and girls, they were all around the same age and, in some cases, they had been friends for years. Christine and Helen were, as usual, at the heart of the crowd. To the others, it was very noticeable that they were happy and smiling.

It was at this point, unbeknown of course to any of this group, that things were about to go wrong. Jacquie Inglis and Toni Kivlin went to the toilet together and emerged a short time later to find that Helen and Christine had been joined by two men. No one can be certain, but it seems entirely likely that the pair standing in the crowded bar talking to the tipsy teenagers were embarking on a carefully laid plan that would lead to the rape and murder of these two innocent girls. If true, this gives a chilling first insight into the character of the men who had the nerve to engage the girls in conversation and quickly befriend them, knowing that their intention was assault, rape and murder. The men would probably have been watching the group before taking the opportunity to move in on Helen and Christine and begin the process of ensnaring them. And, what's more, they'd have been perfectly aware that the girls had friends in the pub who could easily return to be in their company, giving the friends a greater chance of being able to identify, or at least describe the two men chatting to Helen and Christine. Such behaviour demonstrates a coolness, a determination, and an acceptance of risk in pursuit of their gratification.

Jacquie Inglis was later to tell officers that the men appeared to be in fairly intense conversation with Helen and Christine. They appeared unremarkable and certainly gave no one any cause for alarm. One was in his late twenties, of medium height and quite stocky. Jacquie noticed he had piercing brown eyes. His round face had prominent cheekbones and was topped by parted dark hair that lay across his forehead. His flared brown and white striped trousers, brown V-neck jersey and light-coloured shirt were the fashion of the day. The second man was about the same age but slightly taller. He too was wearing the flared trousers that were so popular in the late seventies. Jacquie left the four of them to get on with it and began chatting to another friend who invited them all to go to a party that was going to start quite shortly. She asked Helen and Christine if they

30

wanted to go too. In what was to be a fateful decision, Christine said a definite no and Helen didn't appear to reply. The conversation with the two men was obviously more engaging. One of the men was leaning over the table and then walked to the bar where Jacquie thought he bought the girls a whisky each. It was the last moment she saw her friends alive. Just a few moments after witnessing this scene, the group going to the party left the pub. In the event, like so many of these things, the party they went to fell short of expectations and Toni and Jacquie left in the early hours of the next morning to go to their respective homes by taxi – the end to just another Saturday night out.

It was 10.30 on Sunday morning when Jacquie got the first clue that something was wrong. Helen's Dad, Morain, phoned her to see if his daughter had stayed the night with her. Later that day, a slightly concerned Jacquie went round to the flat where Christine was living, only to discover there was no sign of her or Helen. She went to a telephone box to tell her missing friend's dad. After more phoning round, Jacquie met up with some of their friends from the night before in another High Street pub. They were joined by Morain and Margaret Scott, who by this time, were extremely worried. The group decided it was best to report Helen and Christine missing. The mystery of their disappearance was not to last for long. Shortly after her visit to the Southside Police Station in Edinburgh to make the missing person's report, Jacquie heard a newsflash on the radio saying the bodies of two girls had been found. She immediately phoned the police, and a detective came straight to her house to take a statement. The officer had the painful task of confirming that Jacquie's worst fears had been realised and that, pending formal identification, it was indeed her friends who had been found dead in East Lothian.

The subsequent murder investigation was going to need comprehensive profiles of both victims, so officers spent considerable time unearthing the details of Helen and Christine's short lives. In an inquiry like this, no aspect can ever be dismissed as too small. Most murder victims are known to the killers, so the first step in nearly every murder inquiry is to establish who the friends and acquaintances of the deceased were and who they were last with.

Christine had been largely brought up by her maternal grandmother in a loving and generous family. No doubt she threw up the challenges of many teenagers, but it was clear that, by the time she had reached the age of seventeen, she was an attractive, confident and outgoing young woman with an appetite for life. After she was killed, officers found a diary in Christine's flat. In it were extensive accounts of her life and experiences but they were the innocent thoughts of a child, and none of the details yielded any clues to her killer's identity.

On leaving school, Christine had worked for a time in the city council's Education Department before taking up a post as a typist with a firm of surveyors in Edinburgh.

The information about the girls given here and heard in court during the trials serves to reinforce one simple but very important fact – something that can get buried as a crime is described and discussed in the media and amongst professionals working in the various fields involved. So, it is worth pausing for a moment to remember again that all crimes involve real people; relatives and friends who, often through no fault of their own, find their lives devastated by wickedness and inhumanity. In the case of The World's End Murders, it was not just the dead girls who were affected. It was their family and many friends – the parents who live with the agony of loss every single day for the rest of their lives, and the brothers and sisters who never get over the tragedy and the loss of their sisters' futures. Had their lives not been snuffed out, who knows what Helen and Christine may have achieved? Who knows how many future lives and opportunities were ended that night in October 1977? As I became more acquainted with the details of the World's End inquiries and those of the other murdered victims that eventually were linked to the investigation, the suffering of those left behind screamed out of the files and reports that crossed my desk.

It is a sad fact that many of the relatives of murder victims never recover from their grief. Some die prematurely and are often said by those who survive them to have succumbed to a broken heart. Unable to cope with the grief, some take their own lives, and, in their despair, others turn to the bottle in the hope of finding solace. Yet, in the cruellest of ironies, it is usually the murderers, the infamous, who are remembered by the public. Sadly, notoriety sometimes brings with it a form of immortality.

One of the biggest changes I saw in my police career was the recognition of this fact, and a realisation by the Police Service that more must be done to help the victims of crime and those affected by it. It is right to say, however, that as the later investigations into the events all those years ago began, we found ourselves hampered by the legacy of some old police attitudes.

Until the late 20th century, the difficulties facing those affected by crime were all too often ignored or treated lightly by the investigators. This was because of several reasons. The main one was, of course, cultural. Police attitudes change as those of the rest of society do and, in the old days, victims of crime were sometimes seen as something of a nuisance – a hindrance to the effective investigation and detection of criminals. All too often, they were seen as simply a source of information and their suffering not fully appreciated.

In hindsight, of course, this was short-sighted. Families of victims can be of immense practical assistance to the investigation. They usually only seek courtesy, respect and information and, while there was a traditional reluctance to share any information in a difficult investigation for fear that it might be leaked to the press, this fear was usually misplaced. In many years of investigation, I can think of hardly any families who have betrayed the trust of the investigators and, over all the years since the tragic loss of their girls, the families of Helen and Christine have behaved with the utmost dignity. In the most nightmarish circumstances and in the long glare of publicity, the Scott and Eadie families have carried themselves with great courage and made a significant contribution to the investigations. Their spokesman, Helen's Dad, Morain Scott, was a constant support to the police. Over the years, Helen and Christine's families have gained the utmost respect and admiration of all the investigators.

But this isn't always the case. Not all relationships between the police and the families of victims are as good as those the police shared with the Scott and Eadie families. Sometimes tensions between families and police arise – for example, if people feel they are being denied information, or just not given the courtesy and respect they deserve. Cases from different parts of Scotland that could potentially be linked to the deaths of Helen and Christine were identified, so it was decided that a joint operation, to be known as "Operation Trinity", would be set up to coordinate them. When the deaths of their loved ones were initially investigated, there had been some tension between certain members of the families and the police, so one of the priorities for officers working on Trinity was to establish good relationships with surviving family members from the outset. In line with modern police practice, family liaison officers were appointed, and it was up to them to try and ensure that they rebuilt any broken bridges that the passage of time had done little to mend.

Of course, in recent years the importance of family liaison has been recognised and is now a specialist area of policing with carefully selected officers receiving training to help in this, their most difficult and sensitive role. To get close to, to almost be part of a family in grief, is to share that grief. To follow the case and take the families through from crime to investigation to trial and beyond can be extremely demanding. The role of family liaison officer is not for everyone, and the long-term effects can be stressful, even life changing. I know of several colleagues who have been permanently marked by difficult or harrowing cases. In the sometimes tough world of the officers serving in murder squads, family liaison is sometimes seen as a soft job, a secondary consideration. Experienced officers or those who have done the job themselves know different.

The Family Liaison Officers (FLOs) in our investigation of Helen and Christine did a fine job. I hope the work they have done in the 21st century has gone some way to redress the hurt that must sometimes have been caused through lack of sensitivity in the policing ways of the past.

As I have said, in the World's End case, perhaps because of circumstances, perhaps because of other factors, Helen Scott and Christine Eadie's families had a good working relationship with the police throughout these long and difficult years. Because of the dedication of the officers, over the years, as new initiatives were tried, the family members were amongst the first to be kept informed about what was happening. That made part of the inquiry slightly easier. It should always be remembered that, for many victims and their families, the shock, hurt and pain of crime does not disappear – it simply matures and, like a disfigurement, is constantly present.

Helen's mother, Margaret, died in her mid-sixties, and her surviving relatives were certain that the burden of grief over her murdered daughter played a significant part in her early death. And, by the time we were making progress towards our eventual breakthrough, Christine's gran, who had played such a large part in her upbringing, had also passed away, but her mum, Margaret, and Helen's Dad, Morain, were very much alive. Both were briefed regularly as we tried to ensure they knew of each development before reading about it in the newspapers.

The first inquiry into The World's End Murders had failed to identify the two men who were seen talking to the girls in The World's End. It had also failed to uncover any hard evidence of whether the men had left the pub in the company of the girls. The nearest that was unearthed was the statement of two police officers on duty in the High Street that night and who, by coincidence, were in the street near the bar at about the time Helen and Christine are thought to have left.

Beat constables John Rafferty and George Owenson were on the usual Saturday night detail in the centre of Edinburgh around closing time. As folk were piling out on to the streets at about 11:15p.m., the officers were no doubt keeping a relaxed but wary eye on proceedings, trying to spot where any trouble might be likely to start so that they could intervene before it got out of hand.

We do not know for certain, but it is likely that, since the pair were on patrol in the High Street, they could well have been close to the main door of the World's End around the time the girls and their killers were coming out of the pub and, indeed, may even have seen the four of them. Of course, they had no reason to intervene – it was just another Saturday night, just another crowd of people ranging from merry to downright drunk spilling out onto the pavement.

The High Street then, as indeed now, was always rather gloomy at night. The high buildings and numerous alleyways and side streets mean street lighting is never terribly effective, but the officers clearly saw two girls and two men leaving together. They saw one of the girls trip. The other girl helped her friend back on to her feet and Constable Rafferty recalled they appeared to be bickering about how they were going to get home. He saw what he described as a young man – from the description, almost certainly one of the two men – approach them and offer a lift. A second young man was on hand. In what perhaps was the fateful moment, one girl accepted the lift; the other seemed reluctant, but was nevertheless dragged off by her friend down St. Mary's Street. The officers saw them disappear down the street and thought nothing more of it that night.

As I say, we can't be sure it was Helen and Christine the PCs had seen – they were unable to confirm the girls' identities despite studying several family photographs. Also, because of the everyday nature of what they saw, they had no clear recollection of the two men, except that one of them spoke with what Constable Rafferty said was an out-of-town accent. If that was Christine and Helen, it was the last that anyone, other than their killers, saw of them alive. The next anyone was to know of the two friends was less than twenty-four hours later when Christine's body was found.

# 3

## The First Investigation

The initial investigation into the double killing ran at full tilt from the moment the bodies were found in mid-October 1977 until the end of May the following year.

There were several main lines of inquiry being followed up under the various teams controlled by Detective Superintendent MacPherson, with DCIs Darling and Suddon commanding the two strands of the investigation, one based in East Lothian and the other based in the capital.

Tracing and eliminating patrons of The World's End pub on the night the girls vanished was of prime importance and, given the fact that most murders are committed by people who know or have met their victims, it was a channel of investigation that looked hopeful. But it was more difficult than it first seemed. The World's End was then, as it is now, a busy pub and, being on the tourist route, it has always attracted both regulars and casual customers who pass down the Royal Mile, pop in for a drink and move on. It was no different in the 70s and, on a Saturday night, the pub was full of a mixture of people, some who stayed for the evening, most who called in, had a drink, checked out the action – the girls, the boys – and moved on up the Mile.

Trying to fully establish who was in the pub and when was a tricky exercise. Add to that the difficulty of cross-referencing very different descriptions of the same people and you can start to understand the complexity. If the World's End killings had taken place in 2007, not 1977, there would have been a wealth of technical information to assist the inquiry team. The CCTV footage from the numerous cameras both within the pub and on the streets nearby would have been immensely valuable. The credit card details of customers, who either paid by credit card in the vicinity or drew cash from nearby cash machines, would be retrieved and followed up. Any vehicles checked on the Police National Computer or picked up on the various cameras in and around the city would be traced. Mobile telephone activity in the vicinity could even be scrutinised. Back in 1977, these technologies did not exist. We could not even establish who had used the payphone in the pub that night. The detectives back then had to log timelines and people's positions on a huge paper chart, much as detectives had done a hundred years before. Yet, as we looked back thirty years later, we were amazed just how accurate a job they did and how good some of the descriptions given had been.

At the centre of the pub inquiry were, of course, the two men who had been seen chatting to Helen and Christine and who were believed to have left the pub with them.

There are simple first priorities in homicide investigations: secure the locus, identify the body, establish the cause of death, and trace who was the last person to see the victim alive. The two men seen with Helen and Christine in the pub and who apparently left with them were a natural priority. Not that it was a foregone conclusion that they were the culprits – all sorts of things could have happened between the door of the World's End and Gosford Beach. Nor could the failure of these two men to come forward be taken as a definite sign of guilt. There could have been several reasons why they had not come forward. They may not have known of the incident – though, given the massive publicity, this was unlikely. It is more likely that they should not have been there in the first place – they could have been married and being seen chatting to young girls in a pub would have meant they'd have some explaining to do. There are many reasons why vital witnesses are sometimes reluctant to come forward and it is an age-old problem for the police to coax them to do so. As it transpired, the original inquiry team never traced the two men in the pub with Helen and Christine.

The next problem for the original investigators was to sort out, evaluate and prioritise the mass of information, suggestions and names that came forward in the first weeks after Helen and Christine's murder. There was a genuine mood of public outrage, fanned by an active and imaginative media. There was a sense that this crime, above all others, was beyond belief – it couldn't happen in Edinburgh, it was the stuff of American cop fiction, not reality – and the shock waves rebounded for many months. Frequently, women who were in their teens in the late 70s tell me of the impact of the World's End killings. They were subjected to parental clamp-downs on late nights in the town, the importance of staying with the group was emphasised and, in the pre-mobile phone era, they were encouraged to keep in touch while they were out and about. Taxis did a roaring trade and many a father stayed up to the small hours to make sure a daughter came home safely. That year saw a tangible death of innocence in Edinburgh and the enormous groundswell of emotion led to thousands of pieces of information coming to the hard-pressed incident rooms.

High-profile cases produce an interesting mix of responses. Genuine witnesses come forward but so do well-motivated individuals whose information is irrelevant. Attention seekers appear, as do those with a morbid fascination for the crime. And then there are the ones with malicious intentions, eager to settle a score or do a bad turn to an enemy. Add to that the deranged, the mediums, and those so caught up in the event that they imagine themselves being in key witness roles, and you start to get a picture of an incident room in the first few weeks of a major and high-profile inquiry. In 1977, the media intervention had not reached the twenty-four-hour frenzy we see today but, even so, this was a dangerous time for senior investigators. It is very easy to be drawn up one of the many blind alleys that always await the unwary detective.

George MacPherson, Bert Darling, and Andrew Suddon kept cool heads, for the documents from 1977 clearly indicate their focus and determination not to be distracted. The main lines of inquiry remained on the patrons of The World's End, the two men, and the East Lothian connection. Those close to Helen and Christine, the local boys in their group of friends, were quickly eliminated. Legitimate major lines of inquiry did, however, emerge. Near to where the bodies had been left is the caravan site at Port Seton. Then, as now, this holiday camp attracted many visitors from the west of Scotland. It was largely closed in October when the girls were murdered, but those who frequented it in the summer, perhaps owned caravans there, would know the area and the back roads and might have access to the site even while closed.

A larger and more complex line of inquiry was also emerging in Edinburgh. Naturally, the two men last seen with Helen and Christine were described differently by different witnesses, but all agreed they were smart with short hair. In the late 70s, this was not typical for young men – long hair and straggly moustaches were all the rage – so it was logical that the minds of the inquiry team focused on the military garrison at

Edinburgh Castle, then an operational army base as well as a ceremonial HQ. Young soldiers were regular customers in the High Street pubs – they were smartly dressed and, of course, all had the standard army short back and sides. Given the information available at the time, it was a line of inquiry that had to be pursued, but it was hugely problematic, and it took considerable time and resources to tackle.

Years later, my good friend Dougie Kerr, who retired as a chief superintendent but who had been a young detective on the original squad, told me how challenging the 'soldier' side of the inquiry had been. Like most barracks, Edinburgh Castle saw a constant throughput of solders as they moved to Northern Ireland, Germany, Cyprus and the other operational bases of the army in the late 70s. Tracking them all down, interviewing them and corroborating their statements would have been impossible, so hard decisions had to be made and a highly selective approach taken, with only men who matched certain criteria being interviewed. We now know that it was a red herring and that the energy expended was wasted. It was, however, a task the original squad could not shirk and, scanning the now yellowed original forms, it was obvious they had done the job intelligently and well.

Much work was also done on the description of the clothes worn by the two men. One of them wore very distinctive high-waisted trousers with a row of buttons. This fashion feature was given extensive media exposure with artists' impressions, carried by various newspapers and inquiries carried out as far away as London's Carnaby Street and other leading fashion areas. In a period of bizarre styles, the search came to nothing.

Then, of course, there were the local suspects – the sex offenders and rapists who lived and had offended in the area. One by

Artist's impression of the typical seventies dress style of the men last seen with Helen and Christine.

one, they were traced, interviewed, and eliminated. There were no hot contenders – the scenes of crime and forensic scientists were working on Helen's coat and other objects but there was nothing we could use at the time. Gradually, amidst the thousands of leads, reality dawned – there were no real quality leads left to pursue. Helen and Christine had disappeared from the pub that night and, six months later, a large squad of the ablest detectives of their day, backed by huge public support and active media, were no further forward than they had been on the weekend that the girls' bodies had been found.

I remember the palpable feeling of frustration and self-doubt within the CID at the time. How could a crime of such enormity happen here in Edinburgh, and having happened, how could we fail to solve it?

As the lines of investigation each gradually reached a dead end, the inevitable decision had to be taken. In May 1978, seven months after the crimes, the World's End Murder inquiry, one of the most important crimes to be investigated by Lothian and Borders Police in modern times, was to be wound down until and unless new substantial lines of inquiry were established. It was a big call to make in such a high-profile case, but it was not the end. There was a clear sense of unfinished business and a strong belief that the answer would come, especially from Helen's coat. Looking back, I'm certain it was this mindset of unfinished business that ensured the inquiry was cared for and maintained in such an efficient way.

In those days, before computerised systems, unsolved cases were boxed – literally put in a cardboard box or boxes – and stored in an old records room, where, over the years, they were frequently rifled through for information or old statements. With officers constantly going back over the paperwork, witness statements and police records were seldom returned to their original state. The World's End was always different – the original squad were convinced their work would continue, so nothing was left to chance. All the files were completed, the indexes brought up to date and in the old laboratory on the top floor of the Fettes HQ, Lester Knibb and his colleagues carefully stored all the forensic samples. Helen's coat, samples from the sites where the bodies were found, swabs from the post-mortems and, crucially, all the ligatures, with the knots still in place, were carefully sealed away, awaiting the day when new science would unlock their secrets.

Over the years, bits and pieces of information came in – sometimes it was the name or names of suspects arrested for a serious crime elsewhere and sometimes a piece of gossip or malice. And there was the usual flurry of information that would follow the times when the news was slow and local papers printed their regular 'great unsolved mysteries' articles.

By the 1980s, the responsibility for the World's End had been handed to the East and Midlothian Division for ongoing care and maintenance. As the division for 'where the bodies lay' or had been found, this was the long-established procedure.

\*

The best at their best. Detective Superintendent Ian Thomas and Detective Chief Inspector Allan Jones. Their persistence closed the case.

Reading through the old paper files, it struck me that the successive officers who took responsibility for the World's End could have hardly been of a higher quality. In truth, they had been hand-picked. There was always a feeling that the World's End was special, sacred, and that it was being held in trust until the breakthrough came. The list of officers in charge included some of the most respected of their day: George Ritchie, eventually a head of CID, whose son Andy was destined to be a key player in the 2004 team that would eventually break the case after 2014; Kenny Shanks, a formidable detective, whose family have served Lothian and Borders Police for generations; Detective Inspector Stuart Anderson, who was involved throughout his service; and latterly, Superintendent John McGowan, a fastidious, meticulous and tenacious man who did so much to highlight the case and champion its continued investigation; then finally, Ian Thomas, and the indefatigable Allan Jones, who saw it through to the end.

Long service in the police can sour people – repeated exposure to the worst of human nature can make you cynical, negative and lose faith – but for some this never happens, and they keep their early passion, their idealism and, above all, their belief. The World's End inquiry was served by such people over the years. Any doubts officers newly assigned to the case might have would be quickly dispelled when they read files, examined the photographs and gazed at the last pictures to be taken of Helen and Christine alive – two happy, healthy young girls, barely more than children. That was always enough to stir the spirit and motivate any police officer with pride in the job. And it wasn't all about senior detectives – it never is. The senior detectives take the credit and the blame, their reputations are made or destroyed, but the truth is that it's the rank and file that do the job or not. So it was with the World's End. From top to bottom, through the generations, they never gave up and they just kept going. There were people like Athene Moir, a typist in the incident room off and on for most of the thirty-seven-year investigation. She lived and breathed the inquiry. She was there at the start and, along with Lester Knibb, she was there at the finish. She carried no police rank, she didn't make the headlines, but no one was more dedicated to the tasks than she was.

Then there were detectives like Willie Fleming and Dawn Paterson, who embraced the new age of computerisation to become experts in the HOLMES system. Diligent and utterly dedicated, they epitomised the World's End squad down the long years.

It would be a long nine years after the case was reduced before any substantial new information surfaced to give the investigation new impetus. During that time, the numerous leads that had found their way to the police were dealt with by some of the experienced hands at Dalkeith CID, just east of Edinburgh, many of whom had served on the original inquiry.

We were not to know it at the time, but our decision to keep the case going on a "care and maintenance" basis was important. We were to learn later that a cold case is best solved by keeping it warm. Momentum is everything when a breakthrough comes. To have a squad in and ready to go, briefed and prepared, is a huge advantage.

*

In 1988, the force received what appeared to be the information they needed to make a major breakthrough in the case. They were contacted by an inmate of Edinburgh's Saughton Prison who told them that a cellmate had confessed to him one night that he was responsible for the killings. What made this lead so important was that the man who contacted us had been able to give details of the case that we did not think had been made public. Especially significant was his description of how the bodies had been left.

On the face of it, this was very promising, so a new team was set up and investigations begun. Members of the girls' families were even alerted to the development. This burst of activity coincided with the first emergence of DNA technology as an investigatory tool. It was not the obvious first step it is today, and significant inquiries had been made by the time the suspect was arrested and DNA swabs taken, but hopes were dashed by the scientists who were able to categorically say that while they could not say who the culprit was, they could say who it was not, and the new suspect was not our man.

There were two other significant leads thrown up around the turn of the 1990s that are worth mentioning. One resulted from the decision to send officers to the doors of some of Edinburgh's better-known criminals. During these inquiries, a man came forward sometime about 1992 to say that he had been joyriding in a stolen car in the Aberlady area on the night of the killings and he had picked up a man called John McGrannigan, a well-known criminal and a convicted rapist. Quite why our informant had waited for fifteen years to pass this on was, of course, suspicious, but circumstances and loyalties change. It looked as if we had a lead, and a promising lead at that. Intelligence files revealed that we suspected that McGrannigan's brother, Charlie, had been murdered by a well-known city gangster to silence him. Quite what it was he had to be silenced for was not recorded in the intelligence reports, but officers concluded, not unreasonably, that it just might have been connected to the World's End case. However, once again, after a thorough investigation, John McGrannigan was also cleared by the fledging DNA technology, and we

43

were back to square one.

It may seem odd to some that we bother with any additional inquiries when DNA profiling is available. It's simple – to secure a conviction, we need the best evidence, we need corroboration, we need more than DNA. While DNA profiling may have entered the public psyche as infallible, it is not regarded as such by the courts. DNA analysis is after all a question of expert opinions and statistical probabilities. As such, it is very often subjected to rigorous challenge by the defence. Usually, an approach to the suspect is the last phase of an investigation, done at a time when sufficient evidence has been gathered to justify the detention, questioning and even the arrest of the person concerned.

So, this latest lead was concluded. Our informant, McGrannigan, and the man thought complicit in his brother's death were all interviewed and each of them had their DNA tested. The test results eliminated them once and for all from the inquiry.

However, it was also in 1992 that another tantalising lead came along and, while it was treated less urgently, it remained on file for some time before it was eventually ruled out. A woman came forward to report that her ex-husband had abandoned her and left the country shortly after the killings. To enrich the story, she added that he had owned a pair of highly distinctive trousers like those worn by one of the men seen with Helen and Christine and which had been the subject of considerable publicity. The adage about hell having no fury like a woman scorned did occur to the detectives given the job of following up the lead. Nevertheless, no chances could be taken. An international search was begun and, sometime later, the police in Germany ran the fugitive husband to the ground. The inquiry team was unsurprised when his DNA was checked and he was cleared.

As DNA analysis emerged and became more sophisticated, its use as an investigative tool increased exponentially. While initially it was most frequently used to eliminate suspects, soon it would serve a more positive purpose.

In 1997, a more complex DNA profile was isolated from Helen Scott's coat. It was what we had been waiting for, and prompted a review of the entire case – a fresh look through fresh eyes with the benefit of new science. A famous murder squad detective from New York once said that "sometimes the difference between failure and success is a new thought." The new science was generating some new thinking in the World's End case; we were back on the hunt again.

By this time, the fastidious Detective Superintendent John McGowan was in charge, and he quickly established a base with a small, hand-picked team at Dalkeith police station. The plan was straightforward and logical. They would progress the case through a structured and thorough review of all the old files and then, after drawing up a new list of suspects, they would begin to interview or reinterview those on the list and, where possible, obtain DNA samples to compare with the recently discovered samples from Helen's coat. Exactly twenty years after the murders, John McGowan and his team were ready to start again, but this time, they were not relying solely on interview and alibi – now they had an evidential ace up their sleeve. If they got a sample of the man's DNA, they could be absolutely sure if he was or was not connected to the case.

I was an Assistant Chief Constable working at Fettes Force Headquarters in Edinburgh when this development was going on and the mood was optimistic – the whole force felt that this time we had a real chance to solve the case. If the culprits were in the system and if they were still alive, we would get to them eventually.

After a painstaking review of all the paperwork – literally thousands of documents from the original case – the most promising lines of inquiry were prioritised and details of them were entered into the new HOLMES computerised database. This back record conversion from paper-based to the computerised HOLMES system was laborious and time-consuming, but it was essential to modernise the original inquiry and prepare us for the next step.

The first phase of the investigation was to get DNA samples from the men we knew had been in the World's End after 10:00p.m. on the night Helen and Christine disappeared. We would then do the same with the dozens of named suspects who had been suggested over the intervening years and whose names remained on the files after they had not been fully eliminated. In addition to these priorities, about 1,200 individuals were also flagged on the Police National Computer. They were of lower priority, but if or when they were arrested anywhere in the UK, we asked that their DNA be obtained for elimination.

We seemed to be heading in the right direction but, despite our early hopes, this phase gave us no direct hits. None of our named suspects matched the DNA profile and no one we had traced from the World's End on the night of the murders came close either. Over 200 samples had been sent for costly DNA analysis but, despite the disappointing outcome, it had still been an important exercise – not least because some long-standing inquiries had now been cleared up and the names of some people who had not been fully eliminated in the original investigation had now been removed from the list of suspects. But it wasn't straightforward. We had always been pretty sure that two men were involved in the crime, but we only had one DNA profile. We knew the picture was incomplete. All the pieces of the jigsaw were not on the table.

The planned second phase, an extension of the DNA search, was postponed. In 1999, the East and Midlothian Division of Lothian and Borders was stretched to the limits by an unprecedented series of murders and serious crimes, including a double assassination. Some of the World's End officers had to be temporarily redeployed in order to meet the challenges the force faced. Then the latest champion of the World's End, John McGowan, retired and the impetus was lost for the moment. Such is the fate of historic or cold case inquiries. Urgent current demands must take priority, and this often means that old cases, no matter how important, must be temporarily set aside.

But the World's End was never set aside for long. A chance meeting between the then Detective Sergeant Allan Jones and a visiting lecturer at the Scottish Police College at Tulliallan saw to that.

Allan, a Midlothian-trained detective, was steeped in the World's End inquiry even though the crime had been committed before he joined the police. He had played a part in the latest reinvestigation, and he was convinced that the case was solvable. The lecturer visiting the Police College was Detective Sergeant Andy McKay from the newly formed National Crime and Operations Faculty (NCOF). They fell into conversation and the subject soon turned to The World's End Murders. Allan's enthusiasm was infectious, and Andy McKay soon offered a structured cold case review – a technique pioneered by NCOF, now familiar throughout the world.

The offer was quickly accepted. By this time, the man in charge at Dalkeith CID was Craig Dobbie; then a Detective Chief Inspector, he saw the huge potential of NCOF and worked as quickly as he could to bring their best people north to carry out one of their first comprehensive reviews in Scotland.

It wasn't without risk of course. An independent review meant exposing all our work, good and bad, to scrutiny. But we were confident in our investigations over the years. Expert help should never be refused.

NCOF was as good as their word and, in January 2001, the World's End investigation was subjected to its third thorough examination.

It was clear from the start that the ever-advancing DNA technology was to be the key. All the important non-scientific work that could have been done had been done. The real potential now lay in the forensic samples, particularly Helen's coat and the knots of the gags and bindings, all carefully preserved and undisturbed for over twenty years. Then there was the DNA profile we had already identified. We had to be sure that, as we progressed, this continued to be compared against all databases. It was also decided to widen the search, and through Interpol, ten countries that had significant databases were contacted. The unique profile of the World's End killer was now being searched for from the USA to New Zealand. If he was there, we were confident we would find him. Discussion of why we had only one DNA profile and yet we were of the firm belief that two men had been involved in the girls' rapes and murders will follow in the next chapter.

More locally, all the suspects already cleared were checked and double-checked in case any errors had been made. We all felt we were close, very close, but still we lacked the breakthrough we so desperately needed.

# 4

# The Breakthrough

DNA is a reduced form of the biochemical term "deoxy- ribonucleic acid". It is a complex self-replicating material found in every single cell of the body and has been described as the building block of life. Like fingerprints, no two examples of DNA are identical. But DNA is more useful in solving crimes than fingerprints because, unlike fingerprints, it contains clues as to its ancestral source. That is why, for instance, the late Prince Phillip, Duke of Edinburgh, provided scientists with samples of his DNA when they were trying to identify bones found in a Russian burial pit a few miles north of Yekaterinburg. The bones were thought to be those of the imperial family murdered by the Bolsheviks in 1918. The Duke was not a direct descendant of the Romanovs but, through the complicated interbreeding of the royal houses of Europe, he was related closely enough to them for a balance of probability calculation to be made. In the Russian case, that balance was sufficient to convince the Moscow authorities that the bones were those of Tsar Nicholas II and his family and, because of this, they were accorded a state funeral.

DNA profiling, also known as genetic fingerprinting, did not appear on the police radar until the late 1980s when the importance of the technique became apparent, and detectives started turning to scientists for help in this new miracle aid to detection.

Lothian and Borders Police were at the forefront of forces seeking help in investigations. Like most forces, we had several unsolved high-profile murder cases and officers were keen to explore any avenue that might lead to a resolution.

The first time DNA profiling was considered in the World's End case was in 1988, when the force was exploring a new lead that had been provided to us by a member of the public. That person had supplied specific information involving two identified potential suspects for the murders, and the quality of the lead was such that a substantial inquiry was commenced.

Lester Knibb, the Lothian and Borders forensic scientist who had played such a crucial role at the crime scenes in 1977, took Helen Scott's coat to a company called Cellmark in Cambridge. At the time, Cellmark was blazing a trail in this fast-developing area of technology. The Cambridge scientists managed to isolate and then partially identify a DNA profile contained in semen staining on the garment. Cellmark were not able to give us complete genetic fingerprinting for the source of the staining, but what they were able to tell us was enough to allow the two new suspects to be eliminated. Like all high-profile cases, the vast number of false leads was a feature of the World's End inquiry over the years, and being able to close this one down through the benefit of this new technology was a big advantage.

A fact seldom recognised is that the new science of DNA testing serves just as effectively to protect the innocent as it does to convict the guilty. In the last ten years, numerous 'good suspects' for serious crimes across the country have been quickly eliminated from suspicion by providing a DNA sample. One can only speculate but, in another time, without the assistance of this new science, the result may have been different for some of those suspects.

Returning to the case, it was clear to us as the eighties were turning into the nineties, that DNA technology was advancing at a rapid rate. Its great problem, in the early days, was that testing was a destructive process that rendered the sample useless for further analysis. A difficult decision was taken then not to subject the coat to more testing, as it might leave us without further material if or when the technology improved. We knew how valuable Helen's coat was. The secrets it held were not to be squandered. This was a prudent decision for, in the early days of DNA profiling, many valuable forensic samples were tested to destruction with no result. Had they been preserved until more sensitive testing systems were developed, things may have been different.

Next, it was the turn of scientists employed by our neighbouring force Strathclyde Police. They had committed substantial resources to their forensic science service developing less destructive analytical processes. They worked on the samples for some months before the painstaking examination by scientists Ian Hamilton and Martin Fairly paid off and they were able to identify a DNA match between the semen samples taken from Helen and Christine. We were able to conclude that the same man had sexually assaulted both girls.

As this work was going on in Glasgow, a database of DNA profiles was being established for the whole of the UK. Such was the quality of the latest results that we felt the World's End samples were good enough to go a stage further and be placed on this rapidly evolving database to be compared for possible matches.

The procedures set up to protect the credibility of the database were such that only profiles achieved from a small number of accredited laboratories were able to be included. So it was that the Forensic Science Service in Wetherby, Yorkshire had its initial involvement in the case. This was the move that allowed a full male DNA profile of the girls' attacker to be completed for the first time.

These breakthroughs were remarkable, of that there is no doubt. What was to follow in their wake was breathtaking.

By the first year of the new millennium, the science had evolved to the state that it was felt worthwhile to begin to examine other articles and samples gathered from the 1977 crime scene to see what secrets they held.

\*

In 1977, the care taken of forensic evidence was generally of a lower standard than it is today. Nowadays, as scenes of crime are investigated, the possible presence of what is known as low-copy number DNA is very much at the front the officers' minds. If DNA was a major breakthrough, the discovery of low-copy DNA was extraordinary. The essence of low-copy DNA technology is that microscopic particles of skin, hair, or body fluids, may not yield a full profile or be enough for an exact match, but they could be sufficient to eliminate large sections of the community or point to the probability of a familial link with profiles on the database. In other words, it is not the cast iron certainty of a full match but is rather an indicator, a lead to take investigators and scientists in a particular direction. Low-copy DNA has its risks – in particular, there is the possibility of cross-contamination – but, in the hands of a skilled investigator, its potential is enormous.

\*

50

The discovery of only one DNA profile in the case had long baffled us. Initially, science had identified one man but that had seemed unlikely because of the difficulty one man would have controlling two strong young women. On the other hand, sex offenders tend to work alone. It was with this in mind that Lester Knibb and his scientist colleague, Derek Scrimger, began considering if the new technology involving low-copy DNA would be able to help us. It was always possible that only one man was involved in the sexual attack, but that a second man may have been an accessory and left his mark elsewhere in the crime scene.

Careful thought was given to where low-copy DNA may have survived the initial examination by detectives in 1977 and the passage of time. The conclusion of the scientists was that there was a time capsule within the forensic materials – a place that had been left undisturbed and unexamined since the time when the crimes were committed. That place was the centre of the knots used to bind the girls.

The secrets locked in these bindings had the potential to produce vital clues to the identities of Helen and Christine's killers. Such was the advance in forensic science that, if you had suggested a breakthrough like this was possible to the detectives of the 70s, the response would have been bewilderment and disbelief. However, that was exactly where the next stage of this scientific mystery tour was to take us, and with considerable success.

This part of the story is a great example of how the determination of officers involved in the World's End case has paid off over the years. By this time, the responsibility of the inquiry rested with Detective Superintendent Ian Thomas and the then Detective Inspector Allan Jones. They were typical of a long line of able and dedicated detectives who, over the years, worked with the scientists to keep the World's End case alive. Ian and Allan had come through the same route to hold senior ranks in the CID. They were both career detectives with long experience across a wide range of investigations. Ian's experience was mainly in the city while Allan's service had predominantly been in the rural areas. They were very different individuals, but they shared invaluable traits essential to successful detectives: they were imaginative, energetic and stubborn – but they never, never, gave up. When an obstacle blocked their path, they worked until they found a way round it – and the potential obstacle was sometimes me.

As the investigation ground on, the costs rose and there were always other priorities. Time without number over the years, Ian, Allan or their predecessors would come to me to plead their case for funding. Money was tight, but they always convinced me as to the merits of their case. Their passion and commitment made them impossible to deny. It was just as well for I am convinced that, without them and those who went before them, the World's End case would have remained a mystery to this day.

Ian and Allan had long realised that new developments in forensic science held the key. They had regular formal and informal meetings with colleagues, like scientists Lester Knibb and Derek Scrimger, and people from further afield, ever hopeful of hearing of a new technique, a development that could help this case.

It must have been with a sense of excitement and anticipation that Allan Jones turned up at Wetherby in the spring of 2002 with the carefully preserved tights and belt that had been used to bind the girls. This was only to be partially fruitful. The Forensic Science Service were able to say that yes, there was recoverable and identifiable DNA at the centre of the knots, but there was insufficient material to allow any meaningful progress to be made on the already established but unidentified sample from the semen.

The findings from Wetherby did, however, produce sufficient information for officers to embark on a major new line of inquiry unparalleled since the early days of the case. The total absence of a match on the DNA database led Lothian and Borders Police to go off on what could only be described as an elimination exercise. The profile we had was of sufficiently high quality that the scientists were certain that, if we were able to find a relative of the source of the sample, we would be able to home in on the culprit. So it was that officers embarked on one of the biggest operations in the case since the original inquiry – a venture known as a Familial Search Operation. Swabs were issued to hundreds of men, and they were asked to use them to provide us with a sample of their DNA. All the swabs were analysed and, if everything went to plan, there was a chance that the extended family of the culprit would be discovered.

There were sufficient reference points in the DNA chain of the partially profiled sample that we had for it to be compared to DNA profiles on the national database and near matches extracted. We could then speak to those who were near matches and check their criminal records and those of their families to see if that would lead us to a perfect match. There is little need for me to say here just what an expensive, labour-intensive and painstaking process this kind of work is and, inevitably, for the teams involved in such tasks, morale is at first high, but it begins to flag as time passes without any positive results.

Having drawn a blank in the east of Scotland, it was decided to try the same operation in the west which, because the population is many times greater, would be an even bigger and more difficult job.

It was at this point that the breakthrough in 2004, which had eluded us for twenty-six years, came about. As so often happens in these cases, it was one we were not expecting. In the trawling operation centred on Edinburgh, we had been looking for a general match of nuclear DNA, often abbreviated to nDNA. This is the type of DNA that is most helpful to forensic scientists as it contains more useful genetic information than its counterpart, mitochondrial DNA – it offers a wide range of variables that can be examined.

During the month of January 2004, great effort and thought was put into trying to come up with a different approach to what was a massive task, and one that had no certainty of success. We were advised it would be sensible to isolate the Y chromosome of our DNA sample and use that alone as the control for the testing in the west of Scotland. The point of this approach was twofold. Firstly, unlike other elements of DNA, Y chromosomes do not change from father to son and, secondly, being able to concentrate on checking just one part of the profile would be faster and more cost efficient, so it would allow us to put more resources into following up on potential matches.

So, it was that Allan Jones and his colleagues set off for yet another DNA testing laboratory with specialist techniques, this time in Birmingham, to isolate the Y chromosome in Helen's coat and begin what would inevitably turn into an operation stretching out over many months. Good fortune intervened and two forensic scientists in Birmingham were able to give us the evidence we needed to put a name to the man we had been searching for all these years, but amazingly it wasn't the man who had left the original marks. While they were working on the coat sample to isolate the Y chromosome of the first sample, they discovered what we had suspected all along – there was not just one DNA code there but two. All this time, a second identifiable sample of DNA, in a much smaller quantity, had been there, masked by the more prevalent profile. It was confirmation of what we had believed all along – two men had been involved in the murders of Helen and Christine – and now, for the first time, we had the complete DNA profile of both.

*

One weekend in early spring 2004, I got a phone call from Roger Orr, our head of CID, saying that Ian and Allan urgently wanted to meet me. The importance of the breakthrough can be gauged by the fact that we didn't wait until the Monday to discuss it. Instead, on the Sunday afternoon, we met in my office at Fettes Headquarters. When I was told of the development, Ian and Allan's elation was clear for all to see. This is exactly what they had hoped would happen – because of their ability to shine a light back through time, the scientists had picked out the killers who had evaded normal policing techniques for so long. All their efforts had not been in vain.

Their elation was even more justified when it emerged that the new profile, the one belonging to the long-concealed second man, had matched one that was already on the national register of DNA profiles. We'd got a hit – it meant there would be no familial chain to work along, no difficult cross-referencing to be done and no statistical analyses to be carried out. The profile found in Birmingham was that of Angus Robertson Sinclair.

The name was vaguely familiar to some of us, as he had, we recalled, recently stood trial for a sex killing in Glasgow. The Scottish Criminal Records Office told us that Sinclair already had a prolific history of abduction and violent sex crime. Most importantly, he was safely incarcerated in prison. At long last, we had one of the men involved in the World's End case firmly in the frame. One way or another, we were certain he would lead us to the second.

The low-copy DNA testing of the knots on the items used to bind the girls also indicated the presence of Sinclair. And, elements of three other low-copy DNA profile indications were found – that of each of the girls themselves plus another which matched the dominant DNA profile obtained from the coat. This reinforced the theory that two men had been involved throughout.

So it was that Operation Trinity came into being. Now that we had a suspect, it was time to see if there was concrete evidence of his involvement in any of the other unsolved killings in Scotland that, over the years, had been linked to the World's End case.

Testing of samples recovered from Helen's body also revealed

54

Sinclair's DNA, though in much smaller quantities, which is why it too had been masked for all these years by the dominant sample. In the case of Christine Eadie, it was more difficult. She had been left naked and her outer clothing was never found. However, the bra used to gag her had traces of DNA which could have belonged to Sinclair, and strings of what could have been Sinclair's DNA were also found amongst the unidentified male DNA profile in samples taken from Christine's body.

All in all, the scientists were building up a comprehensive picture of the likely sequence of events all those years ago on that dreadful night in Edinburgh. We now had a number-one suspect who we had discovered already had convictions that would put him right in the offender profile for a likely perpetrator of The World's End Murders. We also had the original DNA profile that we hadn't been able to match on the database, so now the challenge was to try to put a name to it.

We believed this could be done by careful investigation of Sinclair's life around the time of the killings. If we could find out who he associated with, who his friends were, who he might have been with in Edinburgh that night in October 1977, we might be on to something. The next step would be to take this hopefully small group of people, gather DNA samples from each, conduct the analysis and, with any luck, we would find the answer.

But running parallel to the high-tech scientific approach to the case, there would have to be an old-fashioned police inquiry, involving officers interviewing and reinterviewing witnesses from the first inquiry and then building up a massively detailed background knowledge of our suspect. This sort of in-depth investigation is tough enough at the best of times but, given the number of intervening years, it would be taxing indeed. When viewed from 2004, the fact that Bing Crosby had died the day before Christine and Helen were murdered was not the great aid to the memory it had been in 1977.

We would be revisiting evidence that, when it was originally found, may not have been viewed as significant, but now that we knew the identity of one of the killers, had the potential to become vitally important. We were also aware of the fact that it was entirely likely that we would uncover other crimes committed by Sinclair. Quite what those would be was, of course, at that stage, just another mystery but, in the fullness of time, details of any other crimes committed by our man could help us build a better picture, and so it was to be.

The first part of our task was to build up as complete a profile as possible of the man the DNA told us was our prime suspect; the painter and decorator, now a prisoner in his fifties - Angus Robertson Sinclair. This man had already shocked the country with his depraved offending, but his name would soon forever be linked with The World's End Murders.

Angus Sinclair. A small but powerfully built man as he looked in 1982 when he was arrested for a series of rapes and assaults on children.

# 5

## Angus Sinclair

The DNA identification of one of the men at the scene of the World's End killings was the breakthrough in the investigation we had waited a generation for. It had seemed clear on that first Sunday afternoon thirty years ago when the girls' bodies were found that we were almost certainly looking for two men – and they were men of the utmost brutality. It seemed equally certain that anyone capable of such callous acts was unlikely to be a first offender. The abduction and murder of two young women can be no accident. Such coolness of execution is not likely to have been the culmination of events that had started off with innocent intentions and had perhaps somehow got out of hand. It seemed to us that the crime was the premeditated conclusion of a carefully planned operation, or at least the likely outcome.

The eventual isolation of one person's DNA and the match on the police database to Angus Robertson Sinclair took us on a journey through the depths of criminality to a man who allowed nothing to stand in the way of his violent sexual urges, and thereafter, not only showed no remorse for what he had done, but demonstrated over time, utter contempt for his victims.

In his book *The Amber Spyglass,* Philip Pullman wrote, "Good and evil are names for what people do, not what they are." In my experience, this is usually true, in that most murders are not premeditated; they are usually the tragic consequence of a moment's madness or passion – a loss of control that ends a life and changes the lives of many others forever.

Many murderers have no other convictions, are not career criminals and, like their victims, are sometimes simply in the wrong place at the wrong time, in the wrong state of mind. I have sat with a good number of murderers immediately after their arrest. For the most part, they are frightened, nervous, pathetic individuals – more often to be pitied than despised. It's a popular misconception that policemen feel anger, rage and righteous indignation when arresting people for murder – some may, but the usual feeling is one of sadness and regret for the tragic waste of life.

As far as that large percentage of murderers are concerned, Pullman is undoubtedly right, but there are also those who must fall into another category. These include the sadists, the psychopaths, the sociopaths, the multiple killers and, probably worst of all, the child killers – people like the "Moors Murderers", Ian Brady and Myra Hindley, or Robert Black who killed little Susan Maxwell, Caroline Hogg, Sarah Harper, and Jennifer Cardy. In terms of the planning, the repetition, the cruel indifference to suffering and the cool demeanour they show in the aftermath of their crimes, these individuals challenge Pullman's theory. I believe there are evil people – evil people whose actions put them beyond any forgiveness or sympathy – and Angus Robertson Sinclair is one of them.

The catalogue of crime Sinclair had been convicted of by the time our investigation into his background began was already one of the worst in Scottish criminal history. It was a criminal record sufficient to earn him a place in the Premier League of notorious offenders across the UK. Since 1982, Sinclair had been in jail continuously and was unlikely ever to be released. For some reason, however, Sinclair was not widely known to the public and had managed to escape the notoriety that his crimes deserved to have marked him with. Whilst they had all been extensively reported, such was the time span of his offending and the gaps between his arrests that the totality of his crimes seems to have slipped by. It is almost as though the constituent parts of his criminal record had not been added up so that the full range of his crimes was not apparent – until now.

He had, in fact, been known to the police for most of his life, but because of his cunning, his fastidious attention to detail, some degree of luck, and careful selection of victims, I believe that he has escaped the kind of intense police scrutiny he deserved. He got away with too much for too long. It's fair to say a degree of tunnel thinking on our part didn't help, but more on that later.

Let me put it plainly: I firmly believe it is entirely likely that locked away in the mind of this man are details of many more horrific crimes that we will never know of. We certainly uncovered irrefutable evidence of serious violent offending, robberies and non-sexual assaults as part of our inquiry into his past – crimes that all bore the Sinclair hallmark, in that they were calculating in their violence and displayed callous disregard for people's lives and suffering. Who knows what else lies hidden by the passage of time?

Being a criminal is not like a normal career with recognisable routes to the top of your chosen trade or profession. Most crimes, especially violent ones, are unplanned and haphazard. The most successful criminals are never caught. It often amuses police officers to see notorious underworld figures described as top criminals when, in fact, they have spent half their lives in jail. The truth is that their notoriety, by definition, makes them failures. Being caught and having a long criminal record are hardly an indication of success – remember that the next time you see "Mad Findlay" or "Crazy Charlie" on a television chat show. If they were that good, how come they got caught and convicted so often? It is the ones that are never caught, the ones you never hear of, who are the true professionals.

Amongst sexual offenders, however, there is often a clear pattern of escalating seriousness of offence as the perpetrator becomes increasingly more confident in their ability to avoid detection, or as the need for ever greater gratification drives them deeper into depravity. That is not to say that all minor offenders go on to carry out more serious offences. They don't, but the thefts of knickers from washing lines can lead to more serious crimes, and they cannot be ignored. Left unchecked, the park flasher can sometimes go on to become the park rapist if their behaviour is not confronted. Most sex offenders arrested for serious crimes have clues in their backgrounds, pointers to their future behaviour. Some have minor sex crime convictions, and many have been victims themselves. One of the greatest challenges of managing minor sex offenders is the difficulty in spotting the ones who are likely to continue to offend and, worse, those whose offences will escalate and become ever more serious. Social workers and the police are often criticised when it goes wrong. With hindsight, it's always easy to spot the ones who are going to become serious offenders – the tabloid press is very good at it – but, in the real world, it is very hard. Looking at a range of people with similar convictions, it's almost impossible to sit down and do an analysis of the circumstances and predict which men will cease offending, which will stay at the same level, and which will become a major danger to society.

Brought up in some of the toughest areas of Glasgow, Sinclair did not follow any established pattern. His first crimes were of a relatively minor nature and involved theft and housebreaking, albeit at a very young age – he was fourteen at his first court appearance. But, in the Glasgow of the late 50s when he would have been in his mid-teens, these offences would not have been out of the ordinary amongst his peers. It would, however, not be long before the juvenile offender Sinclair would be back in court – as a teenage killer.

As I begin to describe the background of Sinclair and his criminal history, it will quickly become clear just what a very dangerous person he has always been. As I have already said, he shows a contempt towards his victims that is breathtaking. Worse than that, in a criminal career of serious offending stretching back almost forty-five years, he has never once, to the knowledge of officers who have carried out meticulous inquiries into his life, expressed the slightest remorse. This is not just my view and those of other police officers, but the firm conclusion of every professional to have come across him in the criminal justice system since he was twelve years old. Eventually, at the conclusion of our inquiries when he was confronted with his past, he would have the chance to show remorse for what he had done; but, during countless hours of detailed interviews with skilled officers who were thoroughly prepared for their task, there was not a glimmer of contrition. He had nothing to lose – he was serving two life sentences, he was fifty-nine years of age, he knew he was never going to be released – yet he never once showed a sign of cracking. Rather, there was a stony-faced and steady resolve to play the game to the end and, in the finest tradition of the career criminal, admit absolutely nothing.

Sinclair was the youngest of three children born to a couple who lived in the Maryhill area of Glasgow. Mary and Angus Sinclair had a fourteen-year-old son and an eleven-year-old daughter by the time Angus Junior came along. When his third child was born, Angus Senior was suffering from increasingly severe bouts of an illness which was eventually diagnosed as leukemia. He spent a lot of time at the family home in St. Peter's Street, not far from the city centre. Although he was too ill to work, he was able to look after young Angus whilst Mary worked in a nearby tobacconist shop. Angus Senior died just four years after his youngest child was born and Mary Sinclair said she was naturally worried about how he would react to his dad's death. It appeared that he was upset, but his life progressed normally as he went first to nursery and then to the local primary school.

In the background of many sex offenders, there is often a history of them having being victims of sexual abuse before going on to be perpetrators. On the face of it, it's counterintuitive. You would think that, having been the victim of a sex crime and being aware of the long-term solitary suffering that goes with it, the last thing someone would want to do is to carry it on and repeat the victimisation. Yet time and time again we find this is exactly what happens, with victims becoming offenders and on and on, creating a pyramid of suffering. This was not the case with Sinclair. Although he alleged it, we found no evidence to support that he had been a victim. He had a tough upbringing, but no tougher than thousands of others.

The Glasgow of his childhood was a time of upheaval in Scotland's largest city as great social changes were taking place. Huge areas of the inner city were designated as slums and bulldozed, with the residents decanted to estates on the outskirts, as well as the new towns that were springing up across the Central Belt of Scotland. This was the Glasgow of gangs and violence, where murder rates ran far ahead of the rest of the country and local crime lords sorted out their differences with knives and razors and then, increasingly, guns.

It was during Sinclair's teenage years that a period of peace was brought to parts of Glasgow by the unlikely figure of the singer Frankie Vaughan. He became involved with youth work in the east end of the city and ultimately, brokered a deal between rival gangs and persuaded them to join in a weapons amnesty. Sinclair may not have been directly involved in this, but it is important to describe this background to give an impression of the parts of the city in which he grew up. Glasgow was then a place where, in some areas, extreme violence was the currency of everyday life.

The eventual criminal trial would require us to have an exceptionally detailed knowledge of all aspects of Sinclair's life. A simple recitation of his criminal record and any surviving probation reports would not even begin to fill the need we had. We had to find ways to bridge the time gap, to stretch back more than forty years and gather comprehensive details of his life, friends and movements – every scrap of information that could be gleaned to give us clues to his behaviour. As we set off on this task, our investigation was in its early days and it was impossible to gauge the totality of exactly the sort of information we were looking for, but officers knew that any single seemingly unimportant snippet might take on immense significance as the inquiry progressed. This was especially relevant in our search to trace the second man – the elusive source of our original DNA sample.

The first areas to explore were of course his friends and family. There were also the weighty reports drawn up by professionals involved in his various court appearances. Most people connected to Sinclair over the years were well disposed towards us and prepared to do all they could to help clear up these very serious crimes. Lengthy statements were taken from surviving members of his immediate family. As we have already noted, his father died when he was just a young boy and, by this time, his mother was long dead too.

One striking feature of his childhood was the close relationship the young Sinclair formed with his sister's daughter who, for her own protection, I will not name. Family members remember him being very affectionate towards her, and when he was older, using his pocket money to buy her quite generous gifts. His sister saw nothing untoward in this relationship. She recalled that at that time he seemed to be a happy and normal little boy. He would also appear to have been generally well-behaved in class at St. George's Road Junior Secondary School, where he completed his formal education. There was certainly nothing to worry about in his school reports. Even though he'd been in trouble with the police from a young age, they recorded him being of average intelligence and well-mannered.

It was also the clear recall of family members that Sinclair spent a period of time in some sort of residential care, although no one could remember the details of why this had happened, and no official records could be found. It may have been connected to the moody behaviour witnessed by family and teachers after his father's death. In those days, children were put into care for a variety of reasons which, unlike today, did not need to be explained or fully recorded. The stock phrase 'beyond parental control' covered a multitude of sins and often glossed over deep psychological problems. Perhaps the first clue to his future behaviour lay in that decision to take young Angus into care – we will never know. What we do know is that his mother was becoming increasingly concerned.

Sinclair's criminal career started in earnest in 1959, when he was fourteen. His string of petty offences – theft, housebreaking, breaches of probation – are all crimes you could see on a thousand young boys' records as they make the difficult transition through puberty in a bad neighbourhood and with the wrong crowd. But it's the kind of bad start that many boys survive. The vast majority recover – they grow out of their criminal ways and go on to be decent, sometimes even prominent, citizens. As they mature and have their ways mended, usually by a girlfriend or wife, their names disappear from the criminal records, often before they reach the age of twenty.

Because of this perennial trend, the Scottish Criminal Justice System does all it can not to stigmatise young offenders. The Children's Hearing System is criticised by many, and it does have difficulty dealing with the small group of very active offenders; but overall, for the 90% who do not reoffend, it is absolutely the correct response. There are of course exceptions – those who start in their teens and don't stop, those who go on to be career criminals and leave in their wake dozens, even hundreds, of victims. Angus Sinclair was just such a man, and it was at this very early age that the crimes of dishonesty, which were a constant in his background, were overtaken by the sex crimes that were to dominate his life and ensure his infamy.

In 1961, Sinclair appeared at Glasgow Sheriff Court charged with the offence under Scots law of Lewd and Libidinous Practices. This is one of the minor charges available for sex offences and it is usually applied when inappropriate behaviour that falls short of sexual assault has taken place. In what was to be a first sign of his character and nature, he denied the offence which involved an eight-year-old girl who lived just a few doors from Sinclair's family home on St. Peter's Street. Despite his protestations, he was convicted, and his future hung in the balance.

The social consequences were also dramatic. His actions were the talk of the neighbourhood, and he lost his job, his first after leaving school.

While awaiting sentence, Sinclair spent a period in a remand home where the authorities began having their first detailed look at his character without, it seems, any great success. He was again given probation – this time for three years. The probation officers who supervised him found him an enigma. He played the game, worked with the system he knew he could not beat, and he never, ever admitted his guilt. It is not all that unusual for a pubescent boy to be obsessed with sex, but few carry out their fixation to the extremes that Sinclair was to – especially at fifteen years of age.

That fixation with sex turned to utter tragedy just six months later, in July 1961, when he was arrested for the murder of a seven-year-old girl who lived in the same tenement block as his first child victim in St. Peter's Street. Not only was this killing carried out in the same place as the previous attack, but it happened while he was still subject to the probation order for the first offence.

Reading contemporary reports of that case over forty years later was a chilling experience. For someone so young to be capable of such a crime, and then to deny it and calmly try to cover it up as he did, showed that he was cool-headed and detached beyond his years. With the benefit of the hindsight I had that day, it was clear the killing of Catherine Reehill was an ominous sign of what was to come.

The newspapers of the day described what happened. Sinclair, still only fifteen, had been left alone in his home, a tenement flat in St. Peter's Street. He would have been secure in the knowledge that none of his family would be returning for at least three hours. It was a narrow window of opportunity, but it was enough, and it seemed to me that what followed was the execution of a carefully thought-through plan that was carried out with the cold single-mindedness, determination, and the disregard for his victim that was to become Sinclair's signature in later crimes.

The details of this crime were a first illustration of the modus operandi that would be used in later life. The events leading up to the death of the little girl on July 1st 1961 would be mirrored in crimes many years later. There was a carefully laid plan – gain the trust of the victim and then attack with overwhelming violence. Bear in mind that Maryhill in Glasgow in the 1960s was a close-knit and traditional community of working-class families who tended to spend their lives in and around the same areas. The families who lived in the tenements of St. Peter's Street would have been there for years and would have been on first-name terms with every one of their immediate neighbours, and on nodding terms with just about everyone in the neighbourhood.

Minutes after being left alone, Sinclair went out of the house, approached seven-year-old Catherine Reehill, and asked her to run an errand for him. He sent her to the corner shop to buy him some chocolate and instructed her to bring it to his flat. A willing little helper, she quickly ran there and back, only to have Sinclair force himself on her. He tried to have sex with her, but she fought him off, banging her head so badly in the struggle that there was blood everywhere. The details of what happened next do not need to be repeated in graphic terms here – suffice to say that he battered the little girl and raped her.

One of the most telling features of this attack was that, as Sinclair was carrying out his deadly attack, he was interrupted. There was a knock on the door of the flat and Sinclair, in the middle of his murderous assault, opened the front door wide. He appeared totally calm to his caller, a friend and neighbour of similar age, and, after agreeing to meet later that night, Sinclair closed the door and returned to killing. That kind of detachment is very telling. To be caught in the act of murder and be able to divorce yourself so coolly from what is going on so as to appear completely normal is hard to do. One could hardly expect that of a hardened criminal, let alone a boy of fifteen. This was no crime of passion, committed through a loss of reason – it was a cold-hearted plan, carried through with precision.

In his eventual explanation of the crime, Sinclair said that when he realised Catherine was dead, he carried her body out of the flat and down the common stairwell. He left it dumped at the bottom of the stairwell. There was, of course, no evidence to prove his version that she died from an "accidental" blow to the head during the struggle. She may equally well have been bludgeoned by Sinclair. Knowing his character, it is unlikely that Sinclair would have wanted his victim to survive to tell what had happened to her. He always tried very hard to escape blame.

The child's crumpled corpse was found a short time later by a neighbour returning home, and the alarm was raised. The position she had been left in made it appear as if the little girl had fallen down the steep stone stairs. Sinclair was one of the first on the scene and witnesses told how he was heard loudly demanding to know what had happened. The people who rushed to the stair brought by the neighbour's screams could not have been expected to guess at the truth of what had happened. At first, they just presumed little Catherine had fallen down the stairs. Sinclair alone knew how wrong the neighbours' guesses were.

It was not long though before suspicion fell on him – probably because of his very recent past offences. He was detained by police and questioned several times during the following days. He denied all knowledge of what had happened to the little girl, but detectives concluded that he was lying, and he was charged with murder. Later that night, after speaking to his brother, who he had always respected, Sinclair made an admission of sorts. He told officers what had happened and why. He said he had lost control of his sexual urges, there had been a struggle, and Catherine had banged her head.

Here was the first step up the ladder of offending, and a steep one at that. He had, just months before, committed a sexually motivated offence against a young girl. In this latest crime, the offence was grave and the outcome tragic. Looking back all those years, one question stands out – had he already learned that leaving his victim alive would be a mistake? His explanation that Catherine had banged her head appears improbable – there seems to have been a clearly premeditated killing followed by an equally clear attempt to avoid its consequences yet retain some control by his presence at the scene. In the immediate aftermath of the discovery of Catherine's body, Sinclair visited his brother and attempted to establish an alibi. Looking back, it was clear to see that officers in July 1961 were dealing with quite a sophisticated pattern of offending from a very young man.

Whilst on remand, Sinclair was examined at length by psychiatrists. The reports that survived the years remain confidential – suffice to say that he remained detached and seemed not to accept the gravity of his deeds.

*

As we digested the reports into Sinclair that were piling up in the incident room and spoke to people who had had dealings with him over the years, it looked as though we were going to have a tough job getting through to him when we eventually met him.

From the very first days after he was identified by the DNA profile from the World's End crime scene evidence, it was clear that, despite the passage of time and the fact that he was now in jail, Sinclair was not going to be an easy nut to crack.

Much of this early work had been carried out in secret, but my experience of dealing with the press over the years left me convinced that we were not going to be able to maintain that secrecy for much longer. By the time Operation Trinity was up and running, a large squad of officers was being assembled and I had been appointed Officer in Overall Command. As the inquiries grew more extensive and diverse, more officers from across Scotland became involved and a leak, either deliberate or accidental, would almost certainly occur. Inevitably, we would have to go public on the investigation. It might be to our advantage, for there was also the chance that some new information could come our way from the public following the widespread news coverage the inquiry would generate.

The downside would be that we would lose the element of surprise, Sinclair would find out what was happening and know that, sooner or later, we would be knocking on his cell door. It would give him time to prepare himself against what he knew was coming. It was our total determination that, when that day came, the officers interviewing him would know Sinclair as well as they knew their own families. They would know every aspect of his upbringing and offending. They would have a clear idea of his state of mind through detailed and painstaking study of all the various reports compiled over the years. They would also have a good idea of what he was like now. But what would the mindset of the man they would eventually confront be like?

By the time Operation Trinity was up and running, Sinclair had been held in the unit for the detention and treatment of sex offenders at Peterhead Prison on Scotland's north-east coast for some years. The wing of the bleak looking granite building dedicated to this work is universally known as the "Beastie Block". Because of this, most ordinary inmates find Peterhead objectionable, just as they dislike its remote location. Visitors from the Central Belt of Scotland must spend many hours by car or public transport to get there. Eight hours of travel from Glasgow and back and a two-hour visit makes for a long day.

Strangely, however, despite the bleak surroundings, our initial soundings of staff at Peterhead suggested that Sinclair rather liked it there. In fact, it seemed he was something of a model prisoner. One official at the jail, no doubt with tongue in cheek, went as far as to say Sinclair was 'as reliable as some of the staff'. It seemed that quite early on in his stay at the jail he was given trusted inmate status and allowed to work in the kitchen. Within a relatively short space of time, he had earned the respect of the jail authorities and had taken charge of the kitchen, where he maintained a strict regime amongst his fellow inmate workers. He was given responsibility for ordering food and other supplies and in this he showed his characteristic organisational skills and appetite for hard work.

It is well known that sex offenders can often be subjected to a hard time in jail from other inmates. One of the virtues of the Peterhead unit from the inmates' point of view is that all prisoners have similar offending backgrounds and, as such, there is a much reduced chance of the kind of abuse or physical attacks they might face in a mainstream jail.

Sinclair, by all accounts, had adapted well to jail life. He was so confident of his own position in the jail pecking order that he was known to hand out ferocious reprimands to trusty workers in 'his' kitchen if they failed to match his exacting standards.

The picture we were getting of the 2004 Angus Robertson Sinclair was very different from the one that had inevitably been formed from even a casual reading of his criminal record. The older Sinclair took pride in his work and was, in many ways, a model inmate. It was as though he had somehow managed in his own mind to divorce himself from the reality of his background. The merciless sexual predator, who, throughout a long offending career, had shown not one jot of remorse for his action or pity to his victims, appeared to have changed. He was now so trusted by the authorities in the jail and by his fellow inmates that he had a special place in the hierarchy. Inmates sought his advice and counsel, and the judgements he made of their circumstances were characterised as firm but fair.

It was against this background that, in consultation with the senior investigating officers of the forces involved in investigating all the murders that came under the umbrella of Operation Trinity, we decided to go public with details of our operation. I hoped to stop unhelpful publicity that might result from a leak from a source not fully in the picture of what we were doing, and even perhaps bring forward new witnesses to any of the individual cases.

I had no intention of revealing the name of our prime suspect nor even confirming it to reporters, but I was aware that some of the news outlets with well-connected crime reporters knew exactly who our suspect was. At a press conference at police headquarters in Edinburgh, I sat down, flanked by senior officers from the other forces involved, to give an overview of the operation, minus many of the details the press wanted that we needed to protect at this stage. We said we were interested in the unsolved murders of seven young women. At the time of this conference, we were still considering the possible connection of Sinclair to two unsolved murders in Dundee; although, when I sat down that day, there were increasing doubts that these killings were connected to our inquiries. Already, the few potential links with the Dundee murders were beginning to look a little shaky, but the inclusion of those cases in Trinity gave them new impetus and brought forward new lines of inquiry.

The following morning's papers were full of the story, naming Sinclair and giving extensive details on his background. Many experienced journalists in Scotland knew of the cases we were dealing with, and there had been previous speculation concerning Sinclair in some quarters. As the case was not at this stage active, which is to say sub judice and protected by the Lord Advocate's Guidelines and the Contempt of Court Act, the press could say virtually what they wanted without fear of the consequences. Few, if any, mentioned that first killing, that of Catherine Reehill, and we were pleased to see some other sensitive areas of the investigations had escaped the attention of reporters.

As our background inquiries into Sinclair progressed, we uncovered a lot of the detailed information about that first fatal sex attack. Aspects of it were highly unusual and we would find them repeated in later crimes. He had spoken of his sexual activity prior to the killing of little Catherine. Most of it had been conducted in association with other boys. He and one particular friend had been in the habit of having sex with either of two girls who had made themselves available in return for cigarettes. Usually though, it was Sinclair and his friend having sex with the same girl on the same night. He seemed to like to have a chum at hand. There was also a suggestion from Sinclair that one of his friends had warned him of the dangers of sexually transmitted diseases. This obviously struck home, for later he certainly seemed to have had a severe phobia about it – though not severe enough to prevent him continuing his behaviour.

In the Reehill case, the Crown Office, the prosecuting authority, had decided they would not be able to prove premeditation in the killing of little Catherine, and so Sinclair was charged with culpable homicide, the Scots law equivalent of manslaughter. He pled guilty. Before sentence was passed in August 1961, the Judge heard extracts of various reports, one passage of which is chilling in its accuracy. It predicted that no psychotherapy treatment would benefit such a sexual obsession and that young Sinclair would require constant supervision – failure to do this would result in continued sexual offending should he be given the slightest opportunity. These thoughts were prophetic indeed and, as we read them, they echoed down the years.

The Judge, Lord Mackintosh, branded the teenager "callous, cunning and wicked", and ordered that he be detained for ten years.

Reading the stark warnings contained in reports of over forty years ago and knowing what happened during the intervening period were sobering in the extreme. We could never say we had not been warned.

Despite being still only sixteen years old it was clear that, at the time, the authorities had no appropriate place to keep him and he was eventually held in the adult jail in Aberdeen for the first three years of his sentence. Who knows what lessons the young Sinclair was taught by older inmates and how this experience influenced his future behaviour? His time there may have even been the final building block in the creation of Sinclair and the public menace he was to become.

During his stay in Aberdeen, he worked at joinery and net-making, and had a spell in the cookhouse. Those monitoring his progress noticed how he formed firm friendships with older men, recidivists, and displayed a 'thinly veiled disregard for authority or guidance' – a dangerous omen of what was to come. Again, with hindsight, it seems wholly inappropriate that he was sent to an adult prison – young people of Sinclair's age should obviously not be in jail with adult prisoners. These days they would not be in an adult jail except in the most exceptional of circumstances and, if they were, the authorities would ensure they were closely monitored and held for as short a time as possible.

Sinclair stayed in Aberdeen until the mid-60s when he was transferred to Edinburgh with a view to his eventual release. One constant throughout this period of incarceration was a series of regular visits from his mother, Mary, and sister. It seems that they had rather fallen out with Sinclair's brother, who had obviously helped the detectives investigating Catherine Reehill's killing. Sinclair's mother and sister made the long trip to Aberdeen at least once a month to maintain contact.

After three years in Edinburgh Prison, Sinclair was put on to the "Training for Freedom" programme, a scheme designed to ease the passage from life in prison to life back in the community by learning a trade. During this time, Sinclair was allowed periods of home leave and he would stay with his mother at her new house in Bellfield Street in the east end of Glasgow.

There are no official records of the decision-making processes that led to his eventual release, but it is clear that when he walked free from jail in 1968, a very dangerous man was being allowed back onto the streets. It is worth reflecting on the facts that are known about his release from custody because they raise serious issues that still confront us today and are yet to be satisfactorily resolved.

All those involved with Sinclair at this time gave the same bleak assessment of his character. He was judged to be a liar who posed a risk for the foreseeable future. As he served that first custodial sentence, it became apparent that he had shallow emotions and no remorse for his crime. This was apparently seen by some as normal because of his age and the length of time he'd been behind bars. In retrospect, it seems more like an excuse rather than a reason and I would question these factors as a satisfactory explanation for someone's apparent inability to see anything wrong with killing a seven-year-old girl during a violent sexual assault.

Rather than prioritising his emotions and the likelihood of him reoffending, those holding the key to his cell seem to have been more concerned about his ability to find work on the outside, and perhaps their pragmatism is understandable. After all, here was a young man who had already come under negative influences, so they must have deemed it best to get him out of that environment sooner rather than later – and he had developed skills. In the jail in Aberdeen, prisoners could work for a well-established business that made fishing nets for the city's trawler fleet. Sinclair had worked in the net workshop for some time and had become adept at knot tying. This was something that would be of great interest to us later in the investigation.

Overall, it is clear he managed to keep out of serious trouble, though senior prison officers concluded this was largely due to his cunning and his ability to avoid getting caught and to work the system. During his first experience of jail, he had already adapted well to the loss of freedom. His future spells behind bars would see him continue in the same way and become the adaptable model prisoner.

Utilising the "Training for Freedom" programme, Sinclair took a painting and decorating course and obtained City & Guilds qualifications. Under the TFF programme, he would leave prison each morning to work on the outside and return to his cell at night. His first job was with an Edinburgh city centre firm of painters and decorators and so, with supreme irony, Angus Sinclair was first introduced to Edinburgh via the criminal justice system. He got to know the town while training for freedom – who knows how the future may have turned out had he been released from another prison? The law of unintended consequences can surely never have had a more catastrophic outcome.

The dire warnings of all those years before were obviously beginning to fade from memory and the main problem facing Sinclair, by now twenty-two years old, as far as the authorities were concerned, was to get him out and into a steady job that would set him on the straight and narrow. It usually works, but it is less successful for some offenders than it is for others. In fact, it would later be revealed that after his release, in the very first weeks out of jail, he had sex with a girl he knew to be only fifteen, fully aware that it was against the law.

The painting company that Sinclair worked for while he was training for freedom offered him a full-time job on his release, and so he began proper work. He became friendly with other decorators employed by the firm. One was a man who lived just off the High Street in Edinburgh – a few yards from the World's End – and Sinclair visited him at his home as their friendship blossomed.

Sinclair was under a supervision order for three years after his release. During the time he was being supervised, he was in regular contact with probation officers, and we discovered he'd had several girlfriends. Some of these women were traced and interviewed. They told us how Sinclair had bought a small van and he used to take some of them for runs in it throughout Edinburgh and into the neighbouring county of East Lothian, past the spots where Helen and Christine's bodies would be found years later.

Eventually, Sinclair entered into a more stable relationship with a hard-working girl, a student nurse he had met in Edinburgh. Just a month after his twenty-fifth birthday, he married the girl. Her name was Sadie Hamilton, but known to her family as Sarah. Eighteen months later, Sinclair became a father when Sarah gave birth to a son. The couple had, by this time, left Edinburgh and moved back to Glasgow, home city to both. They set up home in Nitshill. It was a good start – a steady job, a child and their own house – but married life for Mr and Mrs Sinclair was anything but smooth. The five-foot-two painter and decorator soon started a string of sexual relationships during their early married life – at least six. This led to periods of separation and, during one of them, he moved in with another woman. Despite this, Sarah felt that by the standards of the neighbourhood they had a normal married life, and his obsession with sex was just part of his nature.

She knew he had been in jail but was not fully aware of the nature of his crimes until many years later. She certainly had no knowledge of the fact that her husband, whilst supposedly out with friends or on fishing trips, had become a violent sexual predator.

During the mid-seventies Sinclair's reputation as a criminal was growing, not as a sex offender, but as a robber. That was about to change.

When he eventually made his next court appearance, it was at Scotland's highest criminal court, the High Court in Edinburgh, in the summer of 1982. There, Sinclair admitted eleven charges of rape and indecency involving eleven girls, ranging in age from six to fourteen, but he vehemently denied assaulting a boy of nine. His rape victims were aged just eight, ten, and fourteen. The other girls had also been subjected to terrifying ordeals over a considerable length of time, which must have left them in a state of trauma – I imagine it had marked them for life. The simple recitation of these facts cannot begin to give even the slightest indication of the suffering Sinclair caused to these unfortunate children and their families.

Each offence was similar. The girls were attacked in the entrances or closes of tenement blocks, either the one they lived in or one near their home. Each time he deployed the same methods. He enticed the girls into these often dark and deserted passageways by stopping them in the street and asking for directions, or asking them to run an errand for him in exchange for money – the same ruse as he had used in the killing of Catherine Reehill. It sent a shiver down our spines; these young girls had been lucky to escape with their lives.

Reading all this years later, it once again highlights a fundamental flaw in our criminal justice system. It is this – here we have someone clearly marked out as a high-risk offender who has been the subject of all sorts of reports, examinations and assessments, most of which offered dire predictions as to his likely future behaviour. But despite it all, he is freed into the community to commit the very acts all those who had contact with him knew he was capable of and predicted likely to perpetrate. Nowhere was there the procedure to intercede or prevent what was, for so many people, a plainly foreseeable disaster.

During Operation Trinity, we would question the chronology of his offending, and why he had switched from the adult victims of 1977 to children. The answer would come later but, regardless of the age of the victims, he was an offender who worked to an established pattern or modus operandi – he was a creature of habit, organisation and remorseless resolve. The alleged offence against the boy didn't fit his usual pattern but, because he admitted the other charges, it was allowed to remain on file. Sinclair would never have admitted a sexual attack on a boy. In the twisted logic of many sex offenders, there is a world of difference between attacks on females of any age and boys. It is a matter of preserving their own self-image – their macho honour.

Before his arrest, these attacks on children had been widely reported in the local press, but investigating officers had deliberately not publicly linked them, not wanting to start a panic. This soon changed: the widespread press coverage given to his court appearance meant that few inmates of Glasgow's Barlinnie Jail would have been unaware of his crimes when he joined their ranks on August 30th 1982. The Judge at Sinclair's trial, Lord Jock Cameron, was famous for his tough, no-nonsense approach to criminals. He had been one of the last Judges in Scotland to pass the death penalty. He sentenced Sinclair to life, recommending he serve at least fifteen years but adding the rider that, in Sinclair's case, he thought life should mean exactly that. Later, we were to wonder why this prolific child sex offender was not considered for the various crimes against adults then being investigated. The risk of tunnel thinking by investigators will be discussed later.

Being jailed as an adult paedophile offender was a tough lesson for the diminutive Sinclair. Despite his constant workouts in the jail gym and a near obsession with fitness, he had been given a severe beating by fellow prisoners on at least two occasions within weeks of his arrival in prison. After that, he was content to remain a protected prisoner under the rules designed to save sex offenders from inmates' jail justice. Even years later at Peterhead Prison's sex offenders unit, where he was by the time Operation Trinity had started, Sinclair's fear of violence from other prisoners remained with him. It was known that he did not relish a move back to the relatively unprotected environment of the general prison population.

As we progressed with the inquiry, we did sometimes reflect that this fear of being put back into the mainstream might work in our favour. The time would inevitably come when Sinclair would have to be formally questioned. This would be a lengthy process lasting for several days and might require Sinclair to be moved to a prison more convenient for this purpose. We hoped, somewhere at the back of our minds, that he might be so keen to stay within his comfort zone at Peterhead that he may decide to make a clean breast of all his crimes and give us a full voluntary confession. He had, on some occasions, been quite forthcoming in the past and been able to admit his guilt when it was clear there was a compelling case against him, and it was in his interests to do so. We realised that any confession he had made had been as a pragmatic response to a hopeless situation – when he thought he had a chance, he admitted nothing.

It became increasingly clear that the picture we were forming in our minds of the 2004 version of Sinclair was of a completely different person to the one jailed twenty years earlier. He seemed somehow to have reinvented himself and it was as though he believed there was no connection between this trusted, organised key figure in the smooth running of Peterhead Prison's kitchen, and the sordid offender that had done so much harm to innocent children. For him to admit his guilt in these killings, it would mean he would have to give up this self-deception and confront the demons of his past. It didn't seem likely, but only time would tell. He would know that one day in the not-too-distant future, he would be speaking to us.

Until that day arrived, it was not possible for us to predict what sort of reception we would get.

It was certain that, no matter what happened, we needed a clear and sophisticated strategy to make sure we got the best out of these eventual interviews. There would be no second chances. A key part of the success of the inquiry would be to carry out detailed profiling of Sinclair, to allow the officers who would eventually be tasked with interviewing him to know their man. They needed to be able to build some sort of bridge to his thinking to quickly establish a relationship which could allow them to get to the truth.

Perhaps unusually against this background of sexual crime, Sinclair's wife stayed in contact with him – not to any great extent but, after a few years, she even began visiting him from time to time. Sarah and their son had, by this time, moved to the south of England, so the journey to remote Peterhead would have been a long and difficult one.

Not long after his arrival at Peterhead, Sinclair had sought entry to the prison's sex offenders' programmes to seek help in overcoming his offending behaviour. It was a ruse; he was still playing the system. We found this particularly interesting because it was a classic example of split personality, or Jekyll and Hyde Syndrome. On the one hand, Sinclair was a model prisoner, trusted with the run of large parts of the jail including the administrative offices. The prison officers had faith in him and he, in turn, had never let them down. Yet, at the same time, there was a very different and dangerous persona in Sinclair. It was concluded that Sinclair was an extremely cold and callous person who still showed not a shred of remorse for his crimes. More worryingly still, he had not changed at all during his sentence. He was still dangerous and manipulative.

So, as one group of professionals were assessing Sinclair as devious and dangerous, others who worked with him day to day saw him in an entirely different light as a trusty, hard-working and reliable individual – a model prisoner in every way.

It was at this time that we first learned that Sinclair had spoken of being a victim of sexual abuse himself. Whether this was true or not, we will never know, but one facet of Sinclair's character was clearly emerging – his devotion to his duties in the prison and his ability as a painter and decorator both pointed to a need for approval. He was a perfectionist because it was a route to self-worth and esteem. A complex character was emerging – on the one hand, he was a violent man, a thief and a sexual predator who exercised power over women by extreme violence and, on the other, he was a perfectionist and a hard worker who sought approval and status by his labours. Angus Sinclair was two very different people, but to what extent did he realise it? Was he in control of both sides of his character? And where did the fault line lie?

The analysis of Sinclair was important, but we had practicalities to consider. What was quite clear to us was the fact that, whilst he may well not have been a model husband by virtue of his affairs, he did not appear to have been committing sexual offences during the early years of his married life. In fact, until 1977, when he was having difficulties in his relationship with Sarah, he seems to have kept himself under reasonable control. But then, for some reason, the balance changed and there was an explosion of offending that culminated in the horrific catalogue of crimes he admitted to in 1982, and The World's End Murders that we were investigating. What the trigger was, perhaps even Sinclair did not know. Was it the difficulties at home or were these domestic difficulties being caused by his descent into the depths of offending? Was it simply an uncontrollable urge or that he had freedom and opportunity? It was clear that he had offended both alone and with an accomplice. What were the factors that influenced that decision?

Whatever the answer to these questions were, one thing was clear – he was dangerous – and experts told us that an accurate assessment of his character was virtually impossible because of his ability to deceive. At times, he may have been less dangerous than others, but he was never safe.

Through the 1990s, Sinclair remained in Peterhead Prison and, despite the view of the Judge, Lord Cameron, in 1982 that he should remain in jail for the rest of his natural life, in the spring of 1997, the release process for Sinclair began again. As is routine, reports were compiled to allow decisions to be made and Sinclair, trying his best to appear open, gave some interesting accounts of his earlier behaviour. He described how his life, after his release from that first ten-year sentence for the killing of Catherine Reehill, revolved round home and work. He painted a picture of how he often put in very long hours at his painting jobs and inferred that his only relaxation was occasional fishing trips. He had few friends – particularly relevant for us later in our investigation was the fact that one of them was his wife's brother, Gordon Hamilton. They spent some time together, fishing and making occasional visits to various pubs.

The presentation of Sinclair prior to him being considered for release from the life sentence is perhaps the most telling of all. He would have to demonstrate that he was no longer a risk to society, and, of course, one of the strong indicators of this would be whether or not he had come to realise the full enormity of his crimes and show that he was truly and demonstratively sorry.

Peterhead Prison pioneered a programme for sex offenders which has won international respect. It aims to get offenders to confront their crimes and realise the dreadful effect they have had on their victims. Bear in mind that this unit in Peterhead was home to Scotland's most serious and prolific sex offenders. His participation in this programme would certainly have been one of the main considerations of the Parole Board when deciding on his suitability for release.

His first application for parole was declined in 1999, with the board concluding that Sinclair's lack of empathy towards his victims was an issue. They may also have feared there was still a risk of his reoffending, or at least that the risk of reoffending had not been eliminated.

His lack of victim empathy was best demonstrated by his clear belief that the little girls he targeted in those attacks in the late 1970s were somehow willing participants. One signature of his offending patterns then was that he would give money to those who he attacked. This clearly allowed him to square his conscience and, in his distorted thought processes, to consider that both parties in the attacks gained something from the experience. Clearly this twisted thinking would have been uppermost in the Parole Board's mind when they turned down his application. It is very common to fail at the first application to the Parole Board. The next time, with another year or so of exemplary reports, he would have a better chance.

That chance never came. Forensic Science was advancing, and Sinclair's past was starting to catch up with him. For the first but not the last time, justice would reach out for Angus Sinclair from beyond the grave.

The brutal sexual murder of diminutive seventeen-year-old Mary Gallagher in Glasgow in November 1978 had been the subject of a major police inquiry with thousands of man hours devoted to attempting to track down her killer. Her body was found on waste ground near a railway station in the Springburn area of the city.

The case, while still open, had long since been on a back-burner after detectives concluded they had explored every possible line of inquiry. Then, in the spring of 2000, officers received credible information, naming a specific individual as Mary's killer, and that person was not Sinclair. The lead was encouraging, and it came from a reliable source, so the inquiry was reopened and a new investigation began into the named suspect, who had not featured in the original inquiry.

The inquiry progressed well, with information being gathered on their new suspect's background and movements, with the eventual aim of arresting him and questioning him over the allegation. As part of that inquiry, old evidence from the crime scene was sent for further forensic examination and the new DNA testing. There was a quick result, and because of the very advances in that science that were to serve us so well later, a perfect DNA profile was obtained. But it wasn't the new suspect who was matched with the crime scene samples from Mary's body, it was another man already on the national database – Angus Robertson Sinclair. Officers quickly checked through their files and discovered that, in the huge database of suspects – thousands of names – he had not featured in the original inquiry. Mary Gallagher had been killed on an area of open ground.

She had been walking across the

Mary Gallacher - murdered on 19 November 1978. Her size gave her an almost child-like appearance. Angus Sinclair was convicted of her murder in 2001.

waste ground during the late evening in the company of a young local boy who she knew. He had run off after their progress was halted by a man standing nearby staring at them. Even though twenty-three years had passed, that boy, now a man, was able to look across the High Court in Edinburgh from the witness box to the dock and identify Sinclair as the man he saw that day as he was walking with Mary. He said how, as a child, he had been terrified by the man's staring eyes.

'He had eyes like dark holes,' he said.

The Jury, or at least most of them, concluded that such was the terror of the eleven-year-old that he was still able to recall accurately the eyes even two decades later as he looked at the greying man with those penetrating eyes now behind gold-rimmed spectacles. The DNA match, of course, was more compelling still, and Sinclair was again sentenced to life imprisonment.

So, by 2001, it was clear that there was more to Sinclair's offending than had first been thought. He was not solely an offender against children. The horrific attacks on the children had been preceded by the murder of Mary Gallagher. The obvious question was: what other crimes could he have committed? There were, after all, several unsolved murders of young women in the 1970s including the World's End killings, and several had taken place on Sinclair's home turf in central Glasgow.

We learned later that some senior detectives in Strathclyde believed that Sinclair was likely to have been responsible for other crimes. For reasons that were never satisfactorily explained, no further examination of Sinclair was made. And no information was passed to us in Lothian and Borders.

The Mary Gallagher trial Judge, Lord Carloway, imposed a life sentence, recommending that Sinclair should stay in jail for the rest of his natural life for what he called a 'callous, brutal and depraved act'.

When it happened, the murder of seventeen-year-old Mary had horrified Scotland and, as details of the killing were recounted at the trial, the passage of time before her killer was brought to justice had done nothing to dilute that horror. She had been strangled with the leg of her trousers and then raped.

At this point, it is very pertinent to note that, if Strathclyde Police had not received the tip-off – incorrect though it turned out to be – Sinclair would not have been convicted of Mary's murder and he may well have been released in 2001. There is no indication that the Parole Board would have said he was fit to be freed, but certainly the fact that the wheels were being put in motion to start the process that may have ended in his release is significant. His conviction in 2001 ensured that this would not happen. The Judge had made it clear. Sinclair had joined the club of a handful of killers in Scotland who would never be released from jail.

One other obvious question arises from the Gallagher case: had a false lead not caused the reopening of the case, would Sinclair have escaped justice for Mary's murder for all time? The answer is that for a time he may have, but eventually it is likely the truth would have emerged. As a consequence of The World's End Murders and several other historical cases, police forces are now routinely examining all unsolved cases and subjecting surviving forensic samples to the latest scientific techniques. The work of these 'cold case' units will surely bring resolution to some of the country's most notorious unsolved cases in the years to come. Many offenders, including rapists and murderers, will find themselves facing justice many years after they thought they had got away with their crimes. The Mary Gallagher case could well have been solved, not in 2001, but eventually.

That said, Sinclair's conviction in 2001 probably saved lives. Had he been released on parole, he would have certainly returned to his old ways.

As soon as Sinclair was convicted and the newspapers were no longer fettered by the contempt of court provisions, they began reporting the new development in the case of Sinclair. They were also speculating that he may have been responsible for other murders of young women in the west of Scotland. They detailed the potential victims as twenty-three-year-old Agnes Cooney, thirty-six-year-old Hilda McAuley, and twenty-year-old Anna Kenny, who were all murdered in 1977 around the same time as The World's End. The fact of the matter was that, whilst Sinclair was an obvious suspect of these killings, little was done to pursue further investigation.

The furor in the aftermath of the 2001 trial eventually died down and the press speculation faded, but it was not the end of interest in Sinclair and speculation as to the unsolved murders. Operation Trinity was to consider all these cases again in 2004. This time, no stone would be left unturned.

# 6

## The Second Man

But we still hadn't found the second man, or rather the first man – the one whose DNA profile we had identified all those years before and for whom we had been searching across the world ever since. We had spent thousands of man hours and hundreds of thousands of pounds in targeted testing, elimination screening and database searches – all to no avail. It had been a frustrating and puzzling exercise. Could it be that our man, the only profile we had identified for years, was a first offender? Was he dead? Or had he stopped offending before the practice of taking DNA samples from offenders had been established? We were desperate to find out and, now that Angus Sinclair had been identified as one of the men present on Helen and Christine's last night, we knew we were closing in.

We were sure that the unidentified man must be an associate of Sinclair. It was logical; the two men last seen with Helen and Christine in the World's End were obviously together – friends out for the night – and, while we were not certain that one of them was Sinclair, there was a very good chance he was. He was a very good likeness of one of the two strangers seen with the girls in The World's End pub. In any case, for two men to have been involved in such a crime and to have kept their dreadful secret for all those years, they had to be close.

As in all searches, we started at the centre and worked outwards, and Angus Sinclair was the centre. Using all the techniques available to us, old and new, we trawled every aspect of Sinclair's life to solve the puzzle – criminal associates, friends, workmates and relatives. It might seem as though this would have been a simple enough process, but it involved looking back almost thirty years with no current information as Sinclair had been in prison since 1982. It was to be yet another difficult exercise.

When the man's identity was finally confirmed, he turned out to be someone closer to Angus Sinclair than we could ever have hoped or imagined. By a process of elimination, we were able to determine, through examining the Y chromosome (the male chromosome) from the original unidentified DNA sample from Helen's coat, that it matched the paternal line of the five brothers of Sarah Hamilton, Angus Sinclair's wife. We eventually established that while being similar, none of the surviving brothers matched the World's End profile exactly. So, there were now two possibilities: the man we were looking for was either another sibling of the brothers, the only missing brother Gordon Hamilton, or someone totally unconnected with them.

As so often in cases like this, it came down to a calculation of probabilities. The scientists had to work out what the chances were of the DNA profile recovered from the bodies of the girls and Helen's coat *not* being that of Gordon Hamilton. By this time, we were being assisted by the National Crime and Operations Faculty, the national group of experts who gave us invaluable help.

One of their scientists gave us the answer.

Dr Jonathan Whitaker, one of the country's foremost DNA experts, was clear – the odds against it being Gordon Hamilton were at least thirty-eight million to one. In the careful language of the scientist, there was an extremely strong possibility that Gordon was the source of the sample.

We were now sure that Gordon Hamilton was the second man at the scene of The World's End Murders. By a process of elimination, Dr Jonathan Whitaker had followed the familial line of the Hamiltons and concluded, beyond reasonable doubt, that the crime scene samples found in the World's End case must have come from Gordon Hamilton. The only problem was that he had died in 1996. So, after all those years, there it was – Angus Sinclair

Gordon Hamilton, an enigma of a man who left little behind to mark his life. This was the best picture we could trace.

had been with his brother-in-law in Edinburgh that night in October 1977. After nearly thirty years, we were sure we had found the two men we were looking for.

To conclude the identification, all we had to do was trace a sample of Gordon's DNA and check it against the crime scene sample – straightforward, or so we thought. Most people leave traces many years after their death, hospital samples, possessions like a watch or a ring they have worn and left with traces of their DNA, clothes they have used or even family photographs they have handled during their lives. Depending on climatic conditions, DNA can survive for many years. We thought that, with a systematic approach, we could surely find some earthly trace of Gordon Hamilton – after all, at that time, he had only been dead for nine years.

The most obvious option was exhumation of Gordon's body – DNA remains detectable in the body for years, especially in bone marrow – but this was quickly ruled out as Gordon had been cremated. Thus began a bizarre, complex and long-running inquiry within an inquiry to track down some remnant of Gordon Hamilton. The search was to intrigue us and frustrate us and it became a fixation for Allan Jones, by that time a Detective Chief Inspector.

Once it became apparent that Gordon's mortal remains were beyond our reach, our next obvious choice was his possessions – a piece of jewellery, a cigarette lighter, a wallet; any article that had been his and that we could prove he had handled frequently and left behind. We drew a complete blank – Gordon had left nothing. Neither his wife nor his family had any keepsake that had belonged to Gordon.

We then decided to follow the medical route. Gordon had had regular illnesses, especially towards the end of his life, so perhaps the local hospital had a blood sample, or maybe samples had been retained from his post-mortem examination. We could find nothing. It was as if all traces of Gordon Hamilton had been erased – as if he had never existed.

By this time the search for a trace of Gordon Hamilton was becoming a personal challenge for the team and, in particular, Allan Jones. It will be already apparent that Allan doesn't give up easily and he wasn't about to now. We had been doing extensive background checks into Gordon's life since his DNA had been identified. We knew he was a strange man; arrogant and bombastic, opinionated, abrasive on occasions yet withdrawn, private and reclusive in other areas of his life. He had been a difficult man to assess – even his brothers and sisters could not paint a vivid picture of him. We even had difficulties getting a photograph of him until we eventually got hold of a faded family snap from his sister's photograph album.

However, we did know something about his work. He had been good with his hands and, from time to time, he did little jobs for friends and relatives – just basic electrical work or painting and decorating. As a last resort, Allan Jones and his team pursued this line of inquiry with vigour. We learned that he had carried out some electrical work in a house in Glasgow some years before he died. He had wired some bedroom lights for a friend, and this had entailed leading electrical cable behind a bedroom wall. This could be just the break we needed. If Gordon had handled the cables and the cables had been sealed behind the wall since that time, it was possible that he had left traces of his DNA.

Allan and his team found the house, got permission from the owners and recovered what we thought might be the cabling, but to no avail – no DNA traces could be found. But Allan Jones did not give up, and the hunt continued when we learned that Gordon had done some home decorating for a relative in Glasgow. We knew for sure that he had wallpapered a room in a flat in the centre of Glasgow and that he had put a polystyrene coving round the edge of the ceiling at the same time. There was little chance of recovering anything from the wallpaper or paint, but we thought that he must have handled the coving strips while putting them in place. If he hadn't worn gloves, perhaps somewhere on the coving there was a vestige of Gordon Hamilton.

In what was a last resort, Allan and his team found the house, deftly retrieved the coving, preserved it carefully and sent it to the Wetherby Forensic Laboratory, then leading in DNA technology. Swabs were taken and to our delight traces of DNA were found. The sample was tiny, but it was enough to make a match with the profile from the World's End sample. At last, we had found Gordon Hamilton.

It all sounds routine when written down. That conclusion, though, was the product of scientific endeavour going back to the day Helen and Christine's bodies were found. At various times, it involved work at the very cutting edge of science. The truth hiding in those samples had been elusive. Witnessing how DNA technology has evolved and helped us, just as it has the entire criminal detection process the world over, was one of the more fascinating parts of Operation Trinity.

But we still had much to do. We had identified Gordon Hamilton as one of our suspects, but we knew little of him. He was long dead and although he was known to the authorities, it was for minor scrapes with the law. We quickly learned that his relationship with alcohol had killed him prematurely but apart from that we knew almost nothing. Importantly, we had no firm evidence of the links between Gordon and Angus Sinclair and, evidentially, this was very important.

If we were to prove that a social relationship between Sinclair and his brother-in-law existed, we would need to conduct lengthy and often difficult interviews with surviving members of Gordon's family of ten brothers and sisters. Foremost amongst those was Gordon's sister Sarah, Angus Sinclair's wife. She, more than any of her siblings, knew the details of Sinclair's relationships with members of her family. It should be put on record that her help to our inquiry was invaluable and allowed us to progress further and faster than we would have without her assistance.

By any definition it is fair to say that the Hamiltons were a troubled family. The children appeared to have been brought up in terror of their domineering and sometimes violent father, and some of them went through adult life the victims of chronic alcoholism that led to the premature death of several, both male and female. Other siblings were persistent offenders and, as such, not the natural allies of the police.

We now know much more about the genetic inheritance of addictive personalities – the predisposition to become addicted to either alcohol or drugs, or both. If one of your parents is addicted, you have four times the chance of becoming addicted yourself; if both your parents are addicts you are eight times more likely. The Hamiltons are a tragic example of a family stricken and almost destroyed by addiction – in their case to alcohol.

It is to the credit of surviving members of this family, most of whom had difficult relationships with alcohol, crime or both, that in the main, they did their best to help us. Despite clearly incriminating himself in the process, one of Sarah's younger brothers volunteered details of the crimes of violence and theft he committed with Angus Sinclair. These offences were to form an important part of the investigation. He perhaps did not tell us the complete truth about his relationship with Sinclair, but he was frank enough to give us some key pointers.

When Operation Trinity was in its early stages, we were pretty sure that the DNA profile belonged to a member of the Hamilton family, but not which one it was. At that time, Gordon Hamilton did not jump out of the family profile as being the most likely candidate for Sinclair's accomplice in killing. According to all who knew him, Sinclair was most friendly with another of Sarah's brothers, who was some six years younger than Sarah. Sarah and her surviving brothers and sisters seemed clear that Gordon and Angus were on little better than nodding terms. The younger brother was by far the best prospect but the chance of him being the second killer was soon eliminated when he provided us with a swab for DNA testing. When the results came back, his DNA clearly did not match the profile of Sinclair's accomplice and he was ruled out as a suspect.

In trying to build an overall picture of Sinclair's involvement in his wife's family, we attempted to establish just how much the Hamiltons, individually or collectively, knew of his past. Sarah, for instance, knew that he had been in jail but was adamant she did not know anything of the details behind her husband's imprisonment other than perhaps having an inkling about it being for a crime of violence.

Sarah first got to know the man who was to cause her so much pain and anguish in Edinburgh, in the late summer of 1969. She was a student nurse and was introduced to Sinclair by a friend of hers who was already in a relationship with him. Not long after that, Sinclair and the friend split up and he took up with Sarah. When Sarah and Angus eventually married, her parents were not at the Edinburgh registry office ceremony. She is certain that, in the months after the marriage, when her new husband met his parents-in-law, he got on well with them, but it seems clear Sarah was ever mindful of the trouble she knew would ensue if her father found out about his past jail term, no matter what the nature of the offence had been. This fear was based on Sarah's sketchy knowledge of Sinclair's crimes. One can only imagine the likely reaction of her father if he ever found out the whole truth about his son-in-law – that he was a convicted child killer.

The complicated family relationships of the Hamilton clan were extremely important to us because of the DNA clues that were going to lead to the solution of the World's End killings. It is fair to say Angus Sinclair polarised the Hamilton family. There were those who detested him and went to any length to ensure they had no dealings with him at all. Sarah's brother Thomas, for example, completely forbade his wife to accept lifts with Sinclair even though she was very friendly with Sarah. To Thomas, Sinclair was a "nonce", prison slang for a sex offender, and, although he had no precise knowledge of his crime, he wanted his family, particularly his wife, to have as little to do with him as possible. However, Sinclair got on very well with another sister-in-law, and it seemed as if they had a close relationship. Somewhere in the middle of this spectrum of emotion and involvement was Gordon. On the face of it, the relationship between Gordon and Angus Sinclair appeared to be little more than a nodding acquaintance – just as other members of the family had described – but, as we were to slowly discover, Gordon was a man with another side to him, a hidden side which was to draw him into a friendship with Sinclair through their shared interests of the darkest kind.

*

Then there was the younger brother, who had been closest to Sinclair. His lifelong addictions to alcohol and crime had left him in a sorry state – we knew he was suffering from severe medical problems and living alone in London. However, when we tracked him down to the bedsit in the west of the capital where he was living, he was very helpful, especially after the severity and nature of the crimes under investigation were made known to him. Without hesitation, he outlined the crimes he and Sinclair carried out and he told us about one particularly brutal offence which would become an important piece of the jigsaw puzzle. The younger Hamilton told us of a crime, no doubt long forgotten by all except the victims, that gave us a real insight into Sinclair's method of operation, and would, we felt sure, tell a lot about the man we wanted to see in the dock. The fact that, by revealing details of this event, he incriminated himself in a serious offence is an indication of how far he was prepared to go to help us.

Heaven knows what the husband-and-wife victims must have thought at first when police came knocking on their door, apparently fired by a new determination to solve the crime that had been committed against them nearly thirty years before. The horrific nature of what happened to the couple in their then home in the Moodiesburn area of Lanarkshire, near Glasgow, meant they would not have forgotten the details of what occurred one awful day in April 1976 – even if they thought the police had.

Elizabeth Black had left her home in a typical tenement-style block of six flats in Bridgeburn Drive to go to her work in a nearby miners' club. It was Friday morning and the day the rent was due to be paid. Her husband,

John, had stayed in bed after a late shift at the factory where he worked, leaving their daughter in charge of the rent money. She wasn't well that morning and had stayed off school. Her mother had told the seven-year-old exactly what to do when the rent man arrived at his regular time later that morning – nothing could go wrong.

The young girl was watching television when there was a knock on the front door at about 10:00am. Having no reason to think that it could be anyone other than the rent man, the little girl opened the door without a second thought, only to be greeted by a terrifying sight. Before her stood two men with stockings over their faces – one was carrying a knife, the other a hammer. The taller of the two men dragged the hysterical youngster up the hallway of the house, holding his knife to her throat, whilst the second man burst into her parents' bedroom and, with a hammer, threatened her now wide-awake father.

Both were bundled roughly into the living room of the house and made to lie face-down on the floor. Quickly, the intruders bound the father and daughter's arms and feet with Sellotape, and both were gagged using the same material. They were then left alone as Sinclair and Hamilton waited for the rent man in another room in the house. Sure enough, before long, there was a knock at the door and the shout of 'Rent man!'. The homeowner could hear a violent struggle as the rent man was overpowered. Mr Black clearly heard the attackers demanding the keys to the safe that rent collectors kept in their vehicles. Then silence. A short time passed, and the taller man came back into the living room and thrust a bundle of notes towards Mr Black saying, "This is for your troubles – sorry about the inconvenience."

As the attackers fled with the rent money, the homeowner was able to break free from his bonds and help his daughter. On cautiously moving through the house, he found the rent collector bound and sitting in a chair in the kitchen. He was bleeding profusely from a head wound and blood was spattered across the floor. Obviously, the unfortunate man had been the victim of a level of violence that was far in excess of what was necessary to commit the crime.

By telling us this incriminating story in the detail that he did, Sinclair's brother-in-law left himself open to prosecution. Fortunately, it was decided that, under the circumstances and due to the long passage of time, it would not be in the public interest to put him in the dock for this serious crime.

This incident was important to us because of the insight it gave into Sinclair's character. It showed his ruthless use of a level of violence that was completely disproportionate to the crime committed. It was Sinclair who had taken a hammer to the rent collector to subdue him, and roughly bound and gagged John Black and his daughter to impose his will.

Ironically, another man had been arrested for the attack. Bizarrely, not long after the incident happened, he was picked out at an identification parade and subsequently put on trial. Thankfully, however, he was acquitted because he had a cast-iron alibi.

Although his brother-in-law spoke about many of the other offences he had committed with Sinclair, it was the robbery of the Moodiesburn rent man that he covered in the most detail. Just as important as Sinclair's appetite for violence was Hamilton's account of his capacity to remain unaffected by using such extreme brutality. Having terrified the father and his seven-year-old daughter and committed a vicious attack on the rent collector, Sinclair appeared back where he should have been only minutes later – on his painting job. He was perfectly calm and controlled, giving nothing away.

Sinclair had been working alongside his brother-in-law just round the corner from the flat when he happened to pick up two bits of information that led to him forming the plan to rob the rent man. He was told you could set your watch by the movements of the rent collector and then, in a different context, he learned that the homeowner would be at home and in bed after his night shift. Sinclair and Hamilton had put down their brushes, left the job and then, after Sinclair had carried out the violent attack, the pair returned. Sinclair was so unaffected by what he'd done that, to their workmates, it must have seemed for all the world as if they had just popped out for a sandwich.

This information gave us a valuable insight into the mind and working methods of Angus Sinclair – methods and behaviours that spanned the range of his offending, both sexual and non-sexual.

But we still had much to learn about Gordon Hamilton and his bizarre connections with some of the other crimes we were investigating.

# 7

## Family Ties

Sarah Sinclair has had to bear three great misfortunes in her life. None of them were of her own making but, despite all her troubles, she always maintained her dignity and always tried to help us where she could. Above all, she needed to protect the new life she created for herself after separating from Sinclair and the nightmare of her old existence. Spouses and families of notorious criminals are in a hellish position. At first there is a natural denial on their part, fostered by an instinct for self-preservation and the knowledge that the conviction of a close relative can bring disaster to the whole family. Sometimes, there is complicity that stops short of actual participation, but is dangerous nonetheless. The desire for self-preservation can close a relative's eyes to the obvious and leave them unwilling to ask the most basic questions for fear of what the answer might bring. As young detectives, we were always told that alibis provided by wives and mothers were never to be weighed heavily. Throughout our contact with Sarah, she convinced us that she was trying her utmost to deal with a difficult situation as best she could.

Many will be surprised that this nurse, who now lives in the south of England and has had nothing to do with Sinclair for many years, remains married to him. The fact is that, while it is clear their marriage ended in all but name many years before, she has simply never got round to divorcing him. Just why a woman who has done so much to build a new life in a different part of the world would remain married to such a man puzzled my team for a considerable period – until they got to know Sarah during many hours of interviews.

From the outset of this inquiry, it was obvious that Sarah Sinclair would be key to the successful outcome of our investigation. The many years that had passed since the commission of these crimes and the need to establish corroboration for all the evidence eventually to be laid before the court meant that we would have to go into minute detail examining every aspect of Sinclair's past, and Sarah would be able to help us more than most other people that had walked through his life. From the outset, we realised the importance of keeping Sarah on our side. However, it was also clear that recalling the everyday details of her married life twenty-five or more years before was going to be a very tough task. That those details were bound up in memories of what for anyone could only be described as a traumatic time would make the recall as painful as it was difficult.

The fact that Sinclair led such a secretive, compartmentalised life allowed him to commit serious offences and kill, yet leave many of those closest to him clueless as to the extent of his crimes. When he went off for one of his weekend painting jobs, Sarah had no reason to believe he wasn't doing what he said he was. At worst, she may have suspected he was pursuing one of his many affairs, but she would certainly have had no idea that he was carrying out the crimes that would be all over the newspapers in the days after he returned home.

Sarah or Sadie Hamilton was just nineteen when she met, fell in love with and married the man she knew as Gus. She was vaguely aware of the fact that Gus had been in jail before their marriage, but she didn't know why and, in fact, did not find out until sometime after the wedding. When eventually she discovered the awful truth and confronted her husband with the details of what she had found out, he admitted he had, as he put it, 'murdered a child'. For her part, Sarah found herself prepared to give him the benefit of the doubt and make allowances for his young age at the time of the crime. The man she married must have managed to project a very different image from what one would expect of a child killer.

Despite making allowances for his earlier behaviour, Sarah quickly realised that Gus Sinclair was a nightmare of a husband. Serially unfaithful and occasionally violent, he'd get involved in robbery, often executed with extreme violence, and he was totally unreliable. Sarah made that assessment based solely on the activities she knew about at the time or had cause to suspect.

It seemed clear to the team who had dealings with Sarah Sinclair that her life had very much been divided into two parts. She was born into straitened circumstances and raised in a dysfunctional family whose lives were largely dominated by petty crime and drink. She'd had a difficult childhood by any standard. From early on, however, Sarah seemed to have been determined to put that behind her and strike out on a different course from the one that seemed preordained for her. The route she eventually took certainly diverged markedly from the one followed by the rest of her brothers and sisters.

As we have seen, it was clear that Angus Sinclair's major personality traits included deviousness and a total lack of empathy for the victims of his crimes. Now we were keen to learn how those characteristics manifested themselves to someone close to him, and who better to help us than his wife?

During her husband's time of offending through the second half of 1977, Sarah had not one iota of a suspicion that he might be guilty of the crimes that shocked the country and had everyone talking about them. Each of those killings in Scotland's Central Belt generated immense publicity, and none more so than The World's End Murders. Years later, all who knew him at that time who we were able to trace were certain that Sinclair showed no outward signs of any involvement in the crimes. He seemed perfectly normal and at one with himself. It was as though he must have been able to kill in the most bestial and depraved way and then, by the time he was back home with his family, behave in what passed for a perfectly normal manner.

The capacity to conceal what was going on from those closest to him may seem astounding but it is not uncommon in criminals who disassociate their crimes with the rest of their lives. They compartmentalise their lives as a defence mechanism and to normalise their existence.

From the Word's End Murders in the autumn of 1977 to the 1978 murder of Mary Gallagher, and through to the sex attacks on children in the next decade, we believed Sinclair had been murdering young women and then raping children. This meant that, in the Central Belt of Scotland between 1977 and June 1982, he had been committing these most brutal of crimes on a regular basis, yet Sinclair had managed to appear perfectly normal to those around him. On top of this appalling list of sexual offences, there were also crimes of dishonesty and violence. Carrying on this kind of lifestyle required highly developed organisational skills – in fact the very sort of skills that would lead to his position of responsibility running the kitchens of Peterhead Prison in later life. In the 19th century, Robert Louis Stevenson famously embodied the split personality of his characters Dr Jekyll and Mr Hyde. In the 20th century, Angus Robertson Sinclair embodied it.

Sarah and Gus had many periods of separation, each one coming in the wake of her discovering his latest affair. Each time, he would talk his way back into the marital home, with Sarah relenting because of a mixture of her feelings for him and a strong desire to do the best for their son.

At our headquarters even we, a hardened group of detectives, wondered about Sinclair's skill in appearing normal despite the horrors that he must have been carrying in his mind. How could it be possible for someone to behave in such a manner and show no outward signs?

If you measure his crimes purely in terms of numbers, Sinclair is not the most prolific killer in recent British criminal history. However, the sheer concentration of his offending places him in a league of his own. The number of victims, women and children, whose lives he ended or left devastated, and the grief and anguish inflicted on their friends and families can scarcely be imagined. That he was able to get away with it undetected for so long is a matter we will discuss later in this book.

Often, crimes like the ones we are dealing with here are solved after a tip-off from a member of the offender's circle after a slip-up by the perpetrator: a shared confidence to ease a troubled mind, or a change of behaviour so out of character as to cause suspicion. The way Sinclair appears to have been able to compartmentalise his life to shut out details of his crimes from his mind and control his emotions meant he gave nothing away, even to those closest to him.

The officers in my team were completely certain that, if Sarah Sinclair had had even a suspicion of what her Gus was doing on his weekends and evenings away, she would have had not the least hesitation in reporting him to the police. If only he had given her that suspicion, if only his guard had slipped even slightly, we were convinced she would have ended it there and then. Sinclair did not give Sarah that opportunity.

When Sinclair was arrested on June 7th 1982, accused of the series of child sex crimes, the effect on his wife was devastating. Their son was eleven at the time, an age when he would have been old enough to have been aware of the general circumstances and enormity of what was going on. The months between Sinclair's arrest in June 1982 and his sentencing at the High Court in August of that year are the last time Sarah had any real interaction with her husband. It was during what would have been one of their last conversations that Sinclair uttered a sentence to Sarah that leads me to believe he may have many more crimes to answer for.

He was on remand to Barlinnie Prison in Glasgow awaiting trial, no doubt passing time reflecting on his likely defence. It was not in his devious nature to admit wrongdoing. Sarah had other ideas, and we know that she told him in no uncertain terms that, if he was guilty of the child sex charges, he should make a clean breast of it. She told Sinclair straight that she did not want to be dragged along with their son into what would undoubtedly be a horrific trial featuring days of little children giving the most distressing evidence. She also expressed to him her growing fear that he may be responsible for other crimes he had not yet been caught for. Sarah must have been worried, knowing what she did about his past, that he may even have killed other children. In the visiting hall of Barlinnie, Gus was challenged as never before and urged to admit his guilt to save his family and victims from the ordeal ahead. Somewhere in the words that followed Gus did exactly that, saying he was indeed guilty of the offences outlined in the charges. He then added that no one yet knew the scale or scope of his crimes. These references haunt all who have had dealings with Sinclair as well as the relatives of the many females that went missing during the years Sinclair was free to stalk the streets of central Scotland. We will probably never know the true extent of his crimes and how many victims, dead and alive, that he left in his wake during that awful time in the late 70s.

While we carried out a detailed examination of all unsolved murders of women in Scotland, there is still the massive grey area of missing persons. In considering dozens of MISPER (missing persons), it chilled me to read frequent phrases like "May have gone away with boyfriend" or "Believed to have run away to London", which often concluded missing persons reports. They constituted a guess, albeit sometimes an educated one, but nevertheless they represent a life being written off in a vague sentence and a haze of uncertainty.

The second of Sarah Sinclair's tragedies is, of course, the fact that her brother Gordon was, for at least part of the time, her husband's partner in crime, even though they didn't seem close. They certainly did not have the protective relationship that one might expect joint perpetrators of such serious crimes to have. I suppose it could be that the knowledge of the crimes they shared did as much to keep them apart as bring them together. It is extremely hard to imagine the relationship that could exist between two human beings involved in such dreadful crimes. Would they, when alone, go over the details of the World's End killings, reliving the satisfaction they derived from the murders, or would they blank it from their minds and never discuss the events of that night? To rationalise their behaviour may have been the way they dealt with it. Whatever they did, neither gave an inkling to those closest to them.

Investigators always think it is in their favour when two people are involved in one crime, particularly a dreadful one. There are many ways this can be a distinct advantage. They may fall out, with one turning so-called King's evidence against the other in the hope of a lesser sentence. With two suspects, you also have twice the chance of something being inadvertently given away during interview.

There is a basic human compulsion to talk about matters that may be weighing heavily on your mind but, as far as we could discover, neither Angus Sinclair nor Gordon Hamilton ever disclosed what took place between them. Hamilton, of course, took his secrets to the grave with him when he succumbed to the effects of his family's curse of alcoholism in 1996.

Whilst we may never know the exact nature of the relationship between Gordon Hamilton and his brother-in-law, one thing is clear – there was bad feeling within the Hamilton family towards both. Gordon Hamilton was found even by those close to him to be pompous and overbearing. There was little contact between Gordon and his parents and siblings after he had left the family home. The family was aware that Gordon had married but beyond that they knew little about him. In fact, such was the distance between Gordon and the rest of the family that, even after Angus Sinclair's arrest, they remained oblivious to many details of his life until our officers made them aware of what had been going on.

We eventually learned that before Gus was detained over the sex attacks on children, he and Gordon had occasionally spent weekends together. They said they were going fishing and, while they were away, they lived in the caravanette camper van Angus had bought – a vehicle that was to play such an important part in our subsequent inquiries. We learned that, despite these lengthy trips away, Angus never brought home any fish – at the time, this would have seemed insignificant, but in hindsight, it was suspicious. These were sensitive issues, and during the early part of Operation Trinity, we were not able to tell Sarah Sinclair of the scope of our inquiries or where they were heading.

Gordon's partnership with Sinclair posed a further problem for us. It was simply that Sinclair had the best kind of co-accused – a dead one. We felt certain he would at best try to minimise his part in the crimes. We knew that even he would find it hard to explain the presence of his DNA – especially in the locations it was found in the World's End case – but, despite this, he and his lawyers were certain to try. He would blame Gordon Hamilton for everything he could and cast himself as the minor assistant. We were certain that sooner or later Gordon would be a convenient scapegoat.

It would be some way down the prosecution process before his legal advisers would have total disclosure of the evidence of the case for that sort of tactic to be deployed. This possibility underlined the need for the interviews we would conduct with Sinclair to be the most carefully planned and executed encounters that would leave nothing to chance, no holes to be wriggled through later. It was unlikely that Sinclair would say much when being questioned, but we had to try to close down opportunities for false defences that would be certain to be conjured up at any future trial. We were right, but it would be a long time until our fears were justified.

We did not think that Sinclair would try to blame Gordon Hamilton right away. For a start, he wouldn't know that we knew about Gordon until the evidence was disclosed and he would certainly not wish to voluntarily lead us to an area in which he may have thought himself vulnerable. We were even uncertain as to whether Sinclair knew that Gordon was dead. More importantly, Sinclair could not have been unaware of the extent of our evidence – especially the damning DNA profiles.

As we gave thought to these matters, I expect our suspect did as well. Sinclair had a good reason to fear DNA technology. After all, it was what had brought him to justice for the Mary Gallagher killing at the very time he thought he was heading for parole and freedom. He must have spent many hours in his Peterhead cell wondering and worrying about what other forensic productions may be lying in laboratories and police storage cupboards waiting to be discovered and bring about the next stage in his downfall. With increasingly sophisticated DNA analysis and cold case reviews taking place across the country, many offenders who had thought they got away with their crimes had good cause to think again.

This is where our contact with Sinclair's family became invaluable. For them, having to put so much energy into trying to recall the minute details of the life of a man they had long wanted to forget about must have been frustrating and difficult. For Sarah, there was an additional problem impacting on her life. As any mother would be, she was desperate to protect her son who, by this time, was a young man.

Over many hours of interviews, from the moment her husband was arrested in 1982 right up to and especially during the preparation of the World's End case, Sarah's memory was put to the test. As various matters took on a new urgency or importance, she would be reinterviewed again and again. Details of cars owned by Gus and how long he had driven them for were hard to recall but the information was vital to us. These recall sessions would be even more difficult for her as she had clearly put such a lot of energy into building a new life far removed from the tough areas of Glasgow where she was brought up and spent so much of her tortured married life with Gus.

One of the other key relationships in Angus Sinclair's life was with Sarah's younger brother. He had lived with them for a while, and we learned that during that time he had been involved with Angus in a variety of crimes.

This Hamilton brother was forty-eight years old when we tracked him down to a bedsit in London. We first spoke to him at the time it had become clear from the DNA evidence that the second World's End killer was certainly a member of the Hamilton family – maybe himself and, if not him, certainly one of his brothers. We were still gathering DNA samples from the surviving siblings so there was always going to be the chance that this man was Sinclair's partner in crime. In fact, when he realised how serious the crimes in our inquiries were, he was open and candid in a way we might not have expected from someone of his background. It soon became clear that he was indeed a partner in crime with Sinclair, but not the crimes we were most interested in. During the time he was staying with his sister, Sarah, and brother-in-law, Gus, the young man had become deeply involved with Sinclair and his violent robberies.

Sinclair had managed to get his young brother-in-law a job with the painting company he worked for in Glasgow. We learned how he and Gus would often return at night to office premises, where they had been painting by day, and steal. These robberies went on undetected for some time. Then Sinclair and the younger Hamilton moved on to till snatches, bursting into a shop or garage and, under the threat of violence, or more often with real violence, making off with the contents of the cash register.

As we had learned from the description of the Moodiesburn rent man robbery, the level of violence used was extreme, and we discovered that Sinclair's favoured tactic was to take a hammer to the head of his victim without threat or warning. Another particularly horrific example of this occurred in Cumbernauld, near Glasgow, when Sinclair had attacked a car salesman's daughter who was carrying a relatively large sum of money. Sinclair had lashed out at the terrified woman with the hammer but fled with no money. After they made their escape, Sinclair lost his temper with his brother-in-law, accusing him of bungling the attack and losing the proceeds.

In another raid on a garage, following information Sinclair had gathered from a prostitute, overwhelming violence was used. Then there was a brutal attack on a man selected at random as he emerged from a pub in Glasgow. In the dark, Sinclair pounced on the man and beat him with the hammer before stealing from his victim, seemingly as an afterthought. It was quite clear that Gus was a gratuitously violent man.

The younger Hamilton appeared to be trying to help us and knew that, in doing so, he was incriminating himself in serious offences. But, the officers who spoke to him felt he was not being entirely frank. There was a suspicion he was holding back. In fact, by checking the stories of other family members, it was quite clear there were areas he was not prepared – or perhaps not able – to go into. He may not have been able to tell as much as he might have once been able, as years of alcohol-related illness had taken their toll on his mental faculties. However, it was hard to determine what had been lost from his memory and what was being hidden away at the back of his mind.

All in all, the Hamiltons were as helpful as they could be about Gus. It was clear that, while they knew of his involvement in crime, they had no idea of his violent sexual offending. His wife's strongest indication of Gus's other side came during a police investigation into the strange case of Edward Cotogno. A Glasgow man, he was a clever, able, but seamy individual who used his photographic hobby to deal in home-produced pornography, much of it involving very young local women. In June 1979 he was found dead in the charred remains of his Glasgow home after a fire. He had met a violent end before the fire had been started and police concluded he had been murdered. Extensive inquiries were carried out over many months, but no culprit was found. Angus Sinclair and Eddie Cotogno were connected, and what happened to Eddie and why remains an intriguing part of this story. At the time of Eddie's death, however, the police knew that Angus Sinclair was one of many of Eddie Cotogno's seedy contacts who had to be traced, interviewed and eliminated – or become a suspect.

At the time of Cotogno's death, Glasgow detectives were frequently at Gus and Sarah's door wanting to speak to Sinclair because they suspected he was involved in robberies or other crimes about the city. On this occasion, they had phoned to make an appointment to see him, and Sinclair had straight away told his wife he thought it would be about the death of a man he knew. He said he could not tell the officers where he was at the time of the killing for unspecified reasons and asked Sarah to provide a false alibi for him and say he had been at home with her. This she did, despite her concerns and fears. Once again, it seems the old rule about not setting too much store by wives' alibis proved true.

We learned that Sinclair had secretly tape-recorded the officers speaking to him, so worried was he about the police investigation. However, we uncovered no hard evidence to connect Sinclair to the death of Eddie Cotogno. But the investigation into his murder got close to Gus and that certainly unnerved him.

The more we found out about Sinclair's life from his family, the more we realised what a difficult situation it had been. One of his first extramarital affairs had been with one of his wife's relatives and it started not long after they married. His wife was kept in the dark about her husband's history by members of both her own family and his – several of whom knew only too well the details of his past.

During Sinclair's married life there had been frequent periods of time when he'd lived away from the family home. Typically, he worked at his painting jobs through the week in and around Glasgow and then went off at the weekends, regularly staying away until the Monday morning. He was away so often that he didn't find out about the birth of his son, which

99

had occurred on a Saturday, for twenty-four or more hours because he was out and about in Edinburgh.

The pressures mounted and eventually, completely frustrated at Sinclair's inability to assume the role of a normal husband and father, the family split. Time passed and healed some of the problems. Sarah knew of Sinclair's numerous affairs, and she had to bear the additional burden of his self-confessed relationships with prostitutes but, despite this, she would allow Sinclair to come back home time and again for the sake of their child.

It was during this rocky period in their marriage that the younger Hamilton moved in with the Sinclairs and his crime career of theft and robbery with Gus began. By then, Sinclair had the caravanette that was to become enormously important to us, as it was the vehicle he owned when the World's End and other murders were committed. It was also about this time that Sinclair developed an interest in photography. It was thought benign until the day his wife Sarah found pornographic snaps of Sinclair and a girl taken with a timer device. This caused a huge family row, but the photos were burnt and his convoluted explanation for having them was accepted. In hindsight, this new behaviour was significant – especially since it linked Angus Sinclair with a like-minded character, the murdered Eddie Cotogno.

Some people might find it difficult to sympathise with Sarah Sinclair – after all, she knew of some aspects of Gus's criminality. That she tolerated it may be seen by some as tacit approval. I do not agree with this view. Like many wives and partners of criminals, Sarah found herself sucked into the vortex by an evil and manipulative man. She struggled free and now she deserves to be able to put this awful part of her life behind her. In truth, Sarah Sinclair is another one of Angus Sinclair's victims. She wasn't murdered, raped or even seriously physically attacked, but she will bear the scars inflicted by him for the rest of her life.

Press speculation made the
links, just as we did

101

# 8

## Operation Trinity

In early 2004, as soon as we had DNA linking Angus Sinclair with the World's End case, we began to examine all other murders and disappearances of young women in the late 70s and early 80s very closely – especially those that bore a resemblance in method or modus operandi to the World's End killings. From the start, we were surprised just how many killings there had been in that very narrow time frame. Later, when "Scothom", the name given to the comprehensive database of homicides of women in Scotland from 1968 to the present, was constructed – a huge and important piece of work done by Strathclyde Police – the picture was even more alarming. We tend to assume that, in the 21st century, we are living in the most violent of times. While comparisons are sometimes difficult, the 1970s was no haven of tranquility either.

After detailed study, it appeared that the cases of three women murdered in the Glasgow area – Anna Kenny, Matilda (or Hilda as she was usually called) McAuley and Agnes Cooney – and two in Dundee – Carol Lannen and Elizabeth McCabe – bore close similarities to The World's End Murders. Together with Helen and Christine, we had a total of seven victims – young women from three areas of Scotland who had all been murdered during the period from August 1977 to February 1980 – and all seven cases remained unsolved.

Because of the three distinct areas in the investigation and the three forces involved, the name 'Trinity' was chosen for our combined investigation and, despite the fact that the Dundee cases were quickly eliminated from the inquiry to subsequently go their own way, the name stuck. I was appointed by the three Chief Constables to be the Officer in Overall Command, tasked with leading the joint effort and ensuring close co-ordination by the different investigation teams from Lothian and Borders Police and Strathclyde Police.

The role of the Officer in Overall Command was a relatively recent innovation, which had come about as a result of the inquiry in the aftermath of the error-ridden "Yorkshire Ripper" case. The first officer to fill the role of OIOC had been my old boss Hector Clark in the investigations into the murders of Susan Maxwell, Caroline Hogg and Sarah Harper. I was aware that I had big shoes to fill. The main criterion for appointment as an Officer in Overall Command was holding the rank of chief officer, having a background in major criminal investigation, and having extensive experience in leading large teams. I was fortunate to be qualified, for I would have hated to miss what I thought would be the last phase of the World's End investigation. It wasn't, however, the easiest of roles. On the one hand, I was ultimately responsible to the Chief Constables and directly accountable for all aspects of the inquiry. On the other hand, it would have been unwise for me to interfere with the individual investigations too much or overshadow the senior investigating officers in the individual cases. They were highly experienced and senior detectives. Detective Superintendents Ian Thomas and Eddie McCusker, backed by Allan Jones in Lothian and Borders, and Colin Field in Strathclyde, were an impressive mix of old heads and young potential. Added to that was the fact that, frankly, they had a lot more recent experience in murder and major crime investigation than I had. In any joint investigation, there will be tensions and competing priorities, with pride and frustration sometimes boiling over, but in the many months we were together, these were always managed and overcome. I had other advantages. I knew most of the members of the Lothian and Borders team, both police and civilian, personally. Lastly, but importantly, I was given a very good, bright young staff officer in Detective Sergeant Stuart Hood, and I managed to take my personal assistant, Jeanette Shiells, with me. Jeanette and I had worked well together for twelve years, and she knew my foibles. These details may sound mundane, but in the careful balancing act of the Officer in Overall Command, they were immensely important.

Running a linked investigation, particularly one focused on historic undetected homicides – cold cases – may sound simple, but it is not. Strict rules and protocols have to be followed if the process is not to become confused and ineffective. For that reason, all police forces in the UK closely follow the 'Cold Case Review Guidance' given by the Association of Chief Police Officers in England and Wales, which is based on the long and sometimes bitter experience of murder squad detectives. It may surprise some people that historic undetected homicides are a problem requiring such a complicated response, but they are. In the ten years up to 1979, there were over 700 cases of homicide where either no one was charged or the accused was acquitted, and that was only in England and Wales.

It is a surprising total, but with new techniques and ever- improving forensic science, many of these cases have been resolved with more to follow. Now, when police forces embark on a historic re-investigation, it is not only with new forensic tools, but with the benefit of the accumulated experience of scores of cases. We now have a better understanding of the value of new forensic techniques, not only in DNA, but in how useful fingerprints, hairs and fibres can be when subjected to new science. The use of lasers, digital imaging and computerised databases all mean that, provided they have been gathered and stored properly, materials recovered from crime scenes, even those considered worthless, can have enormous evidential value. But it is not only in new science that advances have been made. The role of expert independent advisers can be a great advantage. In our case it was an expert forensic adviser, Professor David Barclay, who was of huge assistance, while the advice given by our behavioural psychologist gave us insight into the predicted behaviour of witnesses and suspects, all of which gave us an edge.

A major element in the World's End case was of course the DNA samples and the hairs and fibres recovered from Helen's clothes, and from her coat in particular. But even this was not straightforward, for we had to demonstrate that, over the thirty years they had been in our possession, there had been no opportunity for contamination of the productions. A thirty-year audit trail had to be carried out to prove every movement of the materials and the supervision that attended them. It says much for Lester Knibb and his colleagues that this did not defeat us, for the records had been meticulously kept.

In linking our inquiries, we always followed the latest guidelines and best practice. In TV dramas and fiction, the officer in charge of murder investigations usually confronts the suspect, dazzling all with his or her deductive skill. In reality, the Officer in Overall Command of a linked investigation must pay more attention to policy files and coordinating teams if the investigation is to succeed.

Thankfully, in all these difficult areas we were helped magnificently by the National Crime and Operations Faculty then based at Bramshill in Hampshire. Their knowledge and network of experts provided all the help we needed. The advisory team of experts established to assist us was first class. None of these structures or systems were there to help the detectives in 1977. It would not have occurred to them, even in their wildest dreams, that such methods of working could be possible.

By the summer of 2004, it was clear that we were building a compelling case against Angus Robertson Sinclair for The World's End Murders. There was a growing sense of achievement amongst the teams involved in this major, complex and long-running inquiry. We had started the journey with some hope of reaching our goal, but, in the early days, there were inevitably doubts that we would be able to reach back through the long passage of time and find the supporting evidence we needed to once and for all allow us to achieve justice in this truly iconic case.

Our trump card was the DNA evidence from the World's End killings, but we also had some circumstantial evidence in the cases of Anna Kenny, Matilda McAuley and Agnes Cooney, all young women murdered in the Glasgow area around the same time. We lacked any forensic evidence in these cases, however, and this was crucial.

In the end, it was judged by the prosecuting authority in Scotland, the Crown Office, that we simply didn't have a good enough case to prove the matter beyond reasonable doubt, and this was a bitter disappointment to all of us. It was especially felt by the Strathclyde team, who had done so much to prepare a case against Sinclair for these three murders based on the little evidence that had survived the passage of time. The lengths they went to in trying to make up the evidence gap were remarkable, and their commitment was total.

In the aftermath, much has been made of the lack of forensic evidence in the Glasgow cases. Where were the samples from these cases? Were they lost? Destroyed? If so, why? We will never know for sure what happened to that forensic evidence. We will discuss this later, but before the armchair experts and journalists with perfect hindsight begin their critiques, it is worth remembering the state of forensic science back in the 1970s.

Forensic work on fingerprints, blood, hair, and fibre was already well established, but, although the presence of DNA had been proposed by a Swiss doctor in the 19th century, and Crick and Watson had developed the theory further in 1953, in those days, it was unknown as an investigative tool. Even ten years later, in the late 80s, when I studied at the FBI Academy in Washington D.C. with a faculty with limitless resources and cutting-edge forensic facilities, DNA was only beginning to emerge as an aid to detecting crime.

In the late 1970s, the future of DNA was unknown, and in the early days of the late 80s, forensic samples were often tested to destruction during their examination. This may have happened in the Glasgow cases, or they may have simply been destroyed, having been deemed as being of no further apparent evidential value. During the investigation in 2004–5, the team from Strathclyde Police carried out extensive searches for these samples. No stone was left unturned by Detective Superintendent Eddie McCusker and his team, but without success. It was a major disappointment to these determined and professional officers, but who knows? The missing forensic samples may yet be discovered; they may yet give up their DNA secrets.

Why had the senior detectives of the late 70s not linked the cases back when they were first being investigated and when all the evidence was fresh? The publicity generated by the murders in Edinburgh and Glasgow had been immense. Reading the news clippings of the day, it was clear that there was a public outcry in the truest sense. In addition, some journalists were openly linking the cases and claiming that one man was responsible.

On the face of it, the police were not convinced, but formal linking was, in fact, considered as early as 1980. That year, heads of CIDs from Scottish forces with unsolved murders of young women on their patches held a conference in Perth – a convenient and discreet point for them to gather from throughout Scotland. They met to decide if any joint action should be taken by their respective investigations. Should they be linked either publicly or internally to pool information and speed up detection? In effect, they had to decide whether the crimes were likely to be the work of one man.

No records from those discussions survive but the outcome is known. The senior detectives decided to continue the inquiries as separate entities with no formal element of linkage. This, I rather fear, was a decision taken out of operational and political pragmatism rather than sound policing instincts. When seen from the time of Operation Trinity, I believe the judgement of those senior officers was probably influenced by the ghost of the man known in the press as "Bible John".

*

There had been a series of three killings of women connected to the Barrowlands dance hall in Glasgow during 1968 and 1969. A single culprit had been created in the minds of journalists and, through them, the public at large. The image of a serial killer had been formed and he had been given the nickname of "Bible John" because witnesses in one of the murders had spoken of a strange and creepy individual using biblical quotations in his everyday speech at the dance hall on the night of one of the killings. It was a classic case of the press headline selling the story and driving the investigation. At the time, there was real and widespread public alarm at the thought of "Bible John" stalking the streets of Glasgow looking for his chance to pounce – a 20th century "Jack the Ripper".

The true facts of the case are rather different. Whilst many suspects have been in the frame over the years as a potential "Bible John", it is likely that one man was not responsible for all three killings and there was no "Bible John". This, of course, was not a theory favoured by conspiracists who had rather warmed to the presence of a homicidal maniac. The "Bible John" case has been reopened and reinvestigated on several occasions – a long-dead suspect was even exhumed –, but to this day, there has been no resolution, no real evidence to say that a serial killer ever existed.

The hysteria of this case would still be fresh in the minds of those senior detectives as they met in Perth and I think they came to the decision not to link the cases until such time as they had overpowering evidence to the contrary, at least in part to prevent another "Bible John" character being hyped up by the press. They didn't need anything that could increase the pressure on them or create panic in the community.

What we now know about Angus Sinclair, Gordon Hamilton, the death of Mary Gallagher, The World's End Murders, and the deaths of Anna Kenny, Hilda McAuley and Agnes Cooney should not be used to judge the conclusions of the 1980 conference. The officers in charge then made a pragmatic decision, based on their knowledge at the time. It is easy to be critical in retrospect, but we should remember that our discoveries were brought about by the latest scientific techniques, which were unknown and inconceivable in 1980. Our unearthing of Angus Sinclair relied on techniques that would have been undreamt of then.

In our reviews of the cases being re-examined by Operation Trinity, it was clear that Sinclair had, at no time, featured contemporaneously in any of the earlier Glasgow killings or the World's End case, nor was any reason uncovered to suggest that he should have. By that I mean we did not find any statement or piece of evidence that linked him directly or indirectly to the murders.

In cold case investigations, it is every detective's nightmare that the culprit's identity appeared in the early investigation system – that he or she was there all the time, and the clues were missed. Finding that a killer was questioned but had managed to deceive the interviewers and was therefore eliminated from an investigation is something everyone dreads. Most police officers who have worked on long-running inquiries have been beset by the same problem. As an investigation drags on without a solution, doubts start to creep in. There is an old maxim in murder inquiries that says that the solution usually lies in the first hundred statements – in other words, with those who are most closely connected to the case. Given that murder is usually domestic or by the hand of an associate, this is often true so, in the dark of the night, you can begin to doubt, to question. Did I miss something? Has he got past me?

Over the years, I've kept in contact with several retired officers who had worked on the World's End inquiry. As Operation Trinity began, they knew we had a culprit in our sights, but they weren't really interested in the name. They only had one question – had he appeared in the system of earlier investigations? When I was able to tell them that he hadn't, the relief on their faces was apparent. After all those years, their professional pride was still such that they didn't want to be the ones who had slipped up.

Returning to the present, despite the new science, we still had challenges in the World's End case, for we had yet to prove the association between Sinclair and Hamilton as well as establish their links to The World's End pub and East Lothian.

The other priorities in investigating all five of the murders were common to all the cases. We had to prove the suspect's knowledge of both the abduction and disposal sites and show there had been access to vehicles that could have been used for the disposals. In addition, we would have to reinterview all the significant witnesses who were still alive and traceable and, finally, we had to interview our suspect.

This last objective, the questioning of Sinclair, would be a major exercise, requiring detailed planning and careful execution. That would come at the end of the plans I have outlined, and it would be made more difficult by the fact that Sinclair was already a prisoner and, as such, entitled to all the protection of a man who was not at liberty and therefore not best able to defend himself. You can argue the rights and wrongs of this, but the facts remain – the rules and regulations, the laws, and the strict codes of practice established to protect the innocent also unfortunately protect the guilty.

In 2004, we felt that, overall, the five murders we were dealing with bore such striking similarities that, when viewed together against a background of the circumstances of other unsolved murders of women in Scotland, they were unique. Often a killer will leave some tell-tale sign, a signature that is theirs alone, or perhaps follow a similar pattern of criminal behaviour. This is simply a factor of human behaviour. We all, knowingly and unknowingly, develop patterns of behaviour, some learned in childhood, some adopted and adapted as we learn from life's experiences. It's often said that the best way to predict an individual's future behaviour is to explore their past. This is as true of criminal behaviour as of any other. In these cases, the points of comparison between each murder were significant and bear examination.

Each victim – Helen Scott, Christine Eadie, Anna Kenny, Matilda McAuley and Agnes Cooney – was abducted within an hour either way of midnight on a Friday or Saturday during the second half of 1977. Each victim had been socialising and had been drinking sufficiently for their guard to be lowered. Each victim was taken without a single witness seeing the moment of abduction – a clear sign of careful planning and organisation, especially as they occurred in areas with lots of people going about on busy weekend nights.

Each body was disposed of in a similar way. They were all dumped near quiet roads, out of sight of any nearby highway. This allowed the person getting rid of the body to be certain they would not be seen, and they were then able to make a speedy escape. Even the deposition site of Christine Eadie, near the coast road from Edinburgh to East Lothian, had good sight lines in the hours of darkness to ensure the disposal of the body would not be seen by a passing car. Each girl was tied up – usually both hands and feet, but in one case it was just her feet – and most of the ligatures were made using items of their own clothing. The similarities go on. Suffice to say that, from our standpoint, it all looked compelling – these crimes looked to be unique, to have been committed by the same person, but to prove it, we needed to place these cases in context and compare them with all the other murders of women in Scotland over the period to test their uniqueness.

We were dealing with five murders in six months. Through DNA evidence, we knew, beyond any doubt, that Sinclair was involved in two of them. We also had an assortment of other crimes woven in between the weekend murders that Sinclair was also suspected of. To prove just how unique these murder cases were, Operation Trinity embarked on the largest survey of murders of women in Scotland ever undertaken.

It was all very well to look at the circumstances and say that, superficially, there are strong links between the five murders and conclude they are the work of the same killer. However, we had to prove beyond all reasonable doubt that these killings were unique. In the end it didn't work out, but, in the process, a hugely important database was developed. It was useful for both our own research and future investigations.

It was not only essential to look at the unsolved murders of women, but also to examine all unlawful killings of females to try and show just how singular the five murders were. We needed to go into minute detail, and with all the facts, compile a database. As ever with the Police Service, the enterprise needed a name and so 'Operation Scothom' came into being.

As the database was being designed and built up, the Trinity management team were only too aware of how vital the task facing us was. The decision was taken to make the starting point of our examination some years before Sinclair came on the scene and take it right up to the time for which latest records were available. So, four decades of death were studied in exhaustive depth between the years 1968 and 2003. There was only one rule for membership of this wretched club: the person needed to have been female, dead and have had her death attributed to murder.

As with any enterprise of this nature, it was crucially important to go into it with a highly systematic approach to ensure the results that came out of the other end were true reflections of the facts. Furthermore, it was imperative for the operation to be geared in such a way that all aspects of every murder could be identified and compared with every other killing. We could not fall victim to self-delusion or go looking for the result we wanted to make the pieces fit. Our finished product would have to stand scrutiny, for we could be sure that, if the results of this work were ever to be put before a jury, it was extremely likely that they would be vigorously challenged. The world, and particularly the legal profession, is amply populated by those whose mission is to find fault, so whatever we did had to be substantial enough to withstand all scrutiny.

In this piece of work this was particularly true. As with every aspect of any criminal investigation, we needed to be constantly aware that, one day, a defence lawyer would be going through our work with an eye to discovering inconsistencies, omissions or prejudices that undermined the conclusions. One flaw or one error would render the exercise worthless. We sometimes forget that the defence advocate or solicitor in a criminal case is only responsible for preparing and delivering the best possible case for the defendant. They are not concerned with justice.

Many prominent defence lawyers have made the discovery of procedural irregularities, human errors or simple mistakes in their stock-in-trade. We had to make sure our database was bulletproof. The man given the task to lead this effort was the able and highly experienced Detective Inspector Derek Robertson of Strathclyde Police. He would need all his skill in the coming months.

Much of this work was carried out by officers from the eight police forces of Scotland who were not connected to our investigation. It was essential that the operation was kept as straightforward as possible. We devised a form to be completed for every murder that would ensure each case was looked at in a similar way and the details logged into the computer in exactly the same way, so that accurate comparisons could be made.

It surprised most of us that, during this period (1968-2003), a total of 1,038 women were murdered in Scotland. This figure does not include those who died in the terrorist bombing of Pan Am Flight 103 over Lockerbie on December 21st 1988.

The task was another major undertaking for the whole of the Scottish Police Service in this inquiry, and individual officers in each of the eight areas were responsible for coordinating their force's contribution to the database. It sounds easy but in fact it was a complex job to trace and examine all the files and records, some of which were nearly forty years old.

More than any other crime, murder is the one that has the biggest

111

effect on the community in which it happens. Each case, by definition "the criminal taking of life", is a devastating blow for those most closely connected to it. Whilst murder rightly holds this place as the most abhorrent of crimes, it is fair to say that the different categories have vastly different impacts. The murder of a child stays in the public's mind for a long time, whereas the murder of a criminal rather less so. I highlight this only to demonstrate just how difficult it is to uncover details of each of those one thousand plus murders stretching back so far in time.

We were not just looking at unsolved killings, but at all the murders reported in Scotland. The wide time parameters of the exercise meant that many of the cases we were examining had been investigated, prosecuted, the case closed, and the perpetrator already freed from jail or in some cases dead. Details of many of these murders were hard to track down. To be a worthwhile tool in the prosecution of Sinclair, however, the database had to be a complete examination of every case so each one had to be traced and, eventually, they all were. The Scothom database was a hugely important piece of work, but like many important things in life, it was difficult to achieve. It was also to throw up a problem that we had not expected.

Traceability and accountability were obviously vital for this operation. The exercise was based in Cathcart Police Station in Glasgow, where the responsible officers in each of Scotland's police forces reported. They were briefed to examine these records in minute detail and to extract all the significant factors surrounding each case. They would only have been aware in the most general terms of the importance of their endeavours, but we went to great lengths to ensure they all realised just how crucial the task in hand was. There could be no room for error, corner-cutting or lack of attention to detail.

The database, that was constructed as a result of this painstaking work would, we believed, be of considerable use to police forces in the future. Researchers and criminologists would also be able to consult the findings for academic purposes.

In addition to this research, the pathologists connected to the Scottish police forces went through a similar operation under the guidance of two of the country's senior practitioners from the University of Glasgow. The university lab had detailed knowledge of our case and had already been of immense help.

All the Operation Trinity murders we were examining bore a similar signature in the method of killing and how the bodies were left, but the Scothom database threw up something else. It showed there was the possibility of a sixth killing fitting the pattern. Once a murder is "solved", it tends to slip from the collective memory of the criminal justice system and the press – file closed. So, it was no surprise that the name of Frances Barker meant little to us when we were first told about the striking similarities between her killing and the five murders being examined by us. The only difference was that, in the Barker case, a culprit had been identified, prosecuted and imprisoned for life.

Apart from the murder of Frances Barker and the other five murders, the results from Scothom were exactly what we had expected them to be. As has already been noted, all our victims had been gagged with an item of their own clothing. In the thirty-seven-year period we examined, only three other female murder victims had been gagged but none of them with items of clothing and all three killings had taken place inside buildings of one sort or another. In short, apart from the gag, they bore no similarities to our five cases, rendering the link so tenuous as to be irrelevant. So, what did the murder of Frances Barker mean to our inquiry? Firstly, the circumstances of her death and body disposal were so similar to those of The World's End Murders that her name was immediately added to the list of deaths we were interested in. However, we had to begin a new inquiry into her murder to discover which of four possibilities had come about. I say four because, whatever had happened in this case, that was the sum of the different potential circumstances that had occurred.

To spell it out, there was a limited number of options as to what had happened:

a) - Frances Barker had been murdered by Sinclair and there had been a miscarriage of justice.

b) - Frances Barker had been murdered by Sinclair acting together with the man already convicted of the crime.

c) - Sinclair had been schooled in murder by the man convicted of Frances Barker's death.

d) - The man convicted of Frances Barker's murder happened to use the same MO as Sinclair.

It was clear from the very first time the case came to our attention that, no matter which of these four possibilities had occurred, the case of Frances Barker was going to be problematic for our inquiry. In those early days of our knowing of this murder, I think we all rather hoped option b) or c) would present itself as the eventual outcome. It would be some time before a conclusion could be reached, and a very thorough, painstaking investigation had to be undertaken.

The date of Frances Barker's death, June 11th 1977, would have made her the first victim of the six months of murder. She was thirty-seven and lived alone in a flat in the Maryhill district of Glasgow, having moved out of the family home in the city centre. Frances had worked for a baker in Glasgow for more than four years prior to her death and the company was, in fact, the landlord of her new flat.

The night she met her death she had, like all the other victims, been out socialising and had had a fair amount to drink. I think it would be fair to say that, by the time her sister and other family members she had been with that night helped her into a taxi to go home, she was a little worse for wear.

The taxi driver who dropped her off that night remembered clearly watching his fare as she made a somewhat precarious way towards the door of her close in Glasgow's Maryhill Road. The cabbie did not actually see Frances go into the close because it was a busy Glasgow Friday night and another fare climbed aboard the taxi as soon as Frances got out.

After her murder the police discovered that it was unlikely she would have been able to gain entry to the close that night. She had mistakenly taken the wrong coat from the pub where they had been earlier that night and her house keys had been left in her own coat in that pub.

· Her colleagues at the bakery were no doubt concerned when Frances didn't appear for work the following Monday, nor indeed for the rest of that week, but their concern did not cause them to take any action until Friday – a full week since they had last seen her. They contacted Frances's parents and, later that day, bakery workers and Frances's brother, Tom, went to the flat in Maryhill Road and forced their way in. There was no trace of her and no sign of a disturbance or of anything being out of place.

A full sixteen days later, a man working on his family's farm near Glenboig in Lanarkshire found the badly decomposed remains of a woman lying in a copse next to a farm road. He immediately ran home to get his father and the pair returned a short time later to confirm what the young man had feared – that he had found a body. The police were called and, along with the police surgeon, a careful examination of the scene was made. In what was to become a depressingly familiar pattern over the next few months of 1977, the victim was found to be bound hand and foot, her legs tied together with part of her tights, her arms restrained by her scarf. Her underwear had been used as a gag and this was kept in place by the rest of her tights. Branches and leaves had been scattered over the body to hide it. The area where the body was dumped was similar to the other disposal sites – hidden from view. It was June and the concealment had been made easier by the rich foliage on surrounding trees and bushes.

The post-mortem carried out at the time suggested that Frances had been strangled with some force. There was no evidence of sexual assault, but the body was badly decomposed.

An extensive police inquiry over a period of some weeks failed to find a single witness who had seen Frances after she left the taxi in the early hours of Saturday morning. She had seemingly vanished off the face of the earth.

Reading the old files and cuttings, it seemed that detectives got an early break in the investigations and a man was arrested and subsequently convicted. That man, Thomas Ross Young, is now dead, and it is unlikely that we will ever know the truth of what happened to Frances.

Maryhill, the area where Frances Barker went missing, was Sinclair's home territory. He was brought up on the edge of the district and his mother still lived there at the time of the Barker killing.

Our background inquiries into Sinclair suggested that, on the night of Frances's abduction, Sinclair was probably staying with his mother in Maryhill Road as he was going through one of his frequent separations from Sarah.

The site where the body was found would also have been well known to Sinclair – it was near to the place where a friend used to repair Sinclair's cars. To prove the connection we had interviewed some other associates of Sinclair, and they told us that about the time of the killing, he had been talking about buying and renovating a rundown cottage close to where Frances's body was found. These two strands of information made it abundantly clear that he had a detailed knowledge of the area.

When Frances Barker disappeared, Sinclair was driving a Toyota

115

Carina car, but just a few days later, he got rid of it and bought the Toyota caravanette that was to be his weekend recreation vehicle. At the time of the World's End killings, he still owned the caravanette and we are sure he used it to transport Helen Scott and Christine Eadie to their deaths in East Lothian.

The actual caravanette owned and used by Angus Sinclair at the time of the World's End murders. We traced all its subsequent owners but found it had been scrapped a few months before our enquiry re-opened.

# 9

## The Death of Anna Kenny

The lack of forensic evidence in the Glasgow cases was a huge obstacle from the start. It was clear that, to stand any chance of a successful prosecution, we had to go to extraordinary lengths to establish connections between Sinclair and the scenes of crimes, the places where the women were last seen and where the bodies were found. Fortunately, the original files were intact and from the original statements, we had to trace possible sightings of Sinclair or vehicles he may have driven at the time.

Even with all this done to the very best of our abilities, we knew that the chances were slim. The burden of proof in the criminal court – beyond all reasonable doubt – is a tough standard, as it should be. Without direct evidence or forensics, it was an uphill struggle.

The solution to the 1978 case of Mary Gallagher was brought about through an incorrect tip-off from a member of the public which was to lead to the re-examination of the evidence which, in turn, allowed Glasgow detectives to find an exact DNA match with Sinclair. The three other cases linked to Sinclair by the press in the aftermath of that conviction were not going to be so straightforward.

Samples and productions from the crime scenes in the murders of the three women had, unfortunately, been lost.

It is important to state clearly here the basis for including the account of these three unsolved murders in the narrative of the World's End case. Angus Sinclair was not charged in connection with the deaths of Anna Kenny, Matilda McAuley and Agnes Cooney. These crimes remain unsolved and neither I nor the team who worked with me on Operation Trinity would wish to jeopardise any future prosecution. The fact is, however, that we did reopen these cases and the team from Strathclyde

Police led by Detective Superintendent Eddie McCusker thoroughly re-investigated them. The description of this process is relevant to this story, but it is important to repeat as no one has been charged with these crimes, and no facts or evidence not already in the public domain will be discussed here.

From the start, the reinvestigation of the three cases, bound together by a raft of similarities, came up against a considerable obstacle – the lack of hard evidence.

Strathclyde officers had already reviewed the evidence they had in the cases of Anna Kenny, Matilda McAuley and Agnes Cooney and, shortly after Sinclair's 2001 conviction for the Gallagher murder, they concluded that they could not present a prima facie case against anyone. Without the kind of forensic evidence that had been crucial in the Gallagher conviction, it would only have been possible to present a circumstantial case. There was a powerful set of circumstances but not powerful enough to put to a jury. So it was that Operation Trinity presented probably the last best chance of discovering exactly what happened to the three women and identifying the man, or men, responsible. To overcome the absence of forensic evidence, we were going to have to take a whole new approach to the cases which had already been subjected to extensive investigation and reinvestigation.

It is important to clarify one thing at this point. The 1970s investigations of these three cases were the best they could have been, given the time in which they occurred and the relatively primitive forensic science of the day. Each case was led by officers who were dedicated and experienced and our revisiting of the files turned up no glaring errors or omissions that left these crimes unsolved for so long. These officers did the very best they could with what they had at the time.

The way forward was to establish all possible links and similarities between the three murders and then see whether they matched the circumstances of the World's End case. Then, with analysis of the minute detail of every aspect of all the cases, we would try to establish evidential links between them all, to bind them together.

The chilling fact behind this endeavour was the knowledge that, if we could establish these links and prove that one man or a group of men were responsible for all the murders, it would mean that, in seven months in 1977, he or they had been on a sex killing spree almost unparalleled in British criminal history. If Sinclair was involved, these crimes would

118

have been committed while, to the outside world, he was a hard-working painter and decorator, living what appeared to be a normal life.

By this time in our inquiries, we were already in close consultation with the Crown Office in Edinburgh – the prosecuting authority for Scotland.

The relationship between the police in Scotland, the investigators, and the Crown Office is an interesting one. All prosecutions in Scotland are raised in the name of the Lord Advocate and his or her officers, the procurators fiscal. The fiscals prosecute in the lower courts while counsel known as advocates-depute prosecute in the higher courts. The relationship between the Crown Office, the Lord Advocate and his or her officers and the police is seen as odd and anachronistic by some observers. In fact, it is straightforward and seasoned over hundreds of years, so that everyone knows their roles and responsibilities. It is sometimes seen as too close and cosy and others, from a different perspective, may claim it is an antagonistic relationship, with police and prosecutors appearing to be working to different agendas. In my experience, it is neither of these. The Crown Office rightly preserves its independence and its discretion over whether to prosecute. In a system of independent prosecution, this is the way of the world and, although there are sometimes differences of opinion, the lines of demarcation are clear.

The niceties of the prosecution system were not, however, in the forefront of our minds as we began to examine the three cases. The Strathclyde team was facing the huge task of unpacking three separate thirty-year-old murder investigations – and sometimes it was quite literally a matter of unpacking, as dozens of boxes of old files had to be opened and their contents meticulously examined. These cases had, of course, all been reviewed before but there was no alternative to starting again – going back to the beginning and working slowly through all the evidence, applying the latest investigative techniques. The scale of the task was daunting, but Eddie McCusker and his team set about it in a scrupulous and determined manner.

The case of the first of these victims to be killed, Anna Kenny from Glasgow, was first to be examined and it produced one of the most bizarre twists of any murder investigation I have ever been involved in.

\*

Anna was just twenty when she met her death. She had been on a night out with her best friend, Wilma Sutherland. It was just another ordinary tale of ordinary girls going about their everyday lives. Anna and Wilma seemed to do everything together. They had just started temporary but well-paid jobs on a brewery bottling line in Port Dundas in Glasgow. Previously they had worked together at several different jobs in and around Glasgow and had once left the city for work, again together, for jobs at the Butlin's holiday camp in Filey, North Yorkshire.

So, it was against this background of close friendship that they had arranged to meet up in the High Street of Glasgow, opposite the city's Royal Infirmary, to go out and spend their first wages from the new jobs at the bottling plant. Although they were being paid more than they earned in previous jobs, they didn't have a lot of cash that Friday night, August 5th 1977, but were determined to make the best of it.

A new pub called the Hurdy Gurdy had opened in the Townhead area of Glasgow. It was just the latest thing and the place to be seen for girls of Wilma and Anna's age, and so that was where they headed. After a couple of wrong turnings along the way, the pair eventually arrived at the Hurdy Gurdy, and so began just another Friday night. They stayed in the bar for the entire evening drinking a potent mixture of vodka and beer and chatting to various friends who passed through the pub at different stages of the evening. Towards the end of the night, they fell into the company of two young men, who I will just call Willie and Joe. Willie had gone to the bar in the expectation of meeting up with a friend who, in the event, didn't show up. He knew Joe and was happy to join him and the two girls, Wilma and Anna. It was a decision that would cause him a lot of heartache and trouble over the next few years. Joe was anxious to walk Wilma home but feared she wouldn't go with him if it meant leaving Anna on her own. So it

Anna Kenny - disappeared on 5 August, but her body was not found until 23 April 1979

120

was that Wilma and Joe, and Willie and Anna left the bar that night as couples.

Wilma stayed chatting and kissing Joe in a doorway for a while, having first seen that her by-now tipsy friend Anna was alright with Willie. Willie said that he and Anna kissed for a while, but she made it clear that was it and she was going to go home. Willie was married with a newborn child at home, and so he too thought it best to call it a night and head off as well. When he left her, Anna appeared to be trying to flag down a taxi. He had no way of knowing it, but when Willie caught that fleeting image of Anna, he was the last person known to see her alive.

Just as in the cases of the Edinburgh girls Helen and Christine, no abduction was seen, nothing happened on the night of Anna's disappearance to raise the alarm and it was not until the following morning when Wilma went round to her friend's house that Anna was found to be missing. Later that Saturday afternoon, Wilma, by now distraught with worry, alerted Anna's family and Anna was reported missing. There was no quick solution to this mystery and the longer Anna was missing the more concerned the police and her family became. That said, there was still nothing to suggest for certain that her disappearance was sinister, but the longer it went on, the more all concerned feared the worst.

The response of the police to reports of a missing person in the first twelve to twenty-four hours is crucial. I will discuss this further but it's very often difficult to get it right. Every weekend across the country dozens of mainly young people go missing for a day or a night. Whether it's a party that lasts overnight, a new friendship or a last-minute decision to take a trip, in most cases, the missing person turns up safe and well.

As time went by, however, experience and instinct would suggest to the police that something untoward must have happened to the missing girl and the intensity of the investigation into the mystery that they began made it clear to us that Anna's continued disappearance was taken very seriously.

This brings me back to the vexed question of missing persons, a subject which had concerned me for much of my police service.

It is quite staggering just how many people go missing each year. It's reckoned that, annually, 210,000 people are reported missing in the UK. Two thirds of them are young people and, of course, the vast majority are found or return home – usually within a few days. But a significant number are not traced, do not return home and are never heard of again.

They simply disappear. I believe that, historically, we did not deal with this problem seriously or systematically enough. Times have changed but back then the treatment of missing persons was haphazard to say the least.

Very early on in any missing person inquiry, the police service will make a value judgement on the case and decide the level of resource that is to be allocated. Let me illustrate this with extreme examples. If a child of tender years vanishes, within minutes of the report to police, a major operation swings into place. In fact, after the child abductions and murders by Robert Black, the van driver convicted of three such killings in the 1980s, the importance of a fast response was apparent and detailed plans were drawn up by all police forces as to how to respond to such cases. A strict protocol – 'Operation Child Watch' – was developed.

Now, if abduction is even suspected, within minutes of the police being alerted, major roads are under surveillance both by officers on the spot in cars and through all the technical means to hand. At the other extreme is the disappearance of a troublesome young person, with a history of running away, but who is deemed old enough to look after themselves. In that case, a very different scenario unfolds. If the person is over sixteen, the age when they are entitled to go off somewhere without letting others know, then it's likely that very little will be done immediately to trace them unless there are suspicious circumstances. In cases like these, much valuable time can be lost. If a week or so passes before a non-suspicious missing person inquiry is elevated and prioritised, then the most important time in any investigation is lost. And it's not just time that's lost. Delays mean that forensic opportunities, the recall of witnesses and – most important of all – the impetus are all gone.

At the other end of these puzzles is another mystery. At any given time, there are up to 150 cases throughout the UK where human remains have been found and lie unidentified. Charities do good work in trying to identify them and trace relatives, but many are eventually cremated or buried in unmarked graves – the bleak testimony to lives that have simply fallen between the cracks of an inadequate system.

It can be difficult for the police for other reasons, because there are a significant number of people who, for one reason or another, want to vanish. It may be personal, financial or family reasons that drive someone to disappear but, unless a crime has been committed, there is no reason for the police to be overly involved especially if it seems the individual just wanted to drop out of view. It is sometimes simply the case that the person's life has just become too much for them and they feel a fresh start, unburdened by the baggage of their former existence, is the only way forward. And that's fair enough – after all if no crime has been committed it's no business of the police. However, that does not get away from the fact that we often have no idea what the real circumstances of a missing person are, and sometimes missing persons slip off the radar and fall victim.

It is certain that, in the early days of the missing persons inquiry into Anna's disappearance, some suspicion fell on the boy Willie – not least because of the fact that, in the light of his personal circumstances, he at first denied being with Anna in the minutes before she vanished. Fortunately for him, it was clear from the files on the original investigation that detectives eventually eliminated him from their inquiries and determined that he had nothing to do with her disappearance, not least because his walk home that night had luckily been punctuated with meetings with friends who, when traced, could vouch for his movements. His alibi was complete though his activities that night may well have been the source of considerable domestic stress.

The priority given to this missing person's inquiry was such that it was clearly feared, from early on, that some terrible fate had befallen Anna. The difficulty of detecting the random killer is perfectly illustrated here. Whoever took Anna as she looked for a taxi that night was not seen and extensive inquiries and appeals for help from the public produced no leads. There was no car being driven in a suspicious manner; there were no unexplained sightings of rowing couples; no one saw a struggle; and there was no body, no scene of crime, no weapon, no forensics, no witnesses. Anna had simply vanished.

We had by this time tracked down and finally identified Gordon Hamilton as the man who had left the main samples of DNA at the World's End scenes of crime. Long dead, his was the DNA that we had been trying to identify for years and that we had eventually identified by his familial links with the Hamilton family, Angus Sinclair's in-laws.

As I've already said, Wilma Sutherland had been with Anna in the Hurdy Gurdy on the night she disappeared. When she realised Anna hadn't been home after she'd last seen her in the company of the man she'd left the pub with, Wilma had searched in vain for her best friend. She had raised the alarm and reported Anna as a missing person and, along with family members, had been in the forefront of the hunt for

Anna. So, imagine our surprise when we discovered that Wilma had married Gordon Hamilton just over a year after Anna's disappearance.

They had begun a relationship after meeting one night in the self-same Hurdy Gurdy bar. They had met after Anna vanished but before her body was found many months later in remote Kintyre.

It may never be known what role, if any, Gordon Hamilton played in Anna's disappearance but his connection with the Hurdy Gurdy and Anna's friend, albeit after her disappearance, gave us a tantalising puzzle to consider. Not least was the question about Sinclair's modus operandi. We now knew he had been with Gordon Hamilton at the scene of The World's End Murders yet, as far as we were aware, his other sexual crimes were committed alone. We knew from witnesses that he had certainly been alone in the murder of Mary Gallagher. The exception seemed to be the Edinburgh killings – the difference there of course being the fact that there were two victims.

However, one thing was certain – Wilma Sutherland had, quite unwittingly, married one of the men at the centre of the World's End case. This strange twist became even more bizarre as we uncovered further details. Wilma only went back to the Hurdy Gurdy bar twice after Anna's disappearance and, on one of those occasions, she had met Gordon Hamilton and fallen into conversation with him. It was just before Christmas 1977, and they soon began going out with each other. They got married in October 1978 and some six months later, on April 23rd 1979, Anna's remains were found in a shallow grave in a remote and beautiful area of Argyll at the start of the Kintyre peninsula. Only her skeleton remained but she had been bound just like Christine Eadie in the World's End case. The long period of burial had removed the chances of finding significant forensic evidence.

Was Gordon Hamilton involved in the murder of Anna Kenny? If he was not, did he know who was? Was his meeting and subsequent marriage to Wilma Sutherland sheer coincidence? These are three questions I would dearly like to know the answers to. If he was not involved in the killing and did not know who was involved in Anna's death, then the coincidence of his meeting and marrying Anna's best friend is truly remarkable.

For Wilma, it was clear that her marriage to Gordon Hamilton had been a bad move almost from the start. On looking back, she admitted to us that she was simply at a loss to say why she had entered into this union – her only possible explanation was that the pain and puzzlement of

Anna's disappearance had left her disorientated and vulnerable. Her life with Gordon was difficult to say the very least. He drank heavily, he was violent towards her, and he had extramarital affairs.

He was with her the day police came to their house to tell her that they suspected Anna's body had been found on the West Coast some couple of hours' drive from Glasgow. Hamilton accompanied his wife on visits to Anna's distraught parents. Could a murderer be so detached, so callous, as to sit offering comfort to his victim's family and her best friend, the woman he had made his wife?

During their short marriage, Wilma got to know various members of Hamilton's large family. Her impression of the Hamiltons would have been the same as that of everyone else – a troubled family.

Gordon's role in The World's End Murders had been established by the presence of his DNA and by excluding the other Hamiltons through comparing their profiles with the forensic sample. The scientists told us that DNA testing had shown it was a Hamilton sibling but not one of the living ones. However, much more proof would be needed to finally confirm Gordon Hamilton's role in Helen and Christine's murders. The first step would be to find a sample of DNA that we could prove beyond doubt came from him. He had only been dead a few years, but as I have already described this was still not an easy job.

My years of experience in criminal investigations have taught me that speculating on what might have been is usually a fruitless pastime. At best, it can distract you from the more important task of establishing the facts. At worst, it can mislead and distort the course of an investigation. However, I must confess the motivation behind Gordon Hamilton's marriage to Wilma was the source of much theorising and speculation based on what had to be a simple choice. Was the marriage the strangest coincidence ever, or was it the act of a man callous in the extreme? Or, perhaps, more tantalisingly, the act of a man drawn back to the scene of the crime, compelled to stay close, stay in control, to the extent that he sought a relationship with the person closest to the victim – we will never know.

It is difficult to imagine the tensions that must exist in the relationship between partners in such a crime as The World's End Murders. Did it lead to a lifelong bond between Gordon Hamilton and Sinclair? Did they become confidants, bonded together by their shared experience, or was there distrust and tension? In serious crimes where there are several

125

culprits, the danger is always that one will talk, to gain some advantage or through fear, and betray the secret. Angus Sinclair's history made him a good bet to keep quiet, but Gordon Hamilton must have represented a threat to Sinclair's security. Had he known about his brother-in-law's lifestyle, his heavy drinking and his decline during the 80s, Sinclair must have been concerned about the possibility of Gordon letting something slip. But, by this time, he was in prison and, if he was aware of Gordon's condition, there was nothing he could have done to intervene or influence things.

If Sinclair heard about Gordon's death, he must have breathed a sigh of relief. With the only man who could incriminate him for The World's End Murders dead, his secret was safe . . . or so he thought.

Gordon Hamilton was beyond our reach but what we know of him leaves intriguing questions. Could it really be that Gordon Hamilton was a one-off offender? Was a crime of such savagery as The World's End Murders his first serious offence, and did he then just go back to his everyday life? Could it be that there was a master–servant relationship between the two men in which Gordon Hamilton was the subservient partner? This final possibility seems likely, for throughout his adult life, no one told Angus Sinclair what to do. However, unless new evidence not available to our inquiry comes to light, these questions will have to remain unanswered.

Clues, though, were to be found in what the second youngest Hamilton brother was able to tell us. Unlike his older brother, he had a fairly good relationship with Angus Sinclair. Sinclair had managed to get him a job with one of the painting firms he worked for following his release after his first long prison sentence for the Reehill killing. Then Sinclair gave the boy a second job, so to speak – an apprenticeship as a junior partner in his violent crime enterprises.

The young Hamilton moved into the home where Angus and Sarah were living in Queenslie in the tough east end of Glasgow. He and Sinclair worked away from home from time to time and their friendship was not diminished even after he learned from others of Sinclair's conviction for killing a child. The younger man was of the view that everyone deserved a second chance in life and, anyway, it was a long time ago.

He told officers frankly how he and Sinclair would often return at night to the business premises where they had been painting during the day to steal. This progressed to till snatches at various shops in and around Glasgow. The younger Hamilton admitted that he worried about the extreme violence Sinclair used in these raids.

This member of the Hamilton family also told us that Sinclair had been involved extensively with prostitutes in the Glasgow area and on occasion had used information gleaned from them to select other criminal targets. We were able to verify his accounts of his activities with Sinclair as some of the old crime records still existed. Nobody would ever be prosecuted for these crimes – the passage of time was too great – but they were valuable, nonetheless. They served to establish, beyond doubt, the character and nature of Angus Sinclair as a violent, ruthless, cool-headed man whose offences were premeditated. The traits he displayed in his crimes of violence were also present in his crimes against young girls and in the murders he committed.

As we progressed and began to piece together the jigsaw of Angus Sinclair's life and criminal career, we started to focus on his means of transport. We knew he had to have the use of a vehicle during the World's End abductions and murders, and it had to be big enough to hold four people. Also, Sinclair was travelling fair distances throughout the country so he would need something reliable. As in all serious criminal investigations, we had numerous sightings of vehicles at or near the various crime scenes. Many were vague but some were not and, as it turned out, the cars Angus Sinclair drove in the late seventies were to play a major part in the jigsaw.

We were particularly interested in finding out details of a white caravanette we knew Sinclair had owned in the late 70s at the time of Anna Kenny's disappearance. One such vehicle had been seen by witnesses near the site where her body was found in Kintyre. Other members of the Hamilton family told us that the younger Hamilton had been a passenger in this caravanette on many occasions. He himself had been helpful but we got the feeling that he was perhaps withholding information. Despite his admissions of criminal activity with Sinclair, the team felt certain that his involvement went a great deal further. How much further? That was the question.

The caravanette had become particularly significant to Operation Trinity as we examined links between Sinclair, the area where Anna's body was found and the other crime scenes. The Toyota caravanette would appear to have been Sinclair's perfect murder vehicle. It seemed no accident that the period of his ownership of this vehicle coincided with the dates of crimes we were jointly investigating.

Locating the Toyota caravanette was of huge importance to us. We knew that Sinclair had sold it on shortly after Agnes Cooney had disappeared and, through vehicle records, we began to trace all its subsequent owners. We knew that it was unlikely that a vehicle of its type, which was registered in 1976, would have survived almost thirty years. Nevertheless, we had to make every effort to trace the caravanette or any parts of it. A wealth of forensic evidence could have been hiding in its seat covers and carpets which might have linked it to Helen and Christine or any of the other crimes we were investigating. In the event, we were unlucky. All the subsequent owners of the vehicle were traced – one was even able to provide an actual photograph of it. But we eventually learned that the caravanette had survived until a few years before our inquiry. Although not registered for the road, it had lain on blocks behind the last owner's house – a restoration project that never was completed. Eventually, rust and decay took their toll, and our potential forensic time capsule went to be scrapped. It was tantalisingly close, but all we could do was track down carpets and materials identical to those used in the Toyota. We could use these to make comparisons with fibres found on Helen Scott's clothes, but they were nothing like as good as getting our hands on the real thing would have been. However, we were able to say that there was compelling evidence that fibres found on Helen matched those from the standard fabrics used in caravanettes like Sinclair's.

The caravanette posed another question. It might sound incredible, but it occurred to us that Sinclair's crimes could have been committed simply because he had a means of transport. Did he execute these awful crimes simply because he could?

The murder of Anna Kenny was always going to be difficult to resolve. The length of time between her disappearance and the recovery of her body meant that there was no significant forensic evidence, but there were interesting connections.

The pub Anna left that night, the Hurdy Gurdy, was in the Townhead area of Glasgow, an area of the city Sinclair knew well. His wife's family lived in Stirling Road in Townhead in 1977 and much of the time Sinclair spent with the younger Hamilton and Gordon Hamilton would have been in this district. We also knew that Sinclair had visited the Kintyre area, where Anna's body had been found buried in her shallow grave. He had the right connections, he had the means and, most importantly, we knew he had the will to abduct and murder – he had done it before. It was compelling, but it wasn't enough.

## Two More Glasgow Killings: Hilda McAuley and Agnes Cooney

Taken in sequence, the next unsolved killing we examined was that of Matilda McAuley, another victim of 1977. Matilda, or Hilda as she was known, was separated from her husband and, along with her two young sons, was living at her mother's home when she met her violent death. This is the stark summary of the facts, and it doesn't begin to hint at the immediate life-shattering effect a tragedy like this has on a family. But what often also goes unrecognised is that the consequences of such heartbreak would for generations be felt by those closest to Hilda.

Matilda McAuley - a hard-working mother killed on 2 October 1977

Hilda McAuley was a conscientious and loving parent and, like so many women in her position, to make ends meet, she had more than one job. She did cleaning work at a city centre hairdressers' shop and at a local engineering works. Her main outlet of relaxation was going out with her friends just once a week, usually to the dancing at the famous Plaza Ballroom in Glasgow. It is one of the great sorrows of these cases that Hilda's mother, Martha, died while the death of her daughter was being reinvestigated. Thankfully, she did live long enough to know the process had started. By the time Hilda's mum had died, in the summer of

2004, she had been told by the Operation Trinity family liaison officers that a full examination of the investigation of her daughter's death was underway.

One of the most important factors in any cold case review is the attitude of the victim's family – if there are any surviving. On the one hand, they are often crucial to the success or otherwise of the investigation. Their recollection of the events surrounding the crime can sometimes become more focused by the years. The endless thinking and rethinking about all the facts and circumstances can lead to very different perspectives from those held at the time of the crime, when emotions and passions would have been running high. Loyalties can also change and, in unsolved crimes with domestic connections, this can sometimes lead to a breakthrough. Often, though, the reopening of an old case also reopens old wounds as the hurt and the pain of what happened in the past are once again recalled. It is understandable that, for many families, the overwhelming feeling is that things are best left alone. But, for some families and friends, the continued or revitalised interest in their case is welcomed. It validates the importance of their loved one. And it sends out a powerful message that there is no such thing as an unsolved murder – the police never give up.

The families of The World's End Murders never lost hope and never lost faith in the police. Neither did Martha McAuley. Her daughter's killer was not brought to justice, but I hope that the commitment she saw the Strathclyde team give to the reinvestigation brought her some comfort. We all hoped that our continued efforts gave her some peace of mind during her final days, after so many years of heartache.

Hilda lived with her mother in the Maryhill Road area of Glasgow, the district that kept cropping up during the many facets of this inquiry. It was the centre of Angus Sinclair's territory. Hilda, who was thirty-six when she died, had a bad habit – one that, in the end, may have cost her her life. For convenience, she was in the habit of accepting lifts home from men she had met after a night out in the Plaza. Sometimes they were men she didn't know. Saturday, October 1st 1977, two weeks before The World's End Murders, may have been just such a night.

Hilda had gone out with the intention of ending up at 'the dancing' in the Plaza with three close friends. The four of them had met in the early evening and had a drink in a couple of pubs before arriving at the Plaza shortly after ten o'clock. Jackets were left at the upstairs cloakroom, and they walked down to the dance floor where the little group parted company, as they often did on nights like this. Police would eventually trace and speak to most of the people who were in the dance hall that night and no one saw anything that stood out as unusual. It was just another Saturday night at the Plaza.

Hilda, as far as we could ascertain, spent a lot of the two hours or so that she was in the Plaza on her own. The only fix that officers were able to establish was at about quarter past midnight when the cloakroom attendant remembered Hilda reclaiming her jacket. This woman had got to know Hilda on her regular visits to the dance hall and recalled quite clearly her leaving and told officers she appeared to be sober and showing no signs of being the worse for wear after a long evening.

Hilda had left the Plaza at about the time the place usually started to empty, with revelers heading off to catch the last buses home, so no one paid too much attention to her departure. In fact, no one remembers seeing anything of Hilda either inside the Plaza or outside after she reclaimed her jacket. We may never know exactly what happened in those moments on Sunday, October 2nd 1977 after she left the dance hall. She may have been alone, or she may have been with a man who was offering her one of these convenient lifts home. The next fact that we can be certain about in the story of Hilda McAuley is that she was found brutally murdered some twelve hours later. Sometime, somehow, in those moments after midnight, she met her killer and was carried away.

Hilda's body was found dumped in trees on waste ground at Langbank in Renfrewshire beside what was to become in later years a motorway. In those days, it was the main road between Glasgow and the Clydeside shipbuilding town of Greenock. The area was beside the entrance to a caravan park and was the sort of place that a vehicle could remain unnoticed for some time as traffic raced by on adjacent roads. It was an obscure spot – the kind of place that courting couples might know. It would certainly have required a degree of local knowledge both to know it was there – you wouldn't find the place by accident – and to appreciate what a good place it was for disposing of a body.

As the case of Hilda McAuley was re-examined by the Operation Trinity team, potential coincidences and significant clues emerged from the pages of the old statements they were combing through. That is not to criticise those involved in the original inquiry in any way at all. It is much easier to spot similarities if you know exactly what you are looking for. For instance, we knew by this time that Angus Sinclair owned a very distinctive white caravanette during this period so, while sightings or references to such a vehicle would be significant to us, they wouldn't have been significant to the original inquiry team who had no leads regarding any suspect's vehicles and would have been trying to make some sense of hundreds of car descriptions, some accurate, some vague, without a clue as to the relative importance of any of them.

The small details contained in statements given at the time took on a new meaning for us as we tried to piece together the jigsaw. We had the luxury of being certain what the final picture would look like. We were also aware that Sinclair knew the area well. His sister lived nearby and a former girlfriend of his told us how they used to go for runs in his car to other places very close by. We learned from one of his old criminal pals that, years before, they had travelled to a spot near Langbank for a very specific purpose. They went to test-fire a pistol that they planned to use in future crimes. The exact spot could not be identified but Sinclair's pal remembered it was littered with burnt-out cars that had been dumped as scrap, or by joyriders. We knew that when Hilda's body was found the area nearby was known as a dump site for cars. It was a tantalising connection. The spot was hidden yet accessible from the roads close by.

Hilda's body was found by a father and his two sons out shooting rabbits at lunchtime the day after she went missing. She, like the other victims, had been bound securely, gagged and strangled. Hilda had been left partially stripped and the rest of her clothing in disarray. Some items Hilda was known to have with her when she left home to go dancing were never found. Her coat, handbag, shoes and a hairpiece were missing, and they were the subject of a massive search and public appeals by the original inquiry. By the time Operation Trinity was revisiting the case, the bindings, the gag and Hilda's clothing could not be traced. It was a huge setback for we could only speculate what forensic evidence they might have yielded.

Some documents did, however, survive. The original investigation had been extensive, as had the examination by forensic experts. We were able to make full use of our predecessors' work. Some 1,200 people were interviewed in depth about the night of the disappearance, but despite this intensive operation, they had been unable to find anyone who had seen Hilda McAuley leaving the Plaza Ballroom or at any time afterwards.

Re-examining the case all these years later was, of course, made very much more difficult by the fact that none of the forensic evidence had survived the passage of time. In the World's End case, traces of DNA in items recovered from the crime scenes had led to Sinclair and Gordon Hamilton being identified. In the case of Hilda McAuley, we had no such advantage. Such was our need to trace these items that an inquiry within the inquiry was launched and the Strathclyde team painstakingly retraced the steps of the original investigators – dozens of detectives and scientists over nearly thirty years. No stone was left unturned in the examination of record books and evidence schedules. Even the old cabinets at forensic laboratories were searched. It was a magnificent effort, but it yielded nothing. We contacted surviving detectives and scientists from 1977. This may sound like a bizarre long shot or the plot of TV fiction, but it is more valuable than you might first think. Detectives and scientists tend to remember unsolved cases. When long hours, weeks and sometimes months are devoted to individual cases, it becomes personal, and details of crimes are etched on your memory.

During Operation Trinity, we made great efforts to contact retired detectives and scientists who had been involved in the various cases. We had considerable assistance, and I was hugely impressed by the recall and enthusiasm of these long-retired men and women. It was clear that they still felt an ownership.

By this time, the investigation into Sinclair was being progressed under three main headings. There was the probe into his connections with friends and family, including the various addresses at which he had lived as a free man. There were the vehicles he owned, and lastly, his links with the places where each of the victims were last seen and where their bodies were eventually found.

In the case of Hilda McAuley, the second and third strands of the investigation were coming together. We learned of a car that had been dumped in 1978 in a disused quarry near to where Hilda's body was discovered by the rabbit shooters. A huge amount of time and manpower were expended digging through the scrap and stone lying about in the former Glenboig quarry and, sure enough, Strathclyde Police's hugely experienced underwater search team found the car. Most interestingly, in the boot of the car, we found various lengths of string. Could this be the same kind of string used to bind Hilda McAuley? How would we ever know for certain while the original materials were untraced?

This string, however, provides a wonderful example of just how, with care and attention to detail, it is possible to reach back through time and discover evidence of a vital nature. The actual string from Hilda's body had gone. However, all the documentation of the original forensic investigation survived, and amongst it there was a report from the University of Strathclyde identifying the type of string that had been used. It had been concluded that the string was of a unique manufacture. In fact, there was only one company making this type of string and it was in Co. Kildare, Ireland. In 1977, detectives had discovered a business in Glasgow, Henry Winning & Co. in Caroline Street, that was an outlet for the Irish string.

Then officers were hampered by a lack of suspects. When they had visited Winning's, they found that this product was sold to many tradesfolk all over the west of Scotland. Sales were plentiful and many untraceable. Short of interviewing every person who had access to this string in every company that bought it and then checking their alibis for the night of Hilda's murder, there was no way forward. Even if only 100 balls of this string had been sold, just consider how impossible a task this would be. Not all those balls would be traceable, for a start. Then, for companies that were known to have bought the string, it would have to be established exactly who would have access to it. We were more fortunate as we had a clear focus for our investigation.

So, the Strathclyde team went back to reinterview the man who ran Winning's in 1977 and he recognised the string. He also recalled being interviewed by the original investigation team almost thirty years before. But what was the connection? Next Strathclyde interviewed the boss of the company Gordon Hamilton worked for about this time, a manager of the button-dyeing firm A. M. Robb Ltd. He recalled the string and said they used it for tying up small parcels – and had purchased it from Winning's. Examination of Robb's records found bills from Winning's at this time. For good measure, a second Glasgow company that stocked the Irish twine was also checked and they too supplied Robb's with it. We even managed to find a little parcel which had lain around for all these years unopened, and which was tied up with the very same twine. In the end, this is nothing but an interesting tale, but the story of the string is a very good illustration of the intricacy and depth of our inquiries and how it is possible to fill in seemingly unbridgeable gaps even after nearly thirty years.

Fascinating though these details were, we could not be distracted by them for the main thrust of our investigations at this stage still centred on a detailed re-examination of the five murders, looking at them in the fresh light provided by having a good suspect for two of them – Angus Sinclair for the World's End ones.

*

What we initially thought was the last in the series of killings was that of Agnes Cooney. She was a twenty-three-year-old house parent at a children's home in Bellshill, Lanarkshire, on the outskirts of Glasgow. Agnes was, by all accounts, one of life's caring individuals who took her responsibilities very seriously and went out of her way to help those in need. The last photograph of her shows a cheery, cheeky face full of life and fun.

She was just seventeen years old when her mother and grandmother both died during 1971 and the young Agnes took on the mother role to her five younger brothers and sisters at their home in Coatbridge, Lanarkshire. Everyone who knew her spoke of how well she carried out this difficult surrogate role. Words like "strong", "dependable" and "fiercely protective" were used to describe Agnes.

To fulfil this caring role, Agnes had had to put her ambition to become a nurse on hold so she could stay at home where she was needed. But Agnes also found time to work at a department store in Glasgow until her younger brothers and sisters were older and independent. That day came soon enough though, and it would have been with great excitement that Agnes gave up her job at Bremner's store in Glasgow city centre to begin her nursing training at a hospital in Mauchline in Ayrshire, living in the nurses' home nearby. The caring, committed nature of Agnes's personality is clear from the original statements and reports compiled by officers after her murder in December 1977. This kindly disposition had led her to take up a job as a house parent at a children's home in Lanarkshire when she completed her nursing training and that was the job she was

Agnes Cooney - a warm and caring girl. She was killed on 3 or 4 December 1977

doing when she was killed.

Agnes also spent some of her spare time at a house in Glasgow looking after an aged aunt. She was staying at this address at the time she was murdered. Her father died without the satisfaction of seeing his daughter's killer brought to justice. Her brothers and sisters survived and are still deeply affected by the tragedy.

As in all these cases, the events leading up to the murder were unexceptional – normal people leading normal lives only brought into prominence by a chance meeting with a brutal murderer. On the day she vanished, Agnes had been to see a flat she was considering renting in the Maryhill area of Glasgow with a friend. The pair had done their nursing training together and had become very good friends. Agnes's potential flatmate was going out with a man who was a member of a local band and he joined the two young women as they viewed the flat. The three went on to have supper together at a city centre restaurant and eventually made their way to a club where the band was due to play that night.

The two girls helped the young musician and other members of his band as they unloaded their gear into the Cladda Club in Westmoreland Street in the city centre. After they had set up their amplifiers and speakers, Agnes and her friend settled down to watch the show until it finished in the club about 11 p.m. With the entertainment over, the girls once more lent a hand and lugged instruments and amps back out to the band's van, which was parked outside.

A band member told detectives in 1977 that, as they were packing up, he'd noticed a white Transit-like van with windows at the rear parked across the road. It had taken about fifty minutes or so to load up the band's van and, just before midnight, Agnes was seen leaving the Cladda Club by herself. She seemed to be perfectly normal. She was not upset and had appeared happy as she wished staff goodnight. Not long afterwards, the band members and Agnes's pal realised she had gone without saying goodbye and they were concerned she had just wandered off in an area of Glasgow that was not well known to her.

Agnes's friends first looked round the club and then moved outside to see if they could spot her in the street or standing at a bus stop. There was no sign of her. Later there was a sighting of someone looking very much like Agnes walking in the city centre. Witnesses were to describe her clothing very precisely, leaving officers in no doubt that the sighting was of Agnes walking off into the night and that she was quite alone.

Glasgow is bisected by the M8 motorway and, on either side of it, there are areas of wasteland between the road and the shops and houses. The next series of possible sightings of Agnes were all either on or near this busy route. She appeared to be trying to hitch a lift. There were numerous reports of a woman seen in various locations round the M8. Much of this no-man's-land is made up of a series of underpasses and slip roads which can be daunting enough in daytime but are no place for a young woman alone in the early hours of the morning. Officers worked on the basis that these sightings were of Agnes and they continued to receive further reports of sightings of the lone woman over the next hour or more after she'd left the club. The last was from a motorist who saw someone who may have been Agnes at about 2 a.m. We will never know if any or all these sightings were really of Agnes. In the clamour of publicity following a high-profile murder, there can be many well-intentioned but misleading reports of potential sightings. If it was Agnes, her behaviour was as untypical as it was dangerous. Walking alone in a strange part of town in the dark was risky behaviour for a young woman and Agnes was not a risk taker.

The band members and friends eventually gave up their searches and, believing nothing was seriously wrong, they went their separate ways. What had been puzzling for her friends turned to outright concern when Agnes failed to turn up at work the next morning. Her absence sparked a series of frantic phone calls to friends and family, but all drew a blank as to her whereabouts. Eventually the decision was made to raise the alarm and Agnes was reported missing to the police on the afternoon of Saturday, December 3rd 1977.

She did not remain a missing person for long. At nine o'clock on the morning of Sunday the 4th, her body was found on farmland near Caldercruix in Lanarkshire. A local farmer was driving his tractor along a minor road past his fields when he saw what he took to be a bundle of rags lying about fifteen yards out into the grass. As he continued to drive along the narrow road, it slowly dawned on him that it was probably not just rags but a human body. He raced to his neighbour's farmhouse and raised the alarm. On returning with his neighbour, they confirmed that it was indeed a body lying in the field and the police were called. The farmer told officers he had been working in the area where the body was discovered throughout the previous day and so was certain it had not been there when he'd finished on the Saturday.

Agnes had been bound and gagged with items of her own clothing. The gag was no longer in place when the body was found but the bindings that had been used to hold it in place were still tied round her mouth. She had died from a stab wound.

There was a clear suggestion she may have been alive for a considerable period in between her disappearance from Glasgow city centre in the early hours of Saturday morning and the time she was killed. Had she been kept somewhere for those twenty-four to thirty-six hours and, if so, where?

Again, there was an extensive police inquiry into the killing. It must have seemed obvious to detectives in those days that, if it had been Agnes trying to hitch a lift on or near the M8, in all likelihood, a man had picked her up and he was the one who had killed her. No one came forward to say they had seen her getting into a car and there were few significant sightings at the time of the vehicle that must have been used to dump her body in this relatively remote spot. For our inquiry in 2004, the profile was very similar to the rest. None of the original evidential productions or samples from the initial inquiry had survived the passage of time so we were going to have to go back through this investigation with a fine-tooth comb. Armed with our most recent information, we would have to reinterview surviving witnesses to see if we could add to the knowledge gathered at the time of the original inquiry.

Key amongst our lines of inquiry was the sighting of a newish white van being driven in the vicinity of the deposition site on the Saturday night. Like so many people in major inquiries, the witness had not thought his information important which is why he had delayed in coming forward. By the time he had contacted police, the case of Agnes Cooney was receiving considerable press coverage and even at that stage it was being linked by reporters to the earlier killings and particularly The World's End Murders. The press were noticing the similarities and coming to their own conclusions.

Back then, of course, the white van was just one of many different vehicles people had reported seeing in various places and so it would have been treated accordingly. But, for us, it was extremely important because, when Agnes died, we knew that the vehicle Sinclair was driving was a white Toyota caravanette and it was new.

Yet another of the significant developments came to Operation Trinity as a result of the publicity surrounding our inquiries and the speculation that we were interested in Sinclair. On December 31st 1977, a nine-year-old girl was the victim of a sex assault near her home in Glasgow. The attack had been reported to the police when it happened, but no culprit was ever identified. In 2001 after Sinclair's conviction for the murder of Mary Gallagher, a woman I will call "Joan" contacted the police saying she believed Sinclair was the man who attacked her all those years ago.

This case was very important. The attack on Joan, at the end of December 1977, was not only a very serious crime, but it also marked a change in offending behaviour.

When we first identified Sinclair as one of the individuals involved in The World's End Murders and learned of his later convictions for offences against much younger girls, the crimes for which he was first sentenced to life imprisonment, we wondered why he had changed victim types. What had motivated the change from adult to child victims? The attack on Joan may have been the transitional crime. Horrific though the experience must have been, in hindsight, Joan was fortunate to have survived.

It is clear Sinclair's offending took on a whole new direction after this time although quite why is rather difficult to say. However, it is certain that, during 1977–8, he was driven to murder women. Helen Scott, Christine Eadie and the diminutive Mary Gallagher, who he may have mistaken for a child, – and there may have been others – were all approached late on a Friday or Saturday night, in or after leaving licensed premises, before being abducted and killed. Plus, the way they were all killed bore distinctive similarities. But the attack on Joan heralded an intense period of offending against children and these new victims put him into a very different category of offender. The change from being a rapist and murderer of women to becoming a violent child sex attacker happened very suddenly.

So, what brought it about? In the absence of hard evidence, we can only speculate. Things were changing in Sinclair's life which may have brought about the alteration in his offending pattern. In the face of the publicity about a white van in the weeks after Agnes Cooney's murder, he sold the white caravanette which had been an essential factor in the World's End cases. Worried that eventually the police might identify it, he may have felt it was getting too hot. Whatever he was thinking, the vehicle was certainly sold very soon after Agnes's death.

With the loss of his transport, he might have decided to turn his attention to children because they would have been easier to subdue and control and he would not have needed his van to hold them in. It is sometimes the simplest of things that bring about major events. Sinclair's change in behaviour may have been merely about the loss of his caravanette.

The tenement close where Joan was attacked was just 200 yards from Sinclair's home at Daisy Street and not far from either the Cladda Club or the Plaza Ballroom It was right in the centre of Sinclair's territory, and the case bore many familiar hallmarks. The little girl had been wandering the streets of her home district, waiting for her father to come home and let her into their tenement flat. He was a heavy drinker and Joan often spent hours hanging around waiting for him to roll home from the pub. That day in December 1977, a man had approached her and asked for help in finding a family called Thomson. Ever happy to help, the little girl took on the task and tried two nearby families of that name but discovered neither was expecting a visitor. She returned to the man she later identified as Sinclair with this information. He then asked her to go to another street with him and, once there, he sent her into an unlit tenement close again in search of the mythical Thomson family, who, he said, probably lived on the top floor. She climbed the stairs and, on discovering no one of that name there, began walking back down the dark stair to be met by her attacker on the second floor. There he grabbed her, pinned her to the wall and threatened her with a knife. He then subjected the girl to a terrifying ordeal. Afraid her assailant would kill her, she was crying as quietly as she could and, as the attack continued, she was biting the sleeve of her anorak to stop herself from screaming out loud.

After a while, she heard the front door of the close, two floors below, open. Her attacker jumped up and rearranged his clothing. He then ordered the petrified girl to go to the top landing and not tell anyone what had happened. The man who had entered the close found Joan crying. With her clothing in disarray, it was obvious she had been attacked by the man who had just passed him on the stairs a couple of floors below. He banged on the door of a flat and then ran off to try to catch her attacker but to no avail.

No one was ever charged with this attack. Joan told officers in 2001 that she had gone to an identification parade but had been too frightened to pick out her attacker, even if he had been in the line-up.

Another consequence of this awful experience was that Joan was taken into care on the night of the attack when police found her father drunk and incapable of looking after her. She spent the rest of her childhood in the care of the local council.

No productions from this case had survived – and, this time, even the paperwork had disappeared over the years. When Joan came forward after seeing Sinclair's case in the papers, she was able to give a very full recollection of what had happened and even picked Sinclair's picture out of a large collection of photographs she was shown.

Given the terror of the attack and the tragic family consequences that followed, it says much for this young woman's character that, despite the passage of time, many of the details of that dreadful day were still firmly in her mind, including one that was of special interest to us. She recalled her attacker's trousers had flecks of paint on them.

Reading this case in 2004, the similarities hit us like a sledgehammer. The circumstances and the modus operandi were identical to those of another case we were very familiar with. If you change the names and the dates, you could have been reading the Catherine Reehill case from 1961. The crimes were almost identical with only one important difference – Joan survived.

During the long hours of interviews with Sinclair into various aspects of the case being built up against him, he said little and revealed nothing. When questioned in December 2004 about the attack on Joan, Sinclair was read the girl's account of what had happened to her and, as usual, he gave not the slightest flicker of a reaction to that graphic document. Uniquely, in this instance, he did break from his usual "no comment" stance to concede what had happened to the little girl had been 'quite horrendous'. Cool, detached and cynical? Or could this have been the good Angus Sinclair passing judgement on the bad one?

# 11

## Confronting the Suspect

Every single detail of Operation Trinity was important in its own way. Each order, each inquiry, each review of evidence became another block in the process of building a strong case aimed at bringing justice in these historic cases after a quarter of a century of frustration. Apart from the DNA evidence, no other part of this investigation was potentially more important than the interviews we would conduct with Sinclair.

We had come a long way since my early days in the CID, when it was often a case of accusation and denial until, hopefully, the suspect gave up. Some of the old detectives were masters at winning the psychological battle with suspects. Their techniques differed – some would show the interviewee empathy, others would use the classic good-cop-bad-cop routine, and, in the distant past, it might have been the case of resorting to physical intimidation and brute force. They all worked with some people in some circumstances, but even if the suspect cracked or better still signed a confession in a police notebook, it would usually be retracted on advice of a lawyer and the subsequent court appearance descended into a series of accusations of fabrication and denial.

Before the 1960s, it was usually straightforward, and the court simply accepted the officer's version as a witness of stature and credibility – end of story. But it started to change after the corruption inquiries in the Metropolitan area in the 1960s. The credibility of the police was never quite the same again and later revelations from the West Midlands Serious Crime Squad and many others did nothing to help. These cases of malpractice, corner-cutting and 'fitting-up' were self-inflicted wounds and all were hugely damaging to the entire police service – trust was gone.

In Scotland, mainly because of our unique rules of corroboration, major problems were avoided and there were fewer scandals. Nonetheless, the world had changed, and soon admissions in Scottish criminal cases were viewed with suspicion, times of detention were restricted, and we all had to get a little more professional. It became important that any admission contained specialist knowledge – in other words, something that only the culprit could know such as the location of the body, the stolen goods or the weapon. In such circumstances, the specialist knowledge and the consequent recovery of the evidence were usually persuasive enough to give the confession some credibility.

There were, of course, ways round this as there are with most safeguards but, for the most part, the tightening of the rules, while despised by some old cops, was good for everyone. It offered protection for the innocent suspect who was in the wrong place at the wrong time, forced the police officer to prepare more thoroughly and not simply depend on a verbal admission, and it also protected younger officers from the pressure of older colleagues to "get a result".

Had Angus Sinclair been arrested for the World's End killings in the 1970s, the interviews would have been thorough but crude by comparison to the techniques of the 21st century. Nowadays, for serious cases, interviews are at least tape-recorded and more often videoed as well. They are the subject of intense preparation, and nothing is left to chance. In Sinclair's case, as in other major inquiries, the police are governed by very strict rules of interview, the breaking of which can render any material gathered inadmissible and worthless. This could not be allowed to happen in our case. Sinclair's long experience of the criminal justice system meant he would be very unlikely to be overawed or intimidated by the process. The fact that we had to go public on the investigation many months before seeing him for the first time also meant the element of surprise was gone and he had plenty of time to think things over and prepare for our eventual arrival.

The exceptional circumstances we were dealing with in Sinclair's case meant we needed an exceptional approach to these crucial interviews that, given the number of crimes we were investigating, would stretch over many sessions. He would be questioned about the murders, of course, but also about the robberies and assaults we pulled from the files. A huge planning process was put into establishing a strategy, selecting interviewing officers, training them for the different responses they might get from Sinclair, gathering and collating what are known as interview aids, maps, photographs, sketches to help jog the memory and of course demonstrate the degree of care that has gone into our inquiry.

Early on in Operation Trinity, we turned for help once more to the National Crime and Operations Faculty and got the help of a top criminal psychologist. We had to make sure we were going to get the maximum benefit from the time-limited sessions spent interviewing Sinclair. While the psychologist who helped us cannot be named for legal reasons, she was one of the best. Hugely experienced in the field, she had a long track record of success in dealing with Britain's most dangerous criminals. She was able to form opinions of Sinclair from videoed interviews conducted in 2000 when he had been questioned over the murder of Mary Gallagher. After she'd reviewed each interview the police had conducted with him back then, she made observations and offered guidance on tactics and further plans of action.

We first met Angus Sinclair in a videoed meeting in October of 2004 at Peterhead Prison. The aim of the initial interview was to introduce him to the investigation, give him details of how we saw it progressing over the future weeks and explain to him what his involvement would be. This may seem rather odd to those not acquainted with modern police procedures – a little too polite perhaps. In fact, this approach was suggested as a method of overcoming one of Sinclair's personality traits – one that might stand in the way of successful questioning. Broadly speaking, our psychologist observed that, in the past, Sinclair had been able to take some control of police interviews. He used his self-discipline and contempt for the entire process to intimidate interviewing officers and dominate the exchanges. He also used all sorts of tricks to exasperate interviewing officers to the point where they lost any chance

Angus Sinclair, murderer, rapist and paedophile in 2004.

145

of obtaining meaningful progress. We saw how Sinclair used his eyes very effectively to turn the direction of the interview. He would stare at interviewers in such a way as to make them feel uncomfortable. The inexperienced or unprepared interlocutor would soon find himself on the defensive.

The questioning process of a suspect is a fascinating drama of human interaction and role-play, which, if entered into by either side with unjustified confidence, can lead to disaster. Take, for example, the cocky criminal who thinks he can easily outsmart the police – often you find his tongue gets the better of him and he contradicts himself or makes unintentional admissions as his guard fails. Once that happens, the game is up. Thankfully, most criminals are not very bright or well prepared and often the stress of the event gets to them.

However, the hardened offender who has had years to mull over his story and perfect his replies is a different challenge altogether. Add to that the time lag, Sinclair's controlling personality and his all too obvious ability to deceive and it's easy to appreciate just how difficult we believed the challenge ahead of us was going to be.

One important part of the plan was to select the right officers to carry out the interviews. Many factors had to be taken into consideration. It was important that the interviewers were experienced, but we felt too much experience might work against us. They could not be so set in their ways that they would decline any advice about overcoming the difficulties presented by Sinclair. Nor could they be too senior. In TV police dramas, it's usually the senior detective who confronts the suspect, but this is one area where fact and fiction are miles apart. It's a myth. It would have been ridiculous for me or one of the senior officers from the squad to carry out the interview. For one thing, too senior an officer gives an impression of status or importance to the suspect. To an egotist like Sinclair, this would have been a gift, and a mistake for us. But there was another more practical reason for my non-involvement. The truth was that my interviewing skills were rusty and my techniques well out of date. The other senior officers were more recently practiced but still not as proficient as middle-ranking operational detectives whose experience was current, and techniques bang up to date. In all major case interviews, it is experience, skill and suitability that count, not rank or seniority.

Despite the weight of the forensic evidence that we had, the interview with Sinclair was of the utmost importance and, after careful consideration and lengthy discussions with Ian Thomas and Eddie McCusker, we picked one officer from Strathclyde and one from Lothian and Borders. We felt they offered the necessary experience and the ability to represent us best.

Detective Sergeants Calum Young and Jim Shanley may not at first have welcomed their selection as interviewing officers – after all, it was a huge responsibility with a lot resting on the outcome. Naturally, they gave no indication one way or the other, but they certainly knew that the whole squad was relying on them. The simple truth was that, in the near thirty years of the inquiry, the thousands of jobs undertaken and the hundreds of detectives who had gone before, they were the first to be able to look the World's End suspect in the eye – it would be both a great opportunity and a weighty responsibility. They may have been apprehensive, but we were certain we had picked the correct lead interviewers. Both officers had good reputations and the right skills for the job.

It was unlikely that the sheer power and eloquence of the interview would bring about a change of heart in the suspect to the extent that he would make a full and frank confession, but it certainly was the case that any future prosecution would, in all probability, rely heavily on the videotapes of the interviews to allow the Jury perhaps their only chance of hearing Sinclair's story in his own words and form a judgement on it. In a case like this, the accused very often decides, on legal advice, not to give evidence in court. They know how fatally damaging a good cross-examination can be. Instead, they rely on their counsel saying to the Jury something like, "There is no need for my client to go into the witness box as the prosecution have failed miserably to make a case." While we were not to know it at the time, this is exactly what would happen in the 2007 trial. Thankfully, given the opportunity, the members of a Jury, who often have little legal knowledge but plenty of common sense, usually see this tactic for what it is – a device to keep the accused person from being tested or revealing his guilt in front of their eyes.

The approach we made to Sinclair would be crucial. We had to judge the situation carefully and weigh up all the various conflicting factors, we had to get it right first time. The press, of course, had given wide coverage to our operation and inevitably Sinclair's name had been linked to the inquiry as the main suspect right from the day we first revealed the operation's existence. We were concerned that this speculation and the naming of Sinclair had continued in some of the tabloids despite warnings by the Crown Office. Surprise was going to play no part in our strategy.

From the start we had been gathering information about our suspect's life behind bars and a picture was beginning to emerge. It seemed to us that, in the mind of our suspect, there were two very separate Angus Sinclairs. One was the man of the past – the convicted murderer and sex offender – and the other was the man of the present – a man with a mission, a trusted prison worker, the master of his kitchen and the mentor of his fellow prisoners. By all accounts, Sinclair had indeed become a respected elder statesman among his peers – someone whose advice was sought and usually taken as he oversaw their meals during the long prison days.

To create the optimal conditions, we had a letter delivered to Sinclair in his cell explaining that, later that day, we would be calling to speak to him. Our psychologist had been struck by his courtesy and was convinced that treating him with the same level of courtesy as he offered was the best way forward. The interview sessions stretching out in front of us would be long, detailed and tiring. That was based on him not co-operating. If he began making disclosures, then we faced an even longer but more rewarding task.

Sergeants Calum Young and Jim Shanley took to their brief well. Later that afternoon they sat down in an interview room in the prison and patiently spelled out what was going to happen. They called him "Mr Sinclair" or sometimes "Sir" and he responded as our experts had anticipated. Sitting quietly and seeming relaxed, he made appropriate responses to the initial preamble, saying he understood what was going on. After a while, Calum went on to outline the details of the inquiry and how they affected him. I have watched this section of video over and over again, trying to see if there was even the slightest reaction to any of the information that was being given to him. There was not. First Sinclair was told that he was not suspected of any involvement in the two Dundee murders that had been part of Operation Trinity in the early days but quickly discounted. This was important. If Sinclair felt we were on a fishing trip – a speculative interview accusing him of crimes he knew he did not commit – he would conclude that our evidence was thin and sit back. If, on the other hand, we convinced him of the depth of our knowledge and we were right, there was a chance, albeit a very small one, that he might speak. Then there was another matter – we wanted to demonstrate our fairness and respect for him by showing that we were not simply trying to clear our books of unsolved cases. Judging by his previous interview behaviour, our chances were slim, but we had to try our professional best.

Having told Sinclair the police were not linking him to the killings in Dundee, Calum then said that he was, however, suspected of being involved in other killings – ones that had taken place in Edinburgh and elsewhere in Scotland. 'Do you understand?' Calum asked him. 'Yes,' Sinclair replied in a quiet voice that betrayed no emotion. His single-word answer would be about as revealing as any we would get during what would eventually amount to many hours of detailed interviews.

Sinclair quickly told the officers that he had taken advice from a local solicitor who had instructed him to say that he had no further comment to make on any of the allegations or questions being put to him. Jim and Calum did not let this put them off and, bearing in mind the training they had gone through to help them deal with just such a "no comment" response, they kept going to plan, reminding him every now and then that, if he really wasn't involved in the matters they were asking him about, he should say so clearly, or it could potentially damage his position at any subsequent trial. We were obliged in fairness to do this, remembering that every word, inflection and nuance was being recorded by sensitive video and audio recordings, but it was also a technique to get him talking. The second word is always easier than the first – if you can get a suspect to speak, even if it is just to deny something, that is preferable by far to a stony silence. That way, there is at least some communication and with it comes the chance of a slip-up or something that can be proved to be a lie.

We also thought it important to spell out in simple terms to Sinclair how the sands had shifted over the passage of time. We needed to let him see that people who might have been his friends or allies when he was committing crimes all those years ago were no longer on his side – instead, they were now helping us in a way they would not have dreamt of a quarter of a century or more before.

We hoped to take advantage of Sinclair's comparative isolation over the years. He was no longer in control of his domestic environment, his relatives or his friends. He must have been uncertain about what changes could have taken place and we judged that, for a man with a controlling personality like Sinclair's, this would be uncomfortable.

The interviewers dropped into the conversations details from a statement his sister had made about how he had visited while she was on holiday in Cumbria. There was no great significance in this information

149

other than it demonstrated to him the detail of our inquiry. We also let it be known that members of his wife's family had helped us gather certain information we needed. We wanted him to understand that, for the Hamilton family, covering up for a petty thief was one thing, but helping a sex killer evade justice was not on their agenda.

However, despite the very best efforts of Jim and Calum, it was all to no avail – Sinclair made it clear he was not going to say anything. He was cool, collected and in control and we had little option but to conclude the interview. It was, I suppose, something of a triumph of hope over experience to have expected anything else. A veteran prisoner with little to gain and nothing to lose is hardly likely to invite us to roll the tape for a full confession. But there was a chance he might have done exactly that. He was, after all, serving two life sentences. He was already fifty-nine years old and unlikely ever to be released. What else could they do to him? Even if he had confessed and been convicted of more murders, he would have remained in his comfort zone at Peterhead. Indeed, further convictions may have enhanced his prison reputation in a twisted way, but Angus Sinclair was not that kind of man. The only confessions in his life had come when he was very young or being influenced by his wife and thoughts of family. He had learned his lesson and no such leverage existed now. In short, Angus Sinclair was not the confessing type. He would control the situation by silence. As the interviews progressed, first at Fraserburgh Police Station, then in Glasgow's Govan Police Station, and finally at Livingston – the station that had provided headquarters facilities for Operation Trinity – there were to be just very few clues given along the way.

The biggest of those was at Livingston, some considerable way into the proceedings when we had little to lose. We told Sinclair he was to be questioned over a much earlier killing, the 1970 murder of Helen Kane. This girl had been murdered in Edinburgh some years before the time we believed Sinclair to be active. However, there was a slight connection, as at one time, Sinclair had lived near the area where Helen Kane was last seen. Rather startlingly, he replied to the effect that it had nothing to do with him. He was precise and clear, declaring adamantly, "This one is nothing to do with me." By going further than he had during countless hours of interviews over several months, Sinclair gave us the first real response. Helen Kane's death may have had nothing to do with him but, in saying so, he gave the impression that the other cases may well have been his handiwork. It is, of course, difficult to know exactly what to read into that comment. Was it a fatal slip in an unguarded moment or the natural response of an innocent man or something more subtle? Whatever the reason, it is interesting to contrast this response with the utter silence and detachment of the previous interviews and his performance when he was interviewed about the vicious attack on the rent collector at Moodiesburn – a crime we knew he carried out with his younger brother-in-law.

The investigation was based in the Central Belt, so, after the interview sessions at Fraserburgh had been completed, it made practical sense to transfer Sinclair from Peterhead to Barlinnie in Glasgow. The general pattern of all these interview attempts was the same. He'd be detained under Section 14 of the Criminal Procedure (Scotland) Act and, by the time of the interview at Govan in late November 2004, he was being held in Barlinnie, traditionally one of the toughest prisons in Scotland. As well as moving him for practical reasons, we had also hoped that the change of scene might unnerve Sinclair. He would no longer be in the safe and relatively comfortable surroundings he was used to and in which he enjoyed status and respect. He may have felt nervous, anxious and even vulnerable but, if he did, he certainly didn't show it. He appeared to settle into Barlinnie within hours of his arrival and, after just a few days, he had made such a favourable impression with prison staff that he had won a position of respect. In exactly the same way as he had done at Peterhead, he was working the system perfectly.

So, as usual, manners and courtesy were to the fore as Calum Young, this time with another Strathclyde officer, Joe McKerns, sat down in the interview room at Govan and began the standard formalities. With his name, age and address all noted, a full explanation of the reason for this interview was given. Yes, he understood what they were asking him about. Yes, he understood that, as usual, there were people watching the interview live in another room in the police station. And that was it. His stock reply to any question was "nothing further to say" and he even trotted it out in response to being asked if he knew where Moodiesburn was.

The officers were anxious to move him on from that, the feeling being that even the slightest deviation from his plan may start a little trickle of information that would grow. Once they had established that there was to be no response to the questions over the details of that terrifying robbery in Moodiesburn, the pair of officers switched to a different tack. They began to ask him exactly why it was that he had nothing further to say. In their drive in this direction, Joe and Calum suggested, ever so gently, that Sinclair may not be able to understand what they were asking him about – that they had somehow lost him. They would, ever so politely and apparently unintentionally, question his intellect – give him the impression that they thought he wasn't quite with it. They would leave him feeling he had to say something to assert himself and show that he was in charge of the interview, not them – that the session was on his terms not theirs. It was worth a try, but it did not work. All he would say was something like, "I understand what you are saying, and the response will be that I have nothing further to say."

And so, it went on. They asked why he was saying that he had nothing further to say and got the stock reply. By doing this, he said he was only following the advice of his solicitor. When he was challenged about not having spoken to his solicitor that day and reminded that his solicitor didn't even know he was at the police station being questioned, it made no difference – the rebuff was the same. Throughout this lengthy session, his patience only seemed tried on a couple of occasions. 'Please don't badger me all day,' he said. 'I have nothing further to say.' Knowing the camera and the tape would pick up every nuance, he delivered this remark in a quiet, measured tone.

During those interviews, we deliberately showed Sinclair just exactly how much work had gone into Operation Trinity and made sure he was aware of how much we knew about him, his associates and his habits over the years. For instance, he had been involved with a man I will call James Smith, who had employed Sinclair for a time in his car repair business. Smith had spoken extensively to us about our suspect. He mentioned how Sinclair had once told him that the best way to pick up a woman was simply to approach one in the street. Indeed, Smith said he had actually been in Sinclair's car when he stopped and offered a lift to a woman walking alone in the street at night. But no matter what was introduced, what details we revealed, he remained unflustered and seemingly unconcerned. Always polite, he was apparently content to sit there for as long as we wanted and showed no frustration or irritation at our continuing questions.

Bizarrely, he was even reluctant to discuss a cut on his face. Calum had started to ask him about his general appearance. It was just another attempt to get him talking about anything, but it was based on Calum's keen observation. He had noticed that Sinclair had arrived in the police station with his shoelaces undone. It was no big deal, but it did seem rather odd for a man who, until that point, had been fastidious about his appearance. When asked why he hadn't tied his laces, Sinclair had nothing further to say about it. Then Calum mentioned the cut on his face – had he done it shaving and, if so, when?

'I have nothing further to say,' said Sinclair, so Calum gave him a little verbal nudge to underline the ridiculousness of this stance on such a trivial matter. It worked. With slight embarrassment, Sinclair revealed that he had cut himself shaving the previous morning. There was no breakthrough though, no connection. After this momentary frankness, it was just back to the usual silence.

As this session built towards a climax, Joe laid it on the line to Sinclair – friends from long ago were not friends any more. To underline that point, he slowly and clearly read Sinclair a lengthy extract from his co-accused's confession to the Moodiesburn robbery without identifying the source of the information. There was no hint of a reaction to this – no change in demeanour or expression. Joe went on to ask Sinclair who he thought could have made the statement. When Joe supplied the answer, it was met with apparent indifference from the suspect.

As the questions continued, the officers made it clear to him they would not stop. The questions would go on for weeks or months until they got the answers they needed. Joe cut to the chase. Sinclair should realise his family were helping the police and the detectives of Operation Trinity had built up a massive case against him.

Joe pointed out that, as he had been putting all these matters to Sinclair, the prisoner had allowed himself "a wee wry smile". Why was this? Was it because he knew he did have something further to say or was it because of his disdain for the witnesses' courage in coming forward and saying the things they had? But, as the heat was turned up, Sinclair remained resolute. "I have nothing further to say" was, by this time, his mantra and it was to be his only response.

The frustration of these interviews must be evident to all. They are, however, vitally important to an investigation of this nature. They give us lots of clues and indications if not real answers. Importantly, though, in court much can eventually be made of the fact that the accused was offered the chance to rebut the allegations and chose not to. Questions can legitimately be asked of his version of events in his own defence. "If such and such was the case, why did you not tell the officers at the time of interview all those months ago?" It is a question the Jury has the right to hear asked and answered, if Sinclair were ever to go into the witness box at a trial.

As I have said, the preparations for these question-and- answer sessions were extremely detailed and well thought through. The questioning officers were changed, and all had preparations with carefully briefed officers playing the role of Sinclair to allow the interview teams to gather experience of handling whichever tactics the suspect chose to deploy.

The first of the major sessions took place on November 18th 2004 in the police station in Fraserburgh, along the coast from Peterhead. All too often in the police – and, indeed, in most other walks of life – important operations fall short of expectations because the details have not been properly thought through or the apparently little things have been left to chance. We were determined this would not be the case here and a detailed order was drawn up over a period of days and considered very carefully.

The car used to take Sinclair from prison to police office was wired so that his conversation with accompanying officers could be recorded. This wasn't anything underhand – he was warned this had been done. Thought had been given to the people involved and their likely interaction with Sinclair and so officers were told exactly which seats to occupy in the car – who was next to him, and which officer sat in front.

The interviewing officers, in this case Calum and Joe again, had a detailed interview plan with all the areas to be covered carefully laid out and structured. The vehicles owned by Sinclair were very important to the investigation and so we managed to get pictures of their insides and outsides by tracing people who owned them after Sinclair and, with their help, searching through family photograph albums. The vehicle we were most interested in, of course, was the caravanette that he had owned during the period of these murders. It was the vehicle we had been told he used for his weekend fishing trips with Gordon – the trips that took up the whole weekend but never seemed to produce any fish.

So, after the tape-recorder and video camera were turned on, he was told the subject of this day's session – one of the Glasgow murders. Things took a depressingly familiar direction. "I have nothing further to say" was once more the best we could extract. Until, that is, we got on to the subject of his cars and, for once, he seemed engaged and curious –

154

almost forthcoming. It was truly remarkable. Here we had a man who was determined to hide the dreadful secrets of his past, particularly the serious sex offences, yet, for some reason, he started talking about the cars he owned. Sinclair must have known the vehicles he drove, particularly the caravanette, would be a significant part of our inquiry. He is, when all is said and done, a clever man who knew our investigations had stretched back through time to unearth huge volumes of new evidence relating directly to him. He had little or no idea of what we had discovered, and he had no way of knowing just how important it was for us to establish which cars he owned and when, and yet here he was speaking for the first time as if he was enjoying the recollection – fondly remembering his pride and joy.

In the first part of the interview that day, he stuck rigidly to "I have nothing further to say," even to the point that, at one stage, he burst out laughing as he said it and then apologised for doing so. This indicated to us that the scene was beginning to take on something of the ridiculous, even to him. After a break he spoke a couple of sentences about his jail work, in the kitchens at Peterhead, then stopped himself and, as if reproaching himself, asked for the interview to be cut short because he was saying nothing more.

So, there we have him – disciplined, focused and determined not to talk lest he gives away even the slightest clue that may crack the facade and prompt further revelations. Then, slowly but surely, information started to dribble from him. There was no consistency in his approach. In one question, he would refuse to say even where his son had gone to school and then, in his next answer, he would go into a little detail. Calum, Young and Sinclair ended up doing a verbal dance as, little by little, more and more was squeezed out of him. We weren't getting far, and we were certainly nowhere near a confession – no hints of admissions – but there was a steady trickle of information that allowed us to confirm various minor matters we had been less than certain of and, perhaps more importantly, this allowed Sinclair to realise just how much detail of his life was in our possession. We were able to sit and go through his tax records with him. These clearly showed where he was working and when. Perhaps, for once, the control freak in him slipped a little and, on being confronted with overwhelming evidence on minor matters, he felt comfortable in agreeing with the facts as they were presented to him and, forgetting for a moment to shut up, he sometimes even added a little to what we already knew. Throughout this slightly more productive session, he kept falling back on his "no further comment" line and then, almost in the same breath, he'd make further comment.

For his interviewers, it was extremely difficult to continue with those lengthy sessions and stick to the methods they'd been trained to use when they were up against a wall of silence or a repeated response of "no comment". Their task was frustrating, and at times demoralising, so on the few occasions when Sinclair did open up, the officers would have found it a welcome break.

It went further still. The exact details of the interviews are relatively unimportant, but they deserve further examination if only to establish why we progressed on that particular day. Calum started asking about the places he lived and inevitably that brought in his wife. He agreed that he spent lengthy periods of time separated while they were married and admitted that he took up with other women during these periods. Perhaps deep down a little phrase Calum used at the start of this conversation struck a chord with Sinclair and make him think differently about his situation. Remember that, from the start, we had been at great pains to demonstrate that the people he once regarded as friends and allies may have switched allegiance. One of his accomplices, his partner in the non-sexual crimes, had gone as far as to make formal statements implicating himself in serious offences, such was the change in relationships over the passage of time.

Calum emphasised once more the extent of the investigations we had conducted into his past and told him that we had spoken to a great many of the women he had known over the years. He then told Sinclair that a lot of the women still held him in 'great fondness'. Perhaps this little phrase was sufficient to bring about a bit of a sea change in Sinclair's attitude. Before this moment, the interviewing officers, over all the sessions they had conducted, had given the impression to Sinclair that he was on his own, friendless and alone. Now here were the police telling him some of his old girlfriends still regarded him well.

When he was asked about one of his more long-standing girlfriends, he agreed that he did know her. He said the flat she stayed in wasn't a very nice place and it had no heating or electricity. Then the shutters came down again and questions about her were met with the usual "no comment" reply.

He was then asked about his friend James Smith. Smith was important to us because he told us how his mother's house in Moodiesburn was being painted by Sinclair at the time of the rent collector assault and robbery that we knew he and his younger brother-in-law had carried out just a couple of streets away. So, the interviews went something like this:

'Do you know James Smith?'

'Yes.'

'How did you know him?'

'Nothing further to say.'

'James has spoken to us and given us his version of events.'

'Sorry, I knew James when he worked as a mechanic at the garage where I was a spray painter.'

Then, just as suddenly, all further questions about Mr Smith were met with the usual response of "no comment."

Just as puzzling was Sinclair's willingness to talk about what for him must have been the most difficult subject of all – his sexuality and his relationships with various women. A series of exchanges saw him at once talk about matters right at the heart of the inquiry and then, in the next answer, refuse to answer innocuous inquiries.

'Did you enjoy sex?'

'Yes, I did.'

Then, when asked if he had any preferences, Sinclair laughed as he said, 'No further comment to make.'

He claimed his first sexual relationship after coming out of jail at the end of his sentence for the killing of Catherine Reehill was with a woman in Edinburgh. He refused to say if he lived with her, but did tell us that he got a sexually transmitted disease from her.

He would list the names of his wife's siblings but refuse to say which ones he was friendly with. This was perhaps more understandable as he had committed sexual crimes with one of them and crimes of violence with another.

When reminded, after another break, that the interview was really concerning the events surrounding the death of Anna Kenny, it was back to the "no comment" replies, and so the pattern continued – tiny revelations, followed by 'no comment'.

The officers asked if he had ever been to Argyll and he said he had, but when asked if he had been to Skipness, the scene of the disposal of Anna's body, it was back to the standard "no comment" reply.

Then he came up with an answer to a question that rather bowled

157

us over. Bear in mind that, over many hours of interviews, the only information that had been forthcoming was of a bland, non-incriminatory nature. Some of his answers shed a tiny bit of light into certain areas we were interested in, but that was all. Maintaining concentration and direction over lengthy interviews like this can be demanding and it is all too easy for minds to begin to wander off. I don't know if Calum and Joe were at this stage – three hours or so into that day's session with Sinclair – but, if they had been, they were to snap back quickly. Once again they had reminded him he was being interviewed about the murder of Anna Kenny. A book of interview aids had maps, a picture of the caravanette, the dead girl and even one shot of the Hurdy Gurdy pub where she was last seen alive. Sinclair denied being in the pub at any time and took the opportunity of repeating that he was never much of a drinker. When shown a picture of the pub, he casually dropped into the conversation the fact that he had once been on the roof of the pub – only then it was a bookmaker's shop and Sinclair told the officers he was on the roof trying to break in. What was that all about? Did he think that we would be impressed by his candour about his visit to a building right at the heart of our inquiry? Or was it a distraction to try to establish that he had no fear of admitting his association with the place? Whatever the reason, his talkativeness soon passed, and it was back to "no comment". He had no comment to make on Gordon Hamilton's wife, Wilma, except to say he didn't remember her. We knew of a violent row Sinclair had with Gordon the night before his marriage to Wilma, which ended with neither Sinclair nor Sarah attending the wedding the next day. But this was getting too warm – it was an area much too central to Sinclair's killing spree – and he clammed up again as quickly as he had begun to speak.

Then, six hours into the interview which had only been punctuated with short breaks, the full facts of Anna Kenny's murder as we knew them were put to Sinclair. As usual, I was in a nearby room watching the interview with other senior officers as it took place. The tension building up in the interview room was clearly visible on our TV monitor as the officers summed up the case against him and offered him the opportunity to rebut the allegations one by one. As he declined to reply to the main allegations and sought to dismiss the lesser ones, Sinclair remained as calm and composed as he'd always been. He appeared cold and remote and the whole interview showed him in a particularly bad light, but we needed more, and we didn't have it.

Early in December, Sinclair was again interviewed at Govan police station. The usual recording and monitoring were in place. It was obvious he had realised that he had gone too far in previous sessions and, this time, he stuck rigidly to his "no comment" plan. Our tactics changed slightly to see if we could reach through to how we considered Sinclair perceived himself. We believed he thought of himself as two Angus Sinclairs. There was the bad one of all those years ago – wicked, violent and unreliable – and there was the new one, the good one, the one who was trusted, respected and liked by those around him. Calum and Joe decided they would try to contact the good Sinclair to see if he might be willing to reveal details of the bad one.

This time, they painted a picture of the life of Hilda McAuley for him. They highlighted her hard-working nature and the love she had for her sons. A photograph of the three of them, mother and sons together and smiling, was produced – Hilda's love for her boys was clearly reciprocated. Calum told him how on the night of her murder, the children had helped their mum get ready to go out. They kissed her goodbye and never saw her again. They pointed out the similarities with his own family, even handing him a current photograph of his own son who he hadn't seen for many years. Again and again, Sinclair refused to budge from his "no comment" stance. The familiar scene of questions being asked, and no answers given was played out. Whether it was frustration and anger or guilt I do not know but, during this interview, Sinclair seemed to retreat into himself. He no longer maintained eye contact with the officers, and he sat with his arms folded staring down at the floor. It was as if he had built a defensive cocoon around himself.

At one point in this session, we allowed him a visit from his sister who had been as helpful as she could to us throughout the investigation. We do not know what exchanges took place between Sinclair and his sister, but I believe she tried as hard as she could to persuade him to tell the whole truth for his sake and that of his entire family. It was to no avail and, when the interview continued, it was "nothing further to say" all the way.

During all the interviews when he was asked about the deaths of Helen and Christine, Anna, Matilda and Agnes, Sinclair gave nothing away. Protected by his right of silence, we were met by his stony resistance – just as we had feared we would be. Clearly all his years of imprisonment had done nothing to soften him.

# 12

## Trial, 2007

As the investigation progressed, we felt we were beginning to put together a convincing case. The evidence in the World's End case was strong even though one of our suspects, Gordon Hamilton, was dead. Angus Sinclair had been positively identified through DNA from samples taken from Helen and Christine and strong traces of Sinclair's DNA had also been found in Helen's coat and in the knots and bindings that had been used to secure the girls on that dark night in October 1977. We were indebted for the diligence shown by our scientists in carefully preserving those items since they were recovered from the crime scenes all those years ago. Had they not done so, we wouldn't have had our full DNA profile and would not have traced Sinclair in the first place.

As well as DNA, we had compelling hair and fibre evidence linking Helen to materials used in vehicles similar to the Toyota caravanette we knew Sinclair had been driving at the time, but which had been scrapped a few months earlier. We also had expert opinion that suggested Helen and Christine had not been bound and gagged by the same individual – like so many other habits, knot-tying tends to follow distinctive personal patterns. We thought it was significant that the knots used on Christine were all perfectly symmetrical reef knots while all the knots used on Helen were grannies which suggested a more haphazard approach. When we had considered this aspect of the case, our minds went back to Angus Sinclair's early prison training at Aberdeen, fishing net repair, where consistent and uniform knot tying was essential and would have become second nature to a man tying such knots for so long.

Lastly, we could prove Sinclair's connections with the area of The World's End pub and we had traced one of Sinclair's ex-girlfriends, who told us they had visited East Lothian near the deposition sites. Given the passage of time and without direct evidence or a confession it was as much as we could have hoped for.

In the Glasgow killings, we lacked the kind of forensic evidence we had in The World's End Murders but, nonetheless, the Strathclyde team had built a good case of circumstantial evidence which, when taken together with what we had for the World's End case, would, we felt, present a strong overall case to a jury.

The evidence that we could not, of course, present was that Sinclair had killed and raped before We couldn't say that the use of Mary Gallagher's trousers as a ligature bore striking similarities to all our cases. We couldn't produce evidence about the killing of little Catherine Reehill all these years before or describe the circumstances of the attacks on children in the early 1980s

In England and Wales, evidence of "similar fact" – that the accused has been proven to act in this way before – is admissible and has been crucial in several notable cases. In Scotland, such evidence is not admissible. Sinclair would, therefore, eventually appear in court as an innocent man with the Jury having no knowledge of his background. This aspect of Scots law is to preserve fairness to the accused. It dates, as do so many other fundamentals of the law, to a time when capital punishment meant that there were lives at stake. Nowadays, many of us who have worked in the criminal justice system would view it as archaic – the inability to present such evidence has, in my view, meant that the balance of fairness has swung very much in favour of the accused and away from the victim and public interest.

However, those are the rules of the system, and we knew we had to work within them. As our investigation concluded, we drew up a comprehensive report and submitted it to the Crown Office. It is the job of the Crown Office to decide on prosecution, settle the nature of the charges and then take the case forward to trial.

Many people imagine this is a straightforward, clinical process – that the handing over of the report ends police involvement and begins the prosecution phase. In minor cases it is, but in major cases it is far more complicated than that. In serious or complex cases, a Senior Procurator Fiscal will take an interest from an early stage, sometimes directing lines of inquiry, but usually monitoring the development of the case. At the stage where it becomes apparent that there is a reasonable body of evidence and that the case is probably destined for the High Court, an Advocate Depute is appointed to lead the case for the Crown and to keep abreast of the inquiry. The Advocate Depute's role is crucial, for he or she will ultimately recommend to the Crown Office exactly what charges should appear on the indictment. Then, with the Senior Procurator Fiscal, the Advocate Depute prepares the case for court and leads the prosecution when the case finally appears in the High Court. Some may see this as a blurring of the lines between police and prosecution, but, in fact, it usually works well with each party being very aware of their own role and remit.

From early in Operation Trinity, we had been in detailed consultation with a Senior Procurator Fiscal and, well before our investigations were complete, an Advocate Depute had been appointed to lead the prosecution both in its preparation and through to the eventual trial. We were fortunate that the Advocate Depute we had was one of the rising stars in the Crown Office and he quickly got to grips with the complexities of the five cases. This was no easy task – we had been living with the cases for months, in some cases years, but the Advocate Depute would be starting from scratch.

One of the early decisions he had to make was what should appear on the indictment – in other words, precisely what charges should eventually be brought against Angus Sinclair. During the ten months of our joint investigation, we had amassed a mountain of evidence not just relating to the murders but to several other serious violent and sexual crimes all committed in the late 70s, prior to Sinclair's arrest for the sex attacks on the girls in Glasgow. The crimes we had uncovered were all serious and if they had been current, they would have been prosecuted with vigour. As it was, the passage of time, almost thirty years, meant that their importance had faded. The decision was taken that it was not in the public interest to prosecute Sinclair for those crimes given the length of time that had elapsed.

We fully understood and half expected this decision but, nonetheless, it carried risks. On the one hand, you could see how it would look from the Crown Office's point of view. It could be hazardous to clutter the indictment with less serious crimes when the major issue was the five murders. On the other hand, we felt that these more minor offences painted a background to Sinclair's behaviour and pattern of offending, and there were living witnesses who could have described to the Jury what

162

had happened. It may have been compelling evidence but, ultimately, we accepted it was the Crown Office and the Advocate Depute's decision. He was a very able man and he was the one who would be presenting the case in court, so we respected his judgement.

That left the five murders: the Edinburgh World's End case of Helen and Christine, together with the Glasgow cases of Anna Kenny, Hilda McAuley and Agnes Cooney. By this time, the prosecuting team consisted of the Advocate Depute and a senior Procurator Fiscal from Glasgow who had replaced the Edinburgh Procurator Fiscal to ensure a geographical spread of responsibility – although, as a safeguard, a Senior Procurator Fiscal in Edinburgh retained an interest. It seemed a reasonable idea at the time but later, as things developed, it would prove to be the source of difficulty.

We always knew the viability of the five cases depended on the strength of the evidence in the World's End case. We hoped that together they would stand up in court, but accepted that, separately, the Glasgow cases lacked sufficient evidence. The critical decision had to be made – would they stand together, or would the weakness of the Glasgow cases threaten the World's End case? Although the Crown Office and the police had had close consultations throughout, we knew that this was a decision they and the Advocate Depute would make alone.

Eventually, in spring 2005, the Crown Office decided not to proceed with the Glasgow cases but to serve an indictment on Angus Sinclair charging him with The World's End Murders of Helen Scott and Christine Eadie. It was a terrible disappointment for us all but the bitterest of blows for Eddie McCusker and his team from Strathclyde. It was Eddie's last major investigation and he had worked hard to build a case – no one could have done more – but the Crown Office's decision was absolute and final. There was only one advantage and that was that the strength of the World's End case could not now be jeopardised by weaker cases. Even so, the underlying feeling was one of disappointment. We were convinced we had the right man, but the thirty-year gap and the lack of forensic evidence in the Glasgow cases meant that, despite our best efforts, we would never be able to prove it.

So, after all, we were left with the World's End cases. It wasn't the end result Operation Trinity had been working towards, but in Lothian and Borders, it was hugely important, and we were confident that after all these years we had a very strong case.

As the preparations went ahead, the defence team were given full access to all the documents and papers we'd accumulated over the years. The rules of full disclosure, obligatory in England and Wales, had gradually been accepted as routine in Scotland. This means that the defence has the right to see any evidence we had gathered, which offers them an excellent opportunity to pick holes in an inquiry, especially a historic one like this. It took the defence team a year to review all the evidence, but apart from the delay in going to trial caused by this, we had few worries. We were confident that all the evidence and documents in the World's End case had been properly and professionally cared for over the years. There were flaws but they were minor and understandable in the circumstances.

Eventually the defence had done their preparation and a slot of six weeks was estimated by the Crown Office team as being required for the trial. This was an important and encouraging decision. High Court time is scarce – the courts are overloaded with work – but it was calculated that to lead the whole weight of the prosecution evidence, and to accommodate the defence, a trial of six weeks would be needed.

But things were beginning to change and not for the better. In October 2006, the Advocate Depute, who had been so actively involved with the case for months and who had carefully led the preparations for the trial, was promoted and the responsibility was passed to a new Advocate Depute. At the same time, the lead Procurator Fiscal who had been retained in the Edinburgh office – an able and highly respected individual – was also on the move, leaving the original lead Fiscal based in Glasgow. But by now, he was responsible for the Edinburgh cases of The World's End Murders alone – crimes that were not geographically the responsibility of the Glasgow fiscal's area, and of which there was no deep-seated knowledge or ownership. Bad enough, but there were also practical difficulties as documents had to be ferried back and forward across the country as the lines of communication were extended.

While the various moves in staff were all in theory unconnected to the case, we were alarmed by the changes. The senior and well-regarded Prosecutors who had been involved throughout the investigation – the ones who had made the key decisions and had planned the Crown Office case – would not be in court or play any part in the trial after all. Worryingly for us, there also seemed to be a rejection of, or at least a strong doubt, in the minds of the new prosecution team about the low-copy number DNA evidence that forensic experts from England

164

had identified in the knots of the ligatures used to bind Helen and Christine. This evidence was not enough to provide a complete profile of Sinclair, but did offer a partial one – an indication which we believed would have been compelling to a jury. We knew that low- copy number DNA profiling was controversial, and the forensic science community was divided as to its worth.

We were also aware that, in the background, mistakes made in an Australian case involving the murder of a British man, Peter Falconio, was adding to the controversy over the reliability of low-copy number DNA profiling. Nonetheless, we felt that if this evidence was carefully presented, it would offer strong support to our case because the low-copy number DNA traces, and the different methods of tying the knots, pointed to two people being involved in the binding and gagging with a very strong pointer to Sinclair as being one of them. Ultimately, the Crown Office decided not to lead this evidence, thereby excluding expert evidence of a high quality and leaving the case strong but one-dimensional. In the end, this proved fatal when Sinclair's legal team, at late notice, changed their defence to consensual contact – thus dealing a blow to the single-strand Crown Office case.

By this time, Ian Thomas, Eddie McCusker and I had retired from the police service and Allan Jones had taken responsibility for the police component of the trial. Not that this was of any concern – no one knew more or was better placed to handle the final stages of the police case than Allan. In hindsight, however, I regret that Ian Thomas and I left when we did. However, we had no choice – our police service was completed, and we had other commitments. I had already stayed on for eight months past my planned retirement date, but it left the case light of senior police champions. Ian Thomas and I could only look on anxiously as things started to unravel. It was as if we were watching a train crash in slow motion, powerless to intervene.

There had been too many changes – a new Advocate Depute, a lead Procurator Fiscal who was remote geographically and the rejection of a considerable body of supporting evidence. Separately these issues were concerning but, when put together, they were deeply worrying to those close to the case.

Eventually, over three years after we reopened the case, the trial of Angus Sinclair opened on Monday, August 27th 2007, just six weeks short of the thirtieth anniversary of The World's End Murders. In the new court building, next to the Crown Office in Chambers Street, Edinburgh, not a mile from The World's End pub, he was at last called to account for the murders of Helen Scott and Christine Eadie.

As the date of the trial approached, the liaison between the Crown Office team and the lead officers had been maintained but it came as a shock when, on the opening day, the Advocate Depute made it known that he intended to cut the trial short – from the six weeks originally estimated by the Crown Office to only two. This rang alarm bells for those of us connected to the case – we knew the bulk and the weight of evidence that still remained, and we struggled to imagine how the case could be cut to two weeks without important material having to be excluded. It was, however, a tactical decision which was the Advocate Depute's to make. We were desperately worried, but we just had to live with it.

As the trial drew near, we had speculated as to what Sinclair's tactics would be – his defence had, after all, had over a year to consider their approach. They had also had complete access to all the data, old and new, from the thirty-year inquiry. It seemed to us that Sinclair had three options. The first, pleading guilty on the day, was out of the question. It wasn't in his nature, and in any event, he had nothing to lose by playing it long – after all, he was going nowhere and his expensive legal team was not costing him a penny. The second and more likely option was that he offered no defence, but let the Crown Office prove its case. He had tried this unsuccessfully in the Mary Gallagher case, but it was still worth a try – thirty years is a long time and his lawyers might have picked some loophole in the continuity of evidence that could cast sufficient doubt on the case against him.

In the event, he chose the route we thought he would – he blamed his conveniently dead brother-in-law, Gordon Hamilton, in the special defence of impeachment and furthermore claimed that any trace of his DNA on the bodies of Helen and Christine was as a result of consensual sex. It was always his best chance – everyone he blamed or alleged to be complicit was dead. Gordon Hamilton could not give his version of events and poor Helen and Christine, just seventeen years old when they died, were not there to rebut his hateful suggestion that they had willingly had sex with him.

As we've seen, he had the advantage of no one knowing about his awful past – the Jury had no inkling of the dozen rape victims, or the two other girls proven to have died at his hands. But it was also a

166

risky strategy for, in impeaching his dead brother-in-law and claiming consensual sex with the two young girls, he was placing himself at the scene of the crimes. He had sought to neutralise the power of the DNA evidence but, in doing so, he had implicated himself. This approach also made him potentially vulnerable in other areas. How could he explain his denials and the long silences during the many hours of interviews and then suddenly offer this defence? And it would look odd if he decided not to give evidence himself – after all, an innocent man would surely welcome the chance to deny such awful allegations personally. But, if he did give evidence and forgo his right to silence, he was taking the most awful risk. If he entered the witness box in the High Court, he would have to subject himself to a rigorous examination by the prosecuting Advocate Depute. His usual tactics of sullen silence would not work in the High Court. It was something he had never dared to do before. In all his many court appearances, in all his interviews, he had always hidden behind his right to silence. In the event, he didn't have to face these challenges – the Jury never got the chance to make a judgement on the character and behaviour of Angus Sinclair.

The defence of consensual sex also laid bare the flaw in the Crown Office's approach to the low-copy DNA evidence which would have been powerful in rebutting the suggestion of consent. We had evidence of materials from inside the knots used in tying the girls up that revealed a partial profile of Sinclair's DNA. In one particular sample, a DNA band unique to Sinclair – that is to say one that was not shared by Hamilton, Helen or Christine – was identified. Our experts had calculated a 1 in 390 probability of finding one of those bands elsewhere in the UK's population. This may not seem a lot, but, given Sinclair's admission that he was there, it significantly strengthened that probability.

The low-copy evidence together with the expert witnesses we had who were willing to interpret the knot-tying would have done much to rebut the claim of consent and, when it was made known to us what Sinclair's defence would be, we hoped the Crown Office would reconsider their decision not to present these strands of evidence and would seek to introduce them. In the event, they did not and nor was the evidence of a timeline introduced. This meant there was a potential gap in the understanding of Judge and Jury about the likely time of death of Helen and Christine This led the Judge to conclude that the girls could have been killed at any time up until the discovery of their bodies –

some fifteen to nineteen hours after they were last seen. In fact, we had evidence from pathologists to show that the girls died shortly after they were last seen. Had this evidence been introduced, it would have been harder for Sinclair to credibly claim consensual sexual contact and yet distance himself from the murders.

The disastrous consequences of these omissions would shortly become apparent as the trial of *Her Majesty's Advocate* v *Sinclair* began.

As in every murder trial, the case started slowly – there was some scene setting and time devoted to proving the crime had been committed. The friends who last saw the girls alive came through the court giving their thirty-year-old recollections. It was a strange experience. Having read their statements so many times, we felt we knew them personally but, of course, for us, they were frozen in time, back in 1977. It was odd to see the teenage pals of Helen and Christine stand in the box as middle-aged men and women. Then came the witnesses who'd found the bodies, followed by the first police officers on the scenes – these officers were all now long retired, some for over twenty years.

The defence's tactics became clear – the prosecution's case depended on the DNA evidence and, regardless of Sinclair's claim of consensual sex, there were other considerations. DNA is susceptible to contamination and, back in the 70s, this had not been a consideration so could there not have been some cross-contamination? After all, no protective clothing or face masks were used in those days. It was all designed to create a haze of doubt in the minds of the Jury and it would be hammered home by the defence even if the claim of consensual sex was rejected – thirty years was a long time, witnesses' memories were vague, systems were different, mistakes may have been made, there may be room for doubt and there could be no room for doubt to convict. The standard of proof is clear and set high – to convict, the Jury must be sure of guilt beyond all reasonable doubt. And, in any case, the slight, elderly man in the dock had given an explanation and, as unlikely as it seemed, the Crown Office's case was not structured in a way to attack it.

One of the saddest elements of any murder trial is when the family and friends give evidence and try to describe in words the events that shattered their lives and marked them forever. Morain Scott and Christine's mother, Margaret, spoke of their daughters and gave an account of their last days and the night they left their homes never to return. Both spoke of the impact that the events of October 1977 had on their lives. Then the

168

court heard how Helen's mother had never recovered from her daughter's death and had quickly declined into ill-health and died prematurely. They were not in the witness box long and there were no startling revelations as they went through their evidence, but the feeling of despair was tangible. No words could come close to describing the injury done to the Scott and Eadie families.

The remaining course of the trial was nondescript and brief. Amazingly, the special defence and the claim of consensual sex were seen to neutralise the DNA evidence. This we found unbelievable. Two young women had been found gagged, bound, raped and murdered and the man whose semen is found in them lodges an implausible defence of consent which is accepted without question. It frankly beggared belief.

As the thin list of Crown Office's witnesses came to an end, there was an awful feeling of articlimax. We had put together a strong case, but you wouldn't have known it from the lacklustre presentation in court. Then the final blow fell. We learned that the defence were going to motion for "no case to answer". That is to say that there was no evidence to support a prosecution. It was beyond belief. How could a man whose semen was found in two murdered girls have no case to answer? It defied all logic, and it challenged common sense, but it succeeded. The Judge agreed the defence's motion before a shocked court. The Advocate Depute was not in the court and nor was the lead Procurator Fiscal, who had been largely absent throughout the trial. The trial had ended and there was no right for the Crown to appeal.

All connected to the case felt the blow. Experienced court journalists had never seen the like and, on the Jury benches, there was amazement. Looking at their faces, I doubted if any of this group of ordinary citizens had been fooled by Angus Robertson Sinclair.

The prosecution handling of the case was, at first sight, inexplicable. Why had so much evidence been left out? When considered on cool reflection it was, however, all too easy to see what had gone wrong. As usual, there was no single glaring error – just a series of small events, changes in personnel, questionable decisions over evidence that all combined to weaken the case that went to court. The decision had been taken to strip the case bare and save time by leading on the powerful primary DNA evidence alone. The theory may have been to keep it simple and that to do otherwise would confuse the Jury. In the event, the single pillar of the prosecution case was brittle and was effectively neutralised by Sinclair's special defence. He never had to explain himself or justify his outrageous claims of consensual sex with Helen and Christine. The law protected him from that.

Outside the court Helen's father, Morain Scott, composed to the last and carrying himself with the same dignity as he had for thirty years, spoke for us all: "The law it may have been – justice it was not."

In the aftermath the legal profession at first closed ranks, but the damage had been done, and behind the scenes there was serious disquiet. There were questions in Parliament, and the media covered all aspects of the case and the trial in minute detail. Even the casual observer with an ounce of sense could see that the trial had been a terrible miscarriage of justice, yet the usually outspoken civil libertarians were strangely quiet. It seemed their concern for injustice only extended to those accused, not victims.

And there was another casualty – the reputation of the Scottish Justice System had taken a body blow. Behind the closed doors at the Crown Office this was surely recognised, and to their credit, instead of hunkering down and letting the storm blow over, the Law Officers particularly Solicitor General Frank Mulholland and the then Secretary for Justice in the Scottish Government, Kenny MacAskill, determined to set about the slow and difficult process of putting matters right.

The obstacles were many. It is a strict convention that the Judge and Advocate Depute Prosecutor should not be criticised after the failure of a trial. This is understandable as it serves to protect the independence of Judges and Prosecutors, who, it is assumed, always act in the best interests of justice and the rule of law. The motives of the Judge and prosecuting Advocate Depute in the first World's End trial were never in question – but they got it very wrong. The Advocate Depute should have presented much more of the available evidence to the court, and the Judge should have allowed this evidence to be presented to the Jury. As it was, the failure of the case represented, in the words of one senior legal figure, "The greatest miscarriage of justice in Scotland for forty years." And because of the "double jeopardy" rules embedded in Scots Law there could be no retrial. Angus Sinclair had "tholed his assize", and as the law stood, could not be retried for the same crime.

# 13


# Double Jeopardy


Double jeopardy, put simply, is a procedural defence that forbids a defendant from being tried again on the same or similar charges following a legitimate acquittal or conviction. The origins of the precept lie far in the past, when the death penalty could be applied for several crimes, not just for murder. It was seen as a defence against the arbitrary retrial of an accused until a conviction was secured. In a time before the checks and balances that now apply in the Criminal Justice System, it was a vital safeguard to those who found themselves in the dock. Established as a fundamental guarantee of fairness, by the 21st century the double jeopardy rule was outdated for a few reasons. For a start, the death penalty had long since gone, and the routes for appeal against conviction had increased to ensure all convictions could be thoroughly tested.

Fundamental problems with the concept of double jeopardy were also highlighted by significant developments in many branches of forensic science and investigative techniques, some of which have been described earlier in this book. Suffice to say, these techniques had developed yet further in the thirty years since The World's End Murders. This meant that the evidence available in the 1970s could be augmented out of all recognition by techniques such as DNA analysis, the use of lasers and the latest investigative procedures. In other words, old evidence viewed through a 21st century lens could provide a mass of crucial information that could not have been known at the original trial. With serious crimes like murder and rape, such developments have had enormous consequences, and since the 1990s police forces throughout the western world have been successfully applying these new techniques to previously unsolved or cold cases. But of course, in cases where defendants had already been tried and acquitted, the double jeopardy rule would forbid retrials, regardless of what new evidence might have come to light. In many jurisdictions, including England and Wales, Canada and Australia, the iniquity of this was recognised and the double jeopardy rule was repealed for serious cases where there was new and important evidence. But in Scotland, where the legal establishment tends to be conservative, the double jeopardy rule remained firmly in place, with any challenge sure to be firmly resisted by a legal profession determined to defend the foundations of the highly regarded justice system.

To change the double jeopardy rule required not only the considerable political will to enact legislation but also the support of senior legal figures in Scotland. This was no easy task, and without such a compelling case as The World's End Murders it might never have happened. Several of the key players in the original failed trial in 2007 had clearly been ill-suited to the task, but now things were very different. The Justice Secretary in the Scottish Government, Kenny MacAskill, had been a lawyer by profession long before he entered politics. MacAskill had a deep knowledge and healthy respect for the legal establishment, but that did not prevent him confronting it when necessary or from taking on powerful interest groups when required. He had shown this in his determination to address Scotland's alcohol problems even when it meant conflict with the rich and powerful alcohol industry. Now he was prepared to take on the legal establishment and, galvanised by the outcome of the 2007 World's End trial, he set about gathering political support to change the ancient double jeopardy rule.

Given the pressing programme of legislation, the complexity of the task, and the many other government priorities, it says much for MacAskill's determination that he succeeded in this major change to the law. But political will on its own would not have been enough without the active support and energy of the senior law officers of Scotland, the Lord Advocate Elish Angiolini and the Solicitor General Frank Mulholland.

The offices of Lord Advocate and Solicitor General are among the most ancient and powerful in Scotland. All criminal prosecutions are raised in the name of the Lord Advocate, who is a member of government, and it is the Solicitor General who is responsible for running the business of the Crown Office Prosecution Service. Traditionally, these senior law officers were men who had come through the same public schools and universities to the same top law firms and the Faculty of Advocates, from whose small elite membership the law officers had usually come. After a term or two in office, depending on the fortunes of their political allies, the law officers invariably become High Court Judges. It is astonishing just how long this system had prevailed, and how well most of the incumbents had discharged their duties. Nonetheless, it was ripe for change. Elish Angiolini and Frank Mulholland were part of that change and had come from very different backgrounds from their predecessors. Neither had come through the public school/top university/Faculty of Advocates route (although both latterly became members of the Faculty). Instead, they had worked their way through the Procurator Fiscal Service to the top of their profession. Both were extremely able, fine examples of success through merit, and perhaps because they had come to the top the non-traditional way, were more prepared to challenge the legal status quo.

Both Angiolini and Mulholland had been in post at the time of the 2007 trial, and while they publicly defended the outcome, along with the way the Judge and Advocate Depute handled the proceedings, they undoubtedly both felt disappointed with the outcome, especially Frank Mulholland. The Solicitor General had a long involvement with the World's End investigation, having been senior Procurator Fiscal in Edinburgh and involved in the re-investigation in 2004. A man with a keen intellect, a strong sense of justice and some of the characteristics of a street fighter, one can only imagine his feelings as he watched powerless as the trial in 2007 slipped away. But he was not to be defeated, and in the days immediately following the 2007 debacle he took steps to ensure that, if possible, matters would be set right.

In the first instance he directed that all the evidence in the World's End case be carefully preserved, and the meticulous supervision of all case productions maintained. The immaculate preservation of productions over the thirty years since the crime had been highly unusual and was of huge significance in a prosecution case always beset by defence suggestions of evidence contamination. I'm sure my successors in Lothian and Borders Police would have preserved all the productions anyway, but the immediate order from the Solicitor General sent a powerful message. In a very unusual move, Mulholland also met personally, and maintained contact with, the families of Helen and Christine. He assured them that the investigation into the deaths of their daughters was unfinished business and that if it were possible, he would ensure that justice would be done.

While Justice Secretary MacAskill prepared the political ground, the law officers set about bringing about one of the biggest changes in the Scottish Legal System for over a hundred years.

Shortly after the failed 2007 trial, the Scottish Law Commission was asked to examine the question of the Crown's right to appeal against "no case to answer" rulings. As a result, the Scottish Law Commission recommended that in future the Crown should have the right to appeal 'no case to answer' decisions in serious cases. It was a start – never again could a case with the gravity of the World's End fail for this reason without the possibility of appeal. But this decision did not affect the double jeopardy rule. That would be a bigger challenge.

The enactment of any new statute takes time and needs considerable political support. A change in the law as controversial as the double jeopardy rule met the expected resistance from conservative sections of the legal profession, but point by point it was argued through. It's often said that bad cases make bad laws, in other words that legislation enacted as a result of a specific case often produces flawed legislation. This might well be true, but while the World's End case is often cited as the main reason why the double jeopardy rule was abolished, it was nonetheless a change in the law that was long overdue.

By summer 2011 Elish Angiolini had stepped down as Lord Advocate and Frank Mulholland had replaced her. The same year, all obstructions overcome, the Double Jeopardy (Scotland) Act 2011 was passed into law by the Scottish Parliament with cross-party support, bringing Scotland into line with most other developed legal systems. Very significantly, it was retrospective legislation. Enacting retrospective legislation is unusual, but in the case of the World's End it was of course essential given that the murders were committed decades before. But it wasn't going to be easy. Section 4 of the new legislation states that:

*"A person who, on indictment in the High Court (the original indictment) has been acquitted of an offence (the original offence) may, if the conditions mentioned in Sub Section (3) are satisfied, be charged with, and prosecuted anew for – the original offence or another relevant offence."*

Importantly, the criterion laid out in Sub Section (3) was explicit – a retrial would only be considered by the High Court if:

*"There is new evidence that the person committed the original offence or similar offence, and that the Crown had been granted authority to bring a new prosecution by the High Court."*

In another section it is made clear that the High Court may set aside the acquittal only if satisfied that the case against the accused is strengthened substantially by new evidence.

It was a tough standard to meet. In the World's End case the demand for new material meant that the mass of evidence not presented in the 2007 trial did not qualify. We believed it was important material and were bitterly disappointed that it had not been presented in 2007, but it had been available for that trial and therefore it was not new in 2011. We had to find yet more.

The Scottish Government, Kenny MacAskill the Justice Secretary, and above all the law officers, particularly the Lord Advocate Frank Mulholland, had moved mountains to change the law. It was now the job of detectives and forensic scientists to find new and compelling evidence.

# 14

# New and Compelling Evidence

During the re-investigation of the World's End case in 2004 we had gathered a mass of evidence which clearly pointed to Angus Sinclair and his brother-in-law Gordon Hamilton as being responsible for the deaths of Helen Scott and Christine Eadie. We also had circumstantial evidence to link Sinclair to the deaths of at least three other young women murdered in the 1970s, but the complete absence of forensic evidence meant these cases went no further. We were hugely disappointed that Sinclair would never be called to account for all his crimes, but we were confident that at least we had a strong case with the murders of Helen and Christine. But during the trial in 2007, we watched in horror as much of our evidence was not used by the Crown or heard by the Jury.

As well as the strong DNA evidence linking Sinclair and Hamilton to the girls, we also had compelling evidence that pointed to the nature of the contact between Sinclair and Hamilton and their victims – evidence that would have refuted Sinclair's absurd defence of consensual sex and instead pointed to the direct involvement of Sinclair and Hamilton in the violent murders. We felt that all the evidence painted a complete picture – one which any reasonable Jury would have seen as unequivocal. In the event, during the trial they never got the chance to see the whole evidential picture or even to make a decision based on the sparse evidence they did see.

Among the evidence not used by the Crown was critical low-copy number DNA from the articles of the girls' clothing that had been used to bind and strangle them. As already mentioned, low-copy number DNA is at best indicative rather than conclusive. There was insufficient material found in the post-mortem samples taken from the girls to positively identify a match to Sinclair and Hamilton. Consequently, low-copy number DNA evidence was of less direct value, but still important as background or contextual evidence. On the tights that had been used to strangle Helen, scientists identified particles of DNA from Helen herself, from Hamilton and from Sinclair. The strongest match of course was from Helen – they were the tights she had been wearing the night she was killed. The next strongest match was to Hamilton, with traces of a DNA profile matching Sinclair's making up the remainder. But whereas Helen's DNA profile was complete, Hamilton's and Sinclair's were partial.

On Christine's tights, used as ligatures to bind her, low-copy evidence was even stronger. Once again, the DNA of three people – Christine, Hamilton and Sinclair – was found. Again, Christine's profile was by far the strongest – the tights were hers – and again there were significant traces of DNA particles with matches to Hamilton's and Sinclair's profiles. No other DNA alleles were found on either pair of tights – refuting Sinclair's defence that after having had consensual sex with him and Hamilton, the girls were murdered by someone else.

In 2007 low-copy number DNA evidence would not have been enough to convict Sinclair on its own, but it would have helped complete the picture for the Jury, since it is extremely unlikely that Hamilton's and Sinclair's DNA would have got on to the ligatures other than by their tying them at the time Helen and Christine were murdered.

We had another strong piece of supporting evidence provided by an expert on knots. The study of knots is one of those fascinating but obscure branches of forensic examination, but in my career the opinions of experts in knot-tying have proved immensely useful on several occasions. The materials that are used and the symmetry with which knots are tied are both significant.

From the very start detectives and scientists had seen the knots tied in the ligatures used to bind Helen and Christine as important – so much so that for many years they were carefully preserved, untouched until new technology proved how important they were in terms of low-copy number DNA. But there was something else just as interesting about the knots. Knots on the garments used to bind and strangle Christine were reef knots, whilst granny knots were used in Helen's case. This was important because, being creatures of habit, we usually tie knots in the same way. It is highly unlikely that one person, during the frenzy of a rape and murder, would have used different knots on each victim. Once again this clearly pointed to the involvement of two men. Not until we discovered that Sinclair had been employed making fishing nets during his early years in prison did the significance of this strike us – reef knots are commonly used in making commercial fishing nets. Tying reef knots would have been second nature for him. It was another piece of evidence that was not powerful enough on its own to convict him, but taken with other strong strands of evidence, it would have helped complete the overall picture for the Jury.

And there was one last piece of very sad evidence that the Jury did not hear. Helen's boyfriend had been going out with her for three years, since school days. They were close but had never had sex. During our investigation we had come to realise that Helen and Christine were little more than children, a fact that was poignantly underlined by her boyfriend when he said that Helen had been a virgin on the night she died. The suggestion by Sinclair that she had consensual sex with two men she had met a few hours before her death was as ludicrous as it was repugnant. The simple evidence of Helen's heartbroken teenage boyfriend would certainly have made an impact on the Jury, had they been allowed to hear it.

We had other forensic evidence showing fibres found on the girls' clothing as being identical to the upholstery of the Toyota owned by Sinclair in 1977. We even had some eyewitness identification of Sinclair from outside The World's End pub in October 1977, but again none of this evidence featured in the 2007 trial.

But that was all in the past – it was compelling evidence, at least in our eyes, but it was not new. It had all been available for the 2007 trial so it could not be used as a reason for a retrial under the new double jeopardy legislation. We needed to find yet more fresh and compelling evidence. Fortunately, developments in forensic science were coming thick and fast. And in the police some old champions were still in place. Some new ones, too young to have been involved in the original case, were also keen to play a part in the investigation. The World's End was never an ordinary investigation: so horrifying were the deaths of Helen and Christine that generations of police officers, myself included, saw ourselves as having a personal obligation to settle a debt of honour. This had been true over the years, and it was just as true when the final team of investigators joined the long line of officers who had been involved in the case over three decades. We were all absolutely determined to deliver justice for Helen,

Christine and their devastated families.

Foremost among the investigators was Allan Jones, by 2011 a Detective Superintendent in charge of major crime investigation in Lothian and Borders. Allan had been involved in the case from his earliest service as a police cadet, and as he rose through the ranks he played an active part and was involved in many of the developments as they unfolded over the years. In the late 1990s he led the first DNA screening exercise into the enquiry, involved the National Crime Faculty in their first review in 2001 and then led the consequential DNA elimination swabbing exercise. Allan was one of the senior officers who pushed hardest for the involvement of the English Forensic Science Service, convincing me that the cost, time and political obstacles would be worthwhile. This led to the first identification of the DNA profiles on the items used to strangle the girls which we later matched to Hamilton. Finally, it was Allan by this time a Detective Inspector, with his boss Detective Superintendent Ian Thomas, who persuaded me to agree the funding to take forward the year-long familial DNA swabbing that eventually identified Sinclair. During the 2004 investigation, Allan, then a Detective Chief Inspector, had responsibility for the overarching forensic strategy – an obvious choice given his superb grasp of the case's forensic aspect.

At the conclusion of the 2004 investigation, it was Allan who was left to argue against the "single strand evidential approach" that was the fatal weakness of the prosecution case in the 2007 trial. He saw that without DNA evidence from the ligatures the case would always be vulnerable to the "consensual sex" defence. However, in the end he was forced to concede, then had to watch as our fears were realised and the trial collapsed. No single officer had been more involved in the long investigation, and no officer took the collapse of the 2007 trial harder. But he wasn't finished. Allan is nothing if not resilient; he had proven that over the years and he wasn't about to give up now. Allan wasn't alone in his dedication. His contemporaries, Detectives Andy Ritchie and Jim Shanley, were still very much involved, as was a rising star in the CID in Lothian and Borders, Gary Flannigan. Gary had been a young sergeant attached to the National Crime Faculty when they had helped us so much with our investigation in 2004. Now he was progressing through the ranks and would eventually replace Allan Jones as Detective Superintendent, Major Crime, in Lothian and Borders Police. Eventually Gary, by 2013 a member of the new National Police Force of Police Scotland, would head the last successful phase of the World's End investigation.

But this was still some years away when Allan Jones took stock following the 2007 trial and tried to plot a way forward. By that time the political temperature around the case had risen, and politicians and senior Law Officers at the Crown Office were starting to change the double jeopardy rules.

By this time the World's End case was very widely known, and Allan and his colleagues spoke and made presentations about it at police conferences throughout the UK. Following retirement, I wrote the first edition of this book (2008) and spoke on the investigation to a wide range of groups. This all helped keep the case in the public consciousness and high on the agendas of the police and legal establishment.

Eventually it was at a police conference in England in 2010 that a breakthrough came. Allan Jones was attending and saw a trade display by Cellmark Forensic Service. A commercial company, Cellmark is in the forefront of DNA development and had been involved in the early days of the World's End case. In the interim it had been developing ground-breaking, ultra-sensitive techniques. Allan and his colleagues were determined to see whether these could be of use in the World's End case.

But it was expensive, and before further steps could be taken the Crown Office, as well as Police Chiefs, needed to be convinced. There were, after all, many new, as well as old, cases that competed for scarce resources, and the World's End had arguably had its share. But the murders of Helen and Christine had become totemic and would not be forgotten as long as any avenue of enquiry or new development remained.

With the agreement of the Crown Office a forensic case evaluation was progressed, only fifty hours' work in the initial agreement, but it was a start, as it confirmed the Crown's commitment. The initial case review by Cellmark was so promising that in 2011 the Crown agreed to an overarching forensic strategy which allowed Cellmark to examine all the forensic evidence connected with the case. This was a bold move as it placed the responsibility for this material with a commercial company in England rather than with the newly formed Scottish Forensic Science Service. The decision might have been politically sensitive, but it simply emphasised the cutting-edge work that Cellmark was doing.

Leading the efforts at Cellmark were two scientists, the husband-and-wife team Geraldine and Andrew Davidson. In a piece of remarkable good fortune, they had worked in Scotland, knew the Scottish Justice

System and were even accredited by the Scottish Courts.

While the forensic case was developing, another interesting piece of evidence emerged. During an interview with a long-term prisoner about another case, it was revealed that this prisoner had shared a cell with Angus Sinclair in the period following the 2007 trial. During the long hours behind closed cell doors, it is difficult to avoid conversation, and of course the subject of the World's End came up. Sinclair reputedly made a remarkable statement:

"They didn't have to die."

After the years of silence, at last he betrayed knowledge of Helen's and Christine's deaths. He perhaps thought he was safe in making such a comment after the collapse of the trial, but he was wrong, for as he spoke new forensic developments were emerging which would provide exactly the kind of evidence required to bring him finally to justice.

These developments included Crime-lite®ML, a filtered light source capable of screening for the presence of materials exhibiting fluorescence, which are not always visible under white light, particularly body fluid stains and cellular material. Not only does it identify stains, but it also allows scientists to interpret their distribution and concentrate examination on areas where staining is heaviest. Crime-lite was only introduced to forensic casework in 2009 and accredited in 2011. In the case of the murders of Helen and Christine it proved to be a revelation. Extended Acid Phosphate testing and Sperm Elution were both new techniques for screening for the presence of semen then separating the chemical elements to allow accurate DNA profiling. These new techniques provided a degree of sensitivity unavailable even in 2007, and they are particularly valuable in the examination of old or degraded forensic samples, exactly like the ones in the World's End case.

MiniFiler® was another new DNA technique, which increased the ability to get profiles from very weak or old samples. Highly specialised, it was only developed in 2008, and like the other new technologies seemed purpose-made for our case. And there was more. The techniques for examining low-copy number DNA had improved greatly since 2007, as had the computer software which analysed results and probabilities.

Making use of all these new techniques, the Davidsons began their painstaking examination of the old materials, particularly Helen and Christine's tights and underwear. It had been a long journey full of progress and setbacks but now with all the best people and ground-

181

breaking science focused on the task there was a feeling that at last we would see justice done.

We were not disappointed. Using Crime-lite, Extended Acid Phosphate testing, and Sperm Elution, the tights used to bind and strangle Christine were carefully unwrapped and examined. Samples of DNA from Christine herself, Hamilton and Sinclair were found. Areas of Christine's bra, also used to strangle her, were examined, with the same result.

And so it went on. Slowly Helen and Christine's clothing gave up its secrets. Just as significant, there was no trace of any other person's DNA. We always knew that Sinclair's claim that someone else must have killed Helen and Christine was absurd – now we could prove it.

More importantly the DNA had been found in folds and creases of the garments, which made it obvious that the deposits had been left when the clothing had been ripped and torn to bind and kill Helen and Christine. This showed that not only had Hamilton and Sinclair had sex with the two girls, but had bound and killed them as well. This was the new and compelling evidence we had been searching for.

In March 2014, the Lord Advocate, Frank Mulholland, appeared at the High Court in Edinburgh in the case of *Her Majesty's Advocate* v *Angus Robertson Sinclair* in the first ever application under the Double Jeopardy (Scotland) Act 2011. It was an important moment in Scottish legal history, and a panel of three senior Judges, including the Lord Justice Clerk, sat to hear the application. After a full disclosure of the evidence and lengthy consideration, Lady Dorrian delivered the opinion of the Court.

The Judges had recognised the new evidence as meeting the standards of the new double jeopardy legislation, and given the seriousness of the case, a new prosecution was authorised. It was a legal first. After all the setbacks, and the huge effort by everyone in the Justice System and forensic science community, Angus Sinclair would face justice and once more be called to account for the deaths of Helen and Christine.

The new trial was set for October 13th 2014, almost thirty-seven years after Helen and Christine were brutally murdered. It was to be heard in the new court building in Livingston, West Lothian, a few hundred yards from the old Livingston Police Station, where our 2004 investigation had been based. The case of The World's End Murders had come full circle.

# 15

# Retrial, 2014

# Week 1

On October 13th 2014, the High Court was convened in Court 2 at the new court building in Livingston, West Lothian to hear the case of *Her Majesty's Advocate* v *Angus Robertson Sinclair*. The court building in Livingston is almost as far as you can get from the traditional image of a High Court. It has no dark mahogany or canopied Judge's bench, so typical of the old High Courts in Edinburgh and Glasgow. With light wood used throughout and an air of informality it almost belied the seriousness of the case about to be tried. Livingston had been chosen for several reasons.

First, although only a few miles away from the capital it wasn't in Edinburgh, which was important to help counter the probable defence objection of prejudice due to pre-trial publicity. It is always a problem in notorious cases – and in the case of the World's End it was a serious issue. Since late 1977, acres of newsprint had been devoted to the case, and latterly Angus Sinclair's name had been firmly linked with it. He had been found guilty – if not in a court of law, then in the court of public opinion – in 2007, so it was important that all possible measures were taken to ensure a fair trial. In the three years since the double jeopardy legislation had been passed, many regular commentators on the case, myself included, had refused to say anything about it in order to avoid prejudice. Even so, the Jury in the retrial would be specifically directed by the Judge to ignore all information other than that presented in the court.

But Livingston Court had also been chosen for another reason. As one of the most modern courts in Scotland, it was fully equipped with the latest audiovisual and technical support. The Lord Advocate, Frank Mulholland, would lead the prosecution personally, and he would use the latest technology to lay out a compelling case against Angus Sinclair. Thus, the scene was set in one of the country's most modern courts for one of the oldest cases in Scottish Criminal History to be retried.

Sinclair appeared from custody where he had been continuously since 1981. Now almost seventy years old and heavily bearded, he looked like any other plump little old man, and nothing like the powerful menacing individual he had been in 1977.

Already convicted of the murder of Mary Gallagher and the rape and sexual assault of ten children and young people in the 1980s, he was serving two life sentences, so whatever the outcome of this trial he would spend the rest of his life in prison. Of course, those convictions were inadmissible as evidence – to all intents and purposes, Sinclair appeared as a man without a stain on his character.

Sinclair pled 'not guilty' to the charges of murdering and raping Helen and Christine and, as he had done in 2007, lodged special defences of incrimination, consent and alibi. Once again, he incriminated his dead brother-in-law, Gordon Hamilton, and in a bizarre move claimed that, having met the girls earlier in the evening of their murder, he had consensual sex with them both before leaving them in the care of Hamilton while he went fishing nearby. It was a far-fetched scenario, but it was the only way he could explain why his DNA was found at the crime scene, admit his own presence nearby and yet claim he had nothing to do with the rape and murder of the two teenagers.

The Crown opened the case as it always must in murder trials. The Lord Advocate had to prove that a crime had been committed, and that meant the Jury had to see the photographs of Helen and Christine as they were found that bleak day in October 1977. The old black-and-white pictures still had the ability to shock, and Frank Mulholland was careful to warn the Jury and Helen and Christine's families that the images were disturbing. Also shown were photographs of the articles of clothing used to bind the girls. It was these scraps of material that contained the crucial new evidence. On the second day came another difficult part of any murder trial. Family members had to speak of their dead loved ones, and as they had done in 2007, describe them and recount their last contacts with them. Helen's and Christine's parents must have relived the nightmare thousands of times, and in the courtroom at Livingston, in the presence of the man who killed the girls, they did so again.

Sinclair behaved as he had always done at his various court appearances over the years. In the best traditions of hardened criminals, he sat sullenly listening intently to the evidence while his defence QC, Ian Duguid, picked over the evidence, trying to find faults and inconsistencies in witness statements and during cross-examinations. It's easy to do this in historical and complex cases – memories fade and minor facts become distorted. The burden of proof in a criminal trial in Scotland is to establish guilt 'beyond reasonable doubt', hence the defence's objective is always the same: to sow doubt in the minds of the Jury. But despite this, as the first week of the trial was closing the prosecution was steadily presenting a solid case. Lord Advocate Mulholland was painstaking in his presentation of the facts; nothing was missed, no detail overlooked.

As the trial proceeded and the police witnesses spoke, it was clear that the case had not come to court a moment too soon. Some retired officers that I remembered as being highly capable in the past were now uncertain in their recollections, their memories failing badly with the passage of time. It was obviously difficult for many of the original investigators, who were now mostly over seventy. Although all the documentary and forensic evidence was in place, the Jury still needed to hear from the witnesses themselves.

## Week 2

The second week of the trial opened with the evidence from the pathologists. Despite the passage of time, it was still difficult – especially for the victims' families and friends – to hear once again how the girls had been brutally murdered, and how their bodies displayed the signs of strangulation, suffocation and blunt force trauma to the neck and head. Dr Bob Nagle, one of the pathologists at the time of the crime and now ninety, gave his evidence, supported by Professor Tony Busuttil, one of the best-known forensic pathologists of his generation. While Professor Busuttil had not been involved in the original investigation, he had comprehensively examined all the post-mortem results and his evidence was crucial. He concluded that the same two people had been involved in both murders, so similar were the victims' injuries. After injuries, the Jury were not to know it, but such injuries were Angus Sinclair's signature. A small but powerful man in his youth, he had frequently used extreme violence during his robberies and sexual crimes.

The forensic odontologist, Dr Howard Moodie, followed, giving an opinion about a bite mark on Christine's arm. It was an attacking bite rather than an amorous one. It had been done to hurt and subdue – not during an act of consensual sex.

Then came the expert on knots – the same man who had been ready to give evidence in the 2007 trial but hadn't been called. He compared the symmetry of the reef knots tying Christine with the more haphazard tying of Helen's ligatures. It was in his opinion likely to be the work of two men. It was damning evidence, for it directly contradicted Sinclair's claim to having had consensual sex with both girls but nothing to do with their deaths. Two men had been involved with the tying-up of the girls. Christine had fought and had been bound by someone with experience of tying knots while Helen had shown less resistance and had been bound by a person with little or no knot-tying skill. It all fitted. Sinclair had led the attack and had bound Christine with the reef knots he had learned to tie all those years before in prison. We know from the difference in blood alcohol levels that Helen had died after Christine. Knowing what fate had befallen her friend, Helen must have been paralysed with fear.

DNA was always the foundation of the case against Sinclair, and having heard all the supporting evidence, the Jury now were now presented with complex but crucial interpretation of the DNA samples left on Helen and Christine's bodies and clothing, particularly Helen's coat that dark night in 1977.

The early part of the evidence was both sensitive and disturbing as it focused on the intimate samples taken from the girls during their post-mortem examinations. Of course, it was essential, but it was gruesome in its detail. The main DNA samples found were those of Gordon Hamilton, but there were also traces that matched Sinclair's profile. Sitting in court, Helen's younger brother Kevin, who was present throughout the trial representing the Scott family, listened intently to the details of this very intimate evidence.

The trial was now in the hands of the expert witnesses, scientists whose training and professional reputations demanded the highest standards of objectivity. There are few absolute certainties with such evidence, only degrees of probability, and words must be chosen carefully. On the lining of the coat Helen had been wearing on the night she died were small stains that, when examined, proved to be Sinclair's semen. The statistical probability was one in a billion that the semen was anyone else's. Knowing of this evidence, Sinclair had of course lodged his special defence of consent – that both girls had had sex with him willingly. To anyone knowing Helen and Christine and the characters of Sinclair and Hamilton this was ludicrous – even so, this had been enough to seriously derail the 2007 trial. But this time it was different. All the supporting evidence – the knots, the eyewitness accounts, the traces of DNA on the intimate samples – helped to paint a vivid and precise picture of the events of that night. And the Jury of nine women and six men were taking everything in. They had already visited the lonely spots where Helen and Christine had been found, and by the end of the second week, it was all starting to add up.

## Week 3

The first two weeks of the trial had been taken up proving the crime had been committed and setting the scene. The evidence presented had all been available for the 2007 trial, but much of it hadn't been presented to the court at that time. Week 3 of the prosecution case opened with new evidence. The scientists from Cellmark described the results of new examination of the ligatures used to bind and kill Christine. MiniFiler, the new technique for detecting and enhancing degraded DNA samples, had found traces of Sinclair's and Hamilton's – not full profiles but indicators of their presence. In the case of Helen's ligatures, the evidence was far stronger. On the pants used to gag her were detected strong traces of Sinclair's DNA. It was a billion to one chance against it being anyone else's. The DNA traces found on articles of the clothing used to bind and kill both girls were positive matches for Sinclair and Hamilton, along with the expected traces of the girls themselves. Despite rigorous cross examination, the expert witnesses could not be shaken.

Up till now defence QC Ian Duguid had ably picked round the edges of the Crown case, trying to plant what doubt he could in the minds of the Jury – but he had to do more. And now he did. At the latest possible stage, a forty-seven-page defence document was lodged, setting out forensic opinion that contradicted the Crown's experts. Remarkably, it also laid out what appeared to be Sinclair's recollection of what happened. Breaking his silence of thirty-seven years, he said that he had met the girls the night they were murdered, that he and his brother-in-law Gordon Hamilton had driven them to nearby Holyrood Park where they had had consensual sex, after which he had been driven by Hamilton to East Lothian and dropped off to go fishing, leaving the girls with Hamilton. It was an incredible version of events, but also a high-risk strategy, as it laid the way open to cross- examination by the Lord Advocate.

It was also, however, a foreseeable tactic. Sinclair had remained silent in the past and during the early part of this trial, undoubtedly hoping that some legal technicality might bring it to a halt as it had in 2007. This time, however, there was to be no such escape. Sinclair had lodged special defences, and for them to succeed he had to justify them.

The right of the defence to reveal evidence during a trial at the last moment is one of the inequalities of the justice system. In contrast, the Crown must give notice and full disclosure of all the prosecution evidence well in advance. This allows the preparation of a defence tailored to focus on any perceived prosecution weakness.

The trial was adjourned for twenty-four hours to allow the Crown to study this new evidence, which could have had serious implications were it not for the fact that crucial new evidence from the Cellmark experts was about to be presented to the Jury.

The newest, most important forensic evidence began with an exhaustive introduction to the expertise of the key witness from Cellmark and an explanation of the technology involved. This was vital, as it was an area of evidence that the defence would scrutinise very closely. Although the company was at the cutting edge of the development of DNA science, many of its techniques, although fully evaluated, were new to the Scottish courts. The defence had to create in the minds of the Jury doubt regarding Cellmark's credibility. Knowing this, the Lord Advocate spent hours building a picture of the reliability and international reputation of the work of Cellmark and their main witness, Geraldine Davidson.

The main focus of the Cellmark examination was the ligatures used to bind and kill Helen and Christine, the key elements in proving that

Sinclair murdered them. Regardless of how far-fetched Sinclair's claim of consensual sex was, this claim had to be destroyed. Whilst traces of Sinclair's semen and DNA could be explained, albeit improbably, on the intimate swabs taken from the girls, their presence on the ligatures, particularly where they had been tied during the act of murder, would tell a different story.

Like all scientists, Geraldine Davidson chose her words carefully. All her conclusions were clearly explained, all her estimates conservative and reasonable. Traces of Hamilton and Sinclair had once again been found on the intimate swabs, but no traces of semen had been found on Christine's pants. This meant that if Sinclair was to be believed, seventeen-year-old Christine had *not* put her pants back on after having consensual sex with him and Hamilton before being driven twenty miles to East Lothian. It seems a small point, but it didn't ring true. It was contrary to human behaviour. It didn't add up and the Jury knew it.

The difference between an Investigative Forensic Scientist and an Examining Scientist is important. While the traditional examining scientist subjects evidence to examination and identifies its components, the investigative scientist seeks not only to identify the components but to explain how the material got there and in what circumstances. The interpretation of the DNA on the ligatures was crucial to the case against Angus Sinclair. Traces of his DNA, together with that of Gordon Hamilton, had been found inside the knots. We had known there were traces when we analysed them for the 2007 trial. Now with improved technology and techniques the profiles were stronger, and the inference was clear. The DNA of Sinclair could only have been left when the knots were tied during the act of murder.

The evidence from Geraldine Davidson was painstakingly thorough. Each part of the ligatures was examined separately in minute detail for both semen and other cellular DNA. Each result was interpreted, and probabilities calculated. Statistical evidence demonstrated that the probability that the DNA had come from Sinclair and Hamilton was millions to one.

By the end of the third week of the trial, the court had witnessed a masterclass in the presentation of the evidence in chief by the Lord Advocate and of the giving of evidence by an expert witness. It was painstaking, comprehensive, meticulous, and, as we believed, conclusive.

# Week 4

The prosecution case was concluded by scientist Andrew Davidson, an expert in his own right and the corroborating witness for all his wife Geraldine's findings and conclusions. Like her, he carefully explained their findings and, most importantly, their interpretations.

# Week 5

Now it was time for the defence. Their proposition was that Helen and Christine, two young and sexually inexperienced teenagers who had been out with friends on a Saturday night and had been drinking, but were by no means drunk, had gone off with two much older men they had met just a few hours before. A short time later, in the confines of a small caravanette, both had willingly engaged in vaginal and anal sex with Sinclair and Hamilton, after which they had not put back on their underwear. They had then allowed themselves to be driven miles out of the city, where they were last seen fit and well in the company of Gordon Hamilton, who drove off with them in Sinclair's caravanette after leaving Sinclair to go fishing in the pitch-black autumn night. Even if you knew nothing of the characters of Helen and Christine – even if you knew nothing of Sinclair, Hamilton or fishing, it was all ridiculous. None of it rang true.

If this was not preposterous enough, there was another factor that underlined the unlikeliness of this sequence of events. Sinclair always took a great pride in his cars – in fact it was the only thing he would speak about in the long 2004 police interviews. The Toyota caravanette he owned at the time of the murders was his pride and joy. The idea that Sinclair would give his precious vehicle to Hamilton, known to be a heavy drinker and undoubtedly under the influence that evening, was as unlikely as the rest of his "recollections" of that night.

On day one of the defence case there was a bombshell, when it was announced that Sinclair had elected to give evidence on his own behalf. It was incredible, as he had remained silent during all his police interviews.

He had never taken the risk of giving evidence on his own behalf, and in doing so now forfeited the right of silence and opened himself to cross-examination. He may have believed he had nothing to lose – after all his silence had made no difference during the trial for the murder of Mary Gallagher. Or perhaps he thought he could spin it so that his dead co-accused could take the blame. After all, the whole court had listened to forensic evidence which showed Hamilton's DNA was found in greater quantities than his. Those of us who knew Sinclair would have bet against him giving evidence on his own behalf and we would have been wrong.

The defence led Sinclair in his description of the events of the night Helen and Christine were murdered. Now it was time for cross-examination by the Lord Advocate, who obviously relished the opportunity. Giving whispered responses, Sinclair began slowly and cautiously, answering simply "yes" or "no" to Lord Advocate Mulholland's questions in order to not refer to anything that might incriminate him. It was a high-risk strategy; the Lord Advocate was an experienced Prosecutor. But whilst there were dangers for Sinclair, so were there also for the prosecution. The Lord Advocate had to be careful to make no reference to Sinclair's past or the 2007 trial. To do so would have jeopardised the trial on the grounds of procedural irregularity.

But in the end the problems were all Sinclair's and started early in the cross examination. The post-mortem reports showed clear signs of sexual force on Helen and Christine, injuries inconsistent with consensual sex, but entirely consistent with rape. His responses became mumbled when the awkward questions came and the absurdity of his version of events was laid bare. His account of his fishing trip was riddled with inconsistency, and as the questions from the Lord Advocate became more probing, he was led away from his prepared mental script, instead showing a total lack of empathy for his victims. He admitted he wasn't sure if the girls had consented to sex, and that he had regarded them simply as sexual objects. He accepted that his account of events seemed ludicrous, but when Lord Advocate Mulholland repeatedly asked him to accept responsibility for the murder of Helen and Christine he refused to do so. He came across as cold, callous, detached. Perhaps this was a result of his having been institutionalised for so many years; it was more likely, however, that the Jury was simply getting a glimpse of the real Angus Sinclair.

At the end of the fifth week, the prosecution and defence closed their cases. The prosecution had made a powerful forensic case linking Sinclair and Hamilton to the crimes. The defence had predictably attacked the scientific evidence, and Sinclair had himself spoken; an unexpected turn of events and one which did him no favours. For those of us who had lived with the case for so long it all seemed clear cut, but of course we couldn't see into the minds of the Jury, who knew nothing of Sinclair's dreadful past.

## The Jury's Verdict

Juries are always unpredictable, so the closing speeches of the Lord Advocate and the defence QC would be critical. Depending on the skill of the speaker, these speeches are sometimes what turns a trial one way or the other.

Lord Advocate Mulholland opened by setting out one last time the circumstances of Helen and Christine's deaths. He reminded the Jury that justice in Scotland has no 'sell by date' and that their job was to reach a verdict based on the evidence alone. The prosecution case was then summarised carefully with the key events presented in chronological order – The World's End pub, the last sightings by the High Street beat policeman, the sightings of a caravanette in the Bents Car Park, Longniddry. Then came the graphic descriptions of the finding of the bodies, the deposition sites and the causes of death. Points of law were covered, and the definition of murder explained. Then the full weight of the forensic evidence was underlined and contrasted with Sinclair's recollection of events. There was a final reminder of the strength of the case against Sinclair and Hamilton, and although long dead, Hamilton's role was important – both he and Sinclair had acted in concert, and in doing so were equally guilty.

Lord Advocate Mulholland spoke for over an hour and concluded by reminding the Jury of their duty:

*"It's been thirty-seven years since Christine and Helen were murdered. But Christine's mother and family are still here to see justice. Helen's father and family are also all still here to see justice.*

*Despite the passing of so many years, this case has not been allowed to sit on a shelf and gather dust. The file has never been closed.*

*Instead, the items in this case – the girls' clothes, the ligatures, samples taken from their bodies, even the soil from the field – have all been carefully preserved, returned to with each step forward in technology and science, until now, when using forensic tools such as Crime-lite, we can see the hidden evidential remains of that night in 1977.*

*What we see is Angus Sinclair and Gordon Hamilton all over the ligatures. Angus Sinclair, all over Helen's coat. We also see Sinclair in all the areas where we see Hamilton, bar one. And that is what this case is all about. Sinclair and Hamilton – together – beating, raping and then murdering the girls.*

*This new forensic evidence is added to all the other evidence I have discussed. The totality of this evidence is considerable, powerful and quite frankly overwhelming. It exposes as a lie the incredible story put forward by the accused as to what he says happened that night, a story which on numerous occasions even he agreed sounded ridiculous.*

*The body of Prosecution evidence has not come from forensics alone. It has come from numerous sources – from the families of the girls, from friends of the girls, from police officers at the time, from acquaintances of the accused, from witnesses long since dead but whose statements remain for you to consider, from a knot expert, a dental expert, a soil expert and medical experts. It is on the basis of all this evidence, powerful and overwhelming, that I invite you to find Angus Sinclair guilty of both charges."*

It was a closing speech of the highest quality.

The final defence speech to the Jury was also expertly done. It concentrated on doubts about the forensic science, the passage of time, and the potential for contamination. The verdict was obvious: there wasn't enough evidence and Sinclair should be acquitted.

Finally, on the last day of the trial, the Judge, Lord Matthews, summed up the case in detail, highlighting the points of evidence in detail. It was a necessary end to any High Court trial.

On the Friday of the fifth week, the Jury retired to consider their verdict on the charges of murder and rape. As always there were three verdicts open to them – Guilty, Not Guilty and Not Proven, the last two amounting to the same – the acquittal of the accused.

Regardless of the strength of a case or the number of trials you have sat through, there is always a tension when a Jury retires to reach its verdict. Sitting near me in the court, just behind the families of Helen and Christine, were Allan Jones and Andy Ritchie, two detectives I knew well and for whom this moment represented all they had worked for over twenty years. The Jury took just two hours to deliver its verdict. By unanimous decision Sinclair was guilty on all counts.

Lord Advocate Mulholland moved for sentence, and at this point the Jury learned of Sinclair's past – the culpable homicide of Catherine Reehill, the rapes and sexual assaults on numerous children and the murder of Mary Gallagher. It had obviously been a huge strain and some Jury members wept quietly. After a brief pause, Lord Matthews delivered a brief but devastating sentencing statement – Sinclair was an evil predator who had preyed on women and girls all his life. But despite the gravity of his crimes, the court could not deliver an indeterminate sentence, and a possible parole date had to be designated. The Judge handed down a sentence of thirty-seven years, the longest determinate sentence ever passed in a Scottish court and one which was chosen carefully – one year for every year that Helen's and Christine's families had suffered since that dreadful night in October 1977.

With a nod of the Judge's head Sinclair was taken down and the mood of the court immediately lifted. In an unprecedented gesture the Lord Advocate then publicly acknowledged the thousand officers who had investigated the case over the decades and named all the Senior Investigating Officers, including Allan Jones and myself. Finally, the Judge thanked the Jury and addressed Helen's and Christine's families.

No court proceedings could undo the damage or relieve the pain, he said, but he hoped the families could now begin to heal. He had been listening to a Remembrance Day service just a few days before and had been struck by the familiar words from Laurence Binyan's poem 'The Fallen', which we had all heard so many times:

*"They grow not old, as we that are left grow old: Age shall not weary them, nor the years condemn. At the going down of the sun and in the morning, we will remember them."*

The packed court room emptied, and we quietly left, each with our own thoughts. A short time later Morain Scott, who had so often represented the Scott and Eadie families, spoke to the assembled media outside the court. Justice had finally been done for his beautiful daughter Helen and her friend. On her death bed he had promised Helen's mother to get justice. He had kept his promise.

The trial of *Her Majesty's Advocate* v *Sinclair* was over. At last, after the longest gap between crime and conviction in Scottish legal history at that time, justice had been done. The carefully constructed case had proved overwhelmingly that Helen and Christine had been brutally raped and murdered by Angus Sinclair and his long dead brother-in- law, Gordon Hamilton. It was the first case brought under the new double jeopardy legislation, and it had been the most complex forensic case ever brought before a Scottish court.

For Lord Advocate Mulholland and his team, led by the able Senior Procurator Fiscal, Deborah Demick, it was a triumph. In partnership with the police, they had worked tirelessly to build the strongest of cases, and in doing so had demonstrated the Crown's tenacity and sent a powerful message to the people of Scotland: murder and rape were crimes that would be pursued to the end regard-less of time, cost or legal obstacles.

To Sinclair, it meant not one jot of difference; he was in prison for life anyway. But for Helen's and Christine's families it was the end of a long and tortured journey. Their loved ones could now rest in peace – all the questions about what happened had been answered. And for the police and Crown there was immense relief that after all the years and false hopes they had finished the job. The law had been changed and legal history made, and at the very end, justice had been done for two teenagers who had gone out with friends one fateful night in 1977 and had the tragic misfortune to fall into the hands of two murderous criminals.

# 16

# In Retrospect

It is now almost fifty years since Helen and Christine died, and ten years since Angus Sinclair was convicted of their murders.

Over the intervening time much has changed, especially in the field of Forensic Science, so that the World's End Murders now fall into the category of historic crimes.

There are, however, still questions to be answered about the murders and particularly about the way they were investigated. What did we do right, and where did we fall short? What motivated Angus Sinclair in his murderous rampage and could we have stopped him before we did? And what was so special about these murders anyway?

In some ways it is difficult to understand the notoriety. After all, between 1968 and 2003 well over a thousand women were killed in Scotland. What was so special about the murders of Helen and Christine? Perhaps part of the answer lies in the feeling that their deaths represented a loss of innocence at a time when society was changing rapidly.

In the media their deaths and the emotive 'World's End' epithet struck a chord, while for the police the case was so extraordinary that it got under the skin of many officers who worked on it, myself included. Some cases are like that – the victims or the circumstances stay with you. They haunt you and come to deeply affect you, with every setback only increasing your determination to solve the case.

And of course, for many years we were driven on because we knew we had the key to the puzzle.

We were certain that within the forensic productions – the clothes, particularly Helen's coat – lay the identity of the murderers. But at the time we just didn't have the knowledge or the science to unlock the clues.

We were always confident, however, that one day we would solve the puzzle and identify the men who had killed Helen and Christine. And eventually we did.

## What motivated the murders?

As for Sinclair, this disgraceful human being is in many ways typical of a certain type of offender. Thankfully, we see few like him in a small country like Scotland, but in other parts of the world people like Sinclair are more common and their pathology – that of an organised murderer – is well established. Studies by the FBI, who have had far greater experience than we would ever want with this kind of phenomenon, describe an organised murderer as typically "Male, of average or above average intelligence, a skilled and hard worker, lives with a partner, early offending, controlled mood during the commission of the crime, use of violence, mobility with car in good condition, adaptable – able to change patterns of offending if required and extremely resistant to police interview". They go on to talk of 'Planned offence, the victim a targeted stranger, crime scenes reflect overall control of the victim, restraints used, violence used prior to death, weapon/evidence absent, transports the victim or body a distance from first contact'.

This could be a pen portrait of Angus Sinclair; he ticks all the boxes as a textbook organised killer. He compartmentalised his life, he was intensely secretive, he was a violent thief as well as a sex offender, and like many sex offenders his motives were as much about control and violence as sex. The combination of his offending traits and the complete absence of empathy with his victims made him a danger to women and girls from an early age.

Passing sentence on Sinclair for the culpable homicide of seven-year-old Catherine Reehill in 1961, the Judge, Lord Mackintosh, described Sinclair as 'callous, cunning and wicked – so obsessed with sex that he would not stop short even of taking a life to gratify his lust'. Mackintosh had assessed him with pinpoint accuracy, for Sinclair's behaviour was set by this time for the rest of his criminal career.

Had we been aware at the time of the original investigation of the pattern of Sinclair's earlier killings we would of course have focused on the offender rather than the offence in our hunt for Helen and Christine's killer. As it was, we only became aware of the whole picture in 2004, long after Sinclair had finished his killing and was safely in prison.

197

Another remarkable thing about this case was that, at the time of the World's End Murders, Sinclair was not the only serial killer in Scotland. Also operating at roughly the same time were Robert Black, certainly the killer of four young girls and very possibly more, and Peter Tobin, the murderer of at least three girls and young women. Whilst Tobin's and Black's victims and modus operandi were slightly different from Sinclair's, all three men were of an age, from the same social background, their crimes were sexually motivated, transport played an important part in them, and, crucially, all three evaded detection by conventional investigation. Black was arrested after a long public safety campaign and a stroke of good fortune which saw an observant member of the public report a suspected abduction on a quiet, rural Borders road, and the later return of Black down the same road, by which time a police roadblock had been set up. In an almost unbelievable twist, the officer who arrested Black at the roadblock was the father of his latest victim, who was thankfully recovered, though barely alive, from Black's van. Tobin was arrested after the killing of Angelika Kluk and the concealment of her body in the church in which he worked. And as we know, although imprisoned, Sinclair was brought to justice after over thirty years of painstaking investigation and forensic developments which depended on excellent forensic management atypical of the kind that was usually practised back in 1977.

The coincidence of three such killers operating in a small country at the same time is so statistically improbable as to be almost impossible. At least twelve girls and young women lost their lives at the hands of these men. The obvious conclusion to be drawn from these facts is that we, the Police Service of the day, were ill equipped either to prevent or detect such crimes using the techniques available at the time.

Would it be different today? Much has changed since Sinclair, Black and Tobin killed. Even after Sinclair's failed trial of 2007 there have been huge advances in the investigation of serious crime. Lothian and Borders Police is no more. Gone, too, are the other seven forces that served Scotland, all replaced by the National Force "Police Scotland". While there are mixed views about the Force's structure and controversies around local policing sensitivity, accountability, and the apparent urge to centralise, it is clear to me that whatever else might be unsatisfactory, the management and response to serious crime has greatly improved. The formation of regional Major Investigation Teams, using the most experienced detectives and best techniques means that the most professional response can be concentrated quickly on serious crimes in the vitally important first 24 hours. Largely gone too are the petty jealousies and turf wars that used to obstruct joint working between forces, and which even occurred during periods of the World's End investigation.

Scotland has never been in a better position to meet the increasing challenges of serious and organised crime. But we cannot be complacent, for it is a characteristic of big organisations, including the Police, to eventually suffer from hubris and to come to believe firmly in their own infallibility. We should not forget that the new science that added so much to the World's End came from a small commercial company in England – not our own Scottish Forensic Science Service. The world is getting smaller and there are always lessons to be learned from elsewhere.

Perhaps the most intriguing question for investigators today is how far and in what direction forensic science will develop in the future. The World's End Murders were resolved when technology and methodology developed to the extent that vital evidence could be extracted from materials which were thought to be of no evidential value at the time of the original investigation. The crucial questions are, what currently 'worthless' materials could in future reveal vital evidence, what should we retain, how and where? We cannot keep it all, but if forensic science continues to develop in the way it has over the last thirty years, then we must make sure we are best placed to take advantage of its advances.

Setting aside the failure of the trial in 2007, what could we have done better in the original investigation, and what lessons can we learn?

We didn't resolve the World's End case at the time by traditional policing methods, as it turned out we didn't even come close. But in fairness it's hard to see what else the original teams could have done in their state of knowledge. They followed the leads they had, they kept an ongoing and positive dialogue with Helen's and Christine's parents (a procedure which was not common then), and, most importantly, they scrupulously retained all the relevant documents and forensic evidence so that we, over thirty years later, could capitalise on them.

The first pathological examinations were also inconsistent, with small errors made at both original post-mortems. These too would have consequences as they cast doubt on exact time of death, which thirty years later became a significant factor.

The first phase of the investigation viewed the crimes as local and committed massive resources to local enquiries. The systematic scanning of other crimes in other parts of the country was neither prioritised nor in hindsight carried out thoroughly enough.

Undoubtedly the inter-force conference when the Heads of CID for East and West Scotland met in 1980 missed an opportunity to link the cases of the World's End girls with the three Glasgow murders of Anna Kenny, Hilda McAuley and Agnes Cooney. But even if they had been connected it is doubtful what benefit this would have brought, given the lack of adequate administrative systems at the time. The consequential muddle might actually have been damaging. There again, linking the cases would have ensured that all the forensic productions were retained and stored in one location. This would have prevented the loss or destruction of the forensic evidence in the Glasgow cases, which denied these investigations the enormous benefit of the 21st century science that was key to the success of the World's End case.

### Could we have identified Sinclair earlier?

Could we have identified Angus Sinclair earlier, prevented some of his offences or been able to track down his co-accused Gordon Hamilton in his lifetime? In 1977 Sinclair was not a suspect and didn't feature on the database for the World's End case, or indeed for any of the others. This is no surprise; he was relatively unknown in the late 1970s and had no apparent connection with the area of The World's End pub or East Lothian, where Helen and Christine's bodies were found.

Later, we failed to fully understand the first 1997 DNA breakthrough. This was partly the fault of the scientists not explaining it thoroughly enough, and partly our ignorance of the new science. In the 1997 results there was an indication of the presence of two men – had we been aware of that, further examination might have identified Sinclair a full seven years earlier. This would not have prevented him from murdering again – he was already in prison and his co-accused was already dead. But we would have been on the trail earlier and the Toyota caravanette would still have been available with all its forensic secrets.

Almost twenty years after his death, Sinclair's co-accused, Hamilton, remains a mystery. Unpopular, violent and abusive to his wife, his part in the World's End Murders is essentially all we know about him. Is it possible that this was his only crime? Was he involved with Sinclair in some of his other crimes, and did he also commit offences on his own, between Sinclair's imprisonment in 1981 and his own death in 1996? We can only say that his DNA hasn't been identified at other historic crime scenes, but, bearing in mind how developments in forensic science helped us finally bring Sinclair to justice, who's to know what evidence might yet turn up?

A real opportunity was missed in 2001 when Sinclair was arrested for the 1978 murder of Mary Gallagher. At that time a connection should have been made between Mary's murder and the other outstanding cases in Glasgow and the World's End in Edinburgh. Although members of the Gallagher team suspected Sinclair of other offences, this suspicion was not acted on or shared. It was only with the National Crime Faculty analysis some years later that the link was made clear. The reasons for this grave omission have never been explained. It may have been a question of resources, or simply that, with a busy workload, historic cases were of low priority. Again, no lives were forfeited by this failure, but the Toyota caravanette was still in existence with all its potential for forensic discovery.

After release from prison for the murder of Catherine Reehill, Sinclair's next conviction for sexual crimes was for the rapes and assaults on young girls in the early 1980s. These offences were very different in profile from The World's End Murders, so it is not surprising that no immediate connection was made.

That said, it is remarkable that at the same moment in time that Sinclair was being arrested for multiple serious sexual assaults on children, there was no consideration of a connection to three active investigations into the sexually motivated murders of three young women – Anna Kenny, Hilda McAuley and Agnes Cooney, in the same area.

It was perhaps an example of silo thinking, so prevalent at the time. There was a belief that sex offenders who targeted children were distinct from those who targeted adults, and that sex offenders were themselves restricted to sexual offending. This is of course untrue, many sex offenders are thieves or robbers as well and Sinclair is a good example. Like many highly organised criminals, he lived his life in compartments with his range of criminal activities strictly segregated, thus adding to his sense of control.

So, yes there were opportunities to catch Sinclair both in 1981 and 2001, but by that time his killing spree was over. Thankfully no other young woman's life was forfeited by our failure to detect him earlier.

## Why was the forensic evidence lost in the cases of Anna Kenny, Hilda McAuley and Agnes Cooney?

The loss of the forensic evidence in the three Glasgow cases was disastrous and prevented Sinclair from facing justice for the murders of Anna, Hilda and Agnes. Though they went to incredible lengths to build a case, the Strathclyde team of 2004 could not compensate for this loss.

It is an old truth that to succeed in any enterprise you need good people and good systems. This is especially true of murder investigations.

While the investigators of the 1970s Glasgow cases were highly experienced, the system for the retention of forensic evidence was poor. Instead of retention in laboratory conditions, forensic productions were routinely returned to senior investigating officers, where they were often stored in "bottom drawers". Over the years, as cases piled up, routine spring cleans were carried out. It is likely that the vital forensic evidence in the cases of the three Glasgow murders were simply thrown out as rubbish.

Thankfully the system changed in the 1980s, but this episode is proof of the fact that good people and good systems remain essential.

## How many women and girls did Angus Sinclair murder?

Has Angus Sinclair escaped justice for other serious offences? I am sure of it, but we will never know for certain just how many victims there might be.

It is worth remembering that Sinclair was only at liberty for about 12 years after his first conviction for the culpable homicide of Catherine Reehill, to his arrest for the attacks on children in 1981. We know that he killed Helen and Christine (The World's End Murders) in October 1977, and we have every reason to believe he also killed Anna Kenney, Hilda McAuley and Agnes Cooney during the last six months of 1977. Thereafter, we know he killed the diminutive Mary Gallagher in 1978 before being arrested for the attacks on children which he had carried out over an extensive period in 1980.

It is almost certain that Sinclair was involved in the murder of Frances Barber in June 1977, even though another man (Thomas Ross Young) was convicted of her murder. The similarities between Frances's murder and Sinclair's other murders in 1977 make it highly probable. Sinclair may also have been involved in the murder of the pornographer Eddie

Cotogno in 1978, but since this is way outside his pattern of offending the degree of probability is smaller.

So, what other serious crimes could he have been responsible for? We know that following his release from Edinburgh Prison in1968, he quickly met and married his wife Sadie Hamilton to whom he seemed happily attached from 1970 to 1976. It was only after he left the marital home and bought his abduction vehicle, the Toyota caravanette, that the killings began.

There is, however, one unsolved Edinburgh murder that may be linked to Sinclair, the murder of Helen Kane in 1970.

Helen Kane was a young Edinburgh woman, whose body was found on waste ground in central Edinburgh on May 23rd, 1970. Her death was due to blunt force injury to her head and there were signs of sexual assault. The obvious connection was that Sinclair, recently released from prison, was living in a flat nearby. None of his other victims were attacked in this way so, while his proximity arose suspicion, there was insufficient evidence to link him to this case. No forensic evidence from Helen's death was available by the time we were examining the others.

Angus Sinclair may well have been involved in other sexual crimes and even murder during his short years of freedom, but even if he was not, the crimes we can link him with make him one of the most prolific killers in Scottish history. Given his conviction for the murder of four children and young women, the almost certain link with four more murders and the numerous sexual attacks on children, Angus Robertson Sinclair was arguably among the most dangerous men who ever walked the streets of Scotland in the 20th century.

## What lessons did we learn?

We learned much during the decades of the longest continual criminal investigation in Scottish history and as well as making some mistakes, the many detectives who investigated The World's End Murders got a lot right.

## Systems matter

We learned that systems mattered, and we were fortunate to be able to take advantage of the new computerised administration systems (HOLMES) that came on stream in the mid-1980s. It is unlikely that the old card systems we had used until that time would have coped with the scope of the investigation as it developed.

## Money matters

We were always adequately funded and staffed with able detectives and support staff. This was no small matter over a period of over thirty years. Money is always scarce and current investigations understandably take precedence. During the early phase of DNA analysis, laboratory costs were high. We were fortunate indeed to have a first-class Chief Constable, Sir William Sutherland, from the early 1980s onwards. He made sure we always had the resources to do our job. Other policing areas were not so fortunate.

## Invest in Forensics but not just your own

We learned that there was much to learn from the wider Forensic Science community, not just the big crime laboratories. Cutting edge work is often done in small niche labs. In the end it was just such a laboratory that fully unlocked the secrets of Helen's coat.

## Guard against silo thinking

We began the investigation into The World's End Murders looking for local connections or convicted serious sex offenders who targeted young women. In fact, Sinclair offended over a wide range of crimes, targeting children, then young women, then returning to offend against children, all the while carrying out other crimes of dishonesty and violence. An open mind is essential to success in the investigation of crimes like the World's End Murders.

## Momentum is important

Uniquely, the World's End investigation ran continuously for over thirty years. This momentum was important as a stop-start investigation loses impetus and once stopped is difficult to start again. Even a small care and maintenance team is preferable to closing an investigation. A regular and active review of evidence and new developments can also serve to avoid zombie investigations.

## Have a succession plan

The history of unsolved murders is pockmarked by poor succession planning. A senior investigating officer will retire or move on, taking a wealth of information and ownership of an investigation with them. We were fortunate to have a continuous line of able detectives brought up with the World's End investigation and thoroughly familiar with all its facets. At its conclusion this was of vital importance.

## Families matter

The families of murder victims have an important contribution to make to investigations. We found the involvement and support of Helen and Christine's families invaluable throughout the length of the investigation. They were not only a source of information about their daughters' lives and behaviour, but added much as we worked to maintain public support and the flow of new information.

# 17

# Who solved The World's End Murders?

No one person solved The World's End Murders. Over the course of an investigation that spanned over thirty years, hundreds of police officers, scientists and support staff contributed significantly. Whether it was the front-line detectives, the laboratory staff, the computer operators and technicians or the Force's senior officers who secured the resources – all contributed and were vital to the success of the search for the killers of Helen and Christine. Each formed a component part in the 30-year enterprise, without which the investigation would have failed. But over the years there is a handful of individuals or groups who do deserve special mention.

**Retired Detective Superintendent John McGowan** took charge of the investigation during the middle years when little progress was being made and prospects looked bleak. Having confidence in the developments in computerisation, he championed the time-consuming and expensive back record conversion from the old index card system to the new HOLMES computerised system. Though he retired from the police service before the DNA breakthrough, his vision had modernised the investigation, making it fit to take advantage of developments in forensic science.

Although **Detective Superintendent Allan Jones** joined Lothian and Borders Police after The World's End Murders, he took an early and enduring interest in the case that spanned his entire police service. Always a determined detective, his drive and persistence did much to bring about the final DNA breakthrough.

No one epitomised the tenacity of generations of investigators better than Allan Jones. More than any other police officer he must take enormous credit for bringing the case to closure.

Though not involved in the investigation of the crimes, **Lord Advocate Frank Mulholland** and **Justice Secretary Kenny MacAskill** played a vital role in bringing Angus Sinclair to justice. Following the botched trial of 2007, it would have been easy for both these men to hide behind legal and political conventions, but they did not. Recognising that a miscarriage of justice had taken place, they went to extraordinary lengths to bring about a change to the Law of Scotland in order to see justice done. The willingness of both men to challenge the status quo in the face of trenchant opposition was, in the end, instrumental in the delivery of justice.

At the second trial of 2014, Lord Advocate Mulholland delivered a master class in the art of prosecuting a complex historical case.

Throughout the entire span of the 37 years investigation and court proceedings, **Morain Scott**, father of World's End victim Helen, ably represented his own and Christine Eadie's family. Always staunch in his support of the police, his unfailing presence did much to galvanise generations of investigating officers down the years. Shortly after the murder of his daughter, Morain Scott promised his dying wife that he would see justice done for their daughter Helen. He kept his word.

If any one man or group could be credited with solving The World's End Murders, it could only be **Lester Knibb** and his colleagues from Lothian and Borders Forensic Laboratory. They meticulously recovered the forensic evidence from the crime scenes and protected and preserved them down the years. It was the scientists who had the vision to see the potential of what would eventually prove to be crucial DNA evidence. Put bluntly, The World's End Murders would not have been solved and Angus Sinclair never brought to justice without the actions of Lester Knibb and his scientific colleagues.

Lester Knibb - A meticulous Forensic Scientist who had a vision of the future.

# 18

## Where Are They Now?

All the police officers involved in the investigation are long retired. **Allan Jones** retired as a much-respected Detective Superintendent and is now the Chief Executive of a security company. Retired Detective Superintendent **John McGowan**, now Dr. McGowan, is an academic, researcher and author specialising in early Scottish Police history and structures. Two of the detectives on the Strathclyde side of the investigation, **Colin Field** and **Derek Robertson** became highly regarded Detective Chief Superintendents and are now pursuing careers in the private sector.

**Morain Scott** died in 2015, having lived long enough to see justice done for his daughter Helen and her friend Christine.

**Lord Advocate Frank Mulholland** is now Lord Mulholland, a High Court Judge in Scotland's Supreme Court. **Ex-Justice Secretary Kenny MacAskill** fell from political favour and left the Scottish National Party for the new Alba Party, where he remains as a Member of Parliament.

**Angus Robertson Sinclair** died in prison in March 2019, where he had been detained for forty-seven of his fifty-nine adult years. Despite him only being at liberty for twelve years, he was convicted of four murders of women and girls, numerous attacks on children and is almost certainly responsible for a further four murders.

**Lester Knibb** has retired from the Forensic Science Service but continues to share his knowledge and enthusiasm for science as leader of the Forensic Science Group at the University of the Third Age. From his natural modesty you would never guess the part he played in one of Scotland's most important criminal investigations.

# In Conclusion

This book is written in memory of Helen and Christine, and the other girls who died in 1977. But it is also dedicated to the other victims, the ones we tend to overlook; the families and friends who are left behind. They will never forget, and we should not forget them.

There was a sense of satisfaction in finally seeing justice done in the World's End case, we never saw Helen and Christine simply as murder victims, they were our girls, and we owed them the justice they deserved, but there was never a cause for celebration. Helen and Christine, with all their youth and promise, are still dead. The Glasgow girls, Anna, Hilda and Agnes were denied justice, their families still grieving without even the comfort of closure.

But, through trial and tribulation the long investigation into these dreadful crimes has helped to change the law and has left our justice system fairer and better balanced in the 21st century. That is the positive legacy of this tragic tale, and we can, perhaps, take some comfort from it.

The worst in human behaviour sometimes brings out the best in others. And so, finally, it is right to conclude by saluting the generations of police officers, scientists and support staff who brought The World's End killer to justice. They never gave up, never stepped back, and finally, by imagination and dedication, they succeeded.

They represented all that was best in The Scottish Police Service that I knew.

It was an honour to serve with them.

Tom Wood

Edinburgh

February 2024

The World's End as it is today - a popular tourist pub, just as it was in 1977.

# About the Author

Tom Wood was one of Scotland's most senior and experienced police officers. He is an authority on serious and violent crime and the policing of major events.

He is a graduate of Edinburgh University and the FBI Academy at Quantico, Virginia.

Latterly, he was Deputy Chief Constable and Director of Operations of Lothian and Borders Police. His last role in the police was as Officer in Overall Command of the Linked Murder Investigations into the deaths of numerous young women, including Helen Scott and Christine Eadie (The World's End Murders).

Since leaving the police he has worked in Alcohol and Drug Strategy, Adult and Child Protection and carried out Independent Serious Case and Homicide Reviews. He is now a regular columnist with "The Scotsman" newspaper and writes extensively on crime and justice matters.

His book, *Ruxton: The First Modern Murder,* was shortlisted for the 2021 Scottish National Book Awards.

He lives in Edinburgh.

# Acknowledgements

The writing of this book has been a privilege and a duty, and I am grateful to the many former colleagues who encouraged and helped me in the process. I am particularly indebted to David Johnston, who freely gave his skill and his experience in putting early editions of this book together. I am also grateful to my long-serving and long-suffering PA, Jeanette Shiells, who has typed, altered, and altered again the various drafts and documents.

I wish to acknowledge the considerable input by Ross Fulton into creating the cover for the book, work that was finished off by Skye Galloway, the Ringwood cover designer.

I would also like to acknowledge the fine work of my three Ringwood editors, Megan Gibson, Natasha Chanse, and Annemarie Whitehurst – three young women with brilliant literary careers ahead of them.

Finally, I wish to thank all my friends and family for all they have done to brighten my life. I would also wish to make it clear that even after receiving so much help, any errors, omissions or misconceptions are entirely my own responsibility.

Tom Wood
2024

# More to read:

If you enjoyed *The World' End*, you will most certainly like these other Ringwood books:

## Ruxton - The First Modern Murder

Tom Wood

It is 1935 and the deaths of Isabella Ruxton and Mary Rogerson would result in one of the most complex investigations the world had ever seen. The gruesome murders captured worldwide attention with newspapers keeping the public enthralled with all the gory details.

But behind the headlines was a different, more important story: the ground-breaking work of Scottish forensic scientists who developed new techniques to solve the case and shape the future of scientific criminal investigation.

ISBN: 978-1-901514-84-1

£9.99

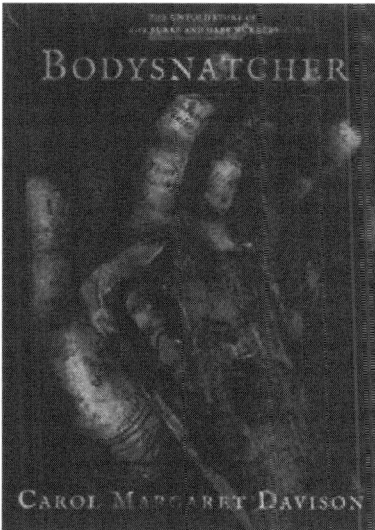

## Bodysnatcher

Carol Margaret Davison

In the late 1820s, two Irish Immigrants, William Burke and William Hare, murdered 16 individuals and sold their corpses for use in anatomical dissections at the University of Edinburgh. Their killings ended when Hare turned King's Evidence, and Burke was hanged.

However, the question of whether their female accomplices, Nelly McDougal and Margaret Hare, were involved, has never been determined. Told by way of alternating confessions, *Bodysnatcher* is both a graphic depiction of one of Edinburgh's most notorious crimes, and a domestic story of a relationship unravelled by secrecy and violence.

ISBN: 978-1-901514-83-4

£12.99

## Cuddies Strip

Rob McInroy

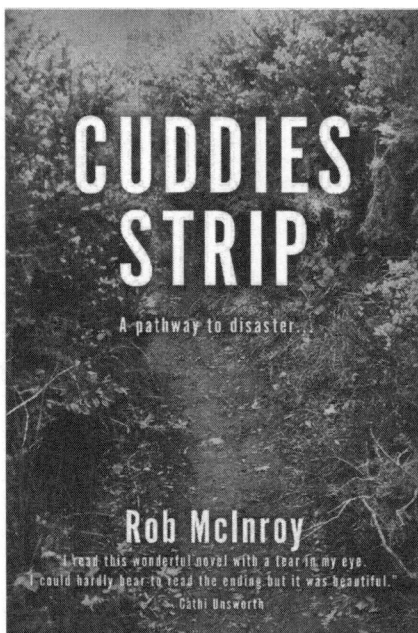

*Cuddies Strip* is based on a true crime and faithfully follows the investigation and subsequent trial but it also examines the mores of the times and the insensitive treatment of women in a male-dominated society.

It is a highly absorbing period piece from 1930s Scotland, with strong contemporary resonances: both about the nature and responsiveness of police services and the ingrained misogyny of the whole criminal justice system.

ISBN: 978-1-901514-88-9

£9.99

## Barossa Street

Rob McInroy

Set in Perth, *Barossa Street* offers, not only a look at the mishandling of justice in the face of 1930's prejudice, but also serves as a commentary of the British public's response to the government's shortcomings. Set on the backdrop of King Edward VIII's abdication and the threat of war. *Barossa Street* is as much a critique of the times as it is a thrilling murder mystery.

With twists and turns down every street, follow Bob Kelty in this suspenseful thriller to see whether he can solve the latest who-done-it and find that much needed relief from the trials of life.

ISBN: 978-1-901514-41-4

£9.99

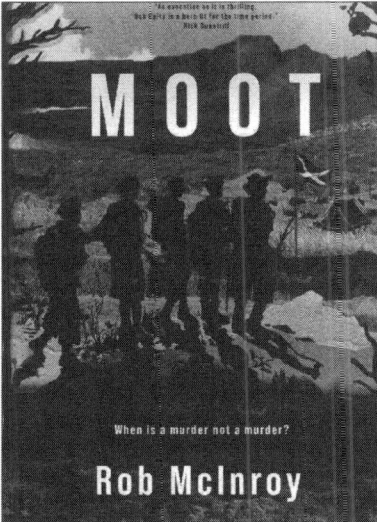

## Moot

Rob McIlroy

July 1939, and 3,500 young men from around the world arrive at Monzie Castle in Perthshire for the third international Rover Scout Moot. In the shadow of looming war the Moot seems to be a last gasp of international friendship and fraternity. But among them is a murderer.

Bob Kelty discovers a dead body in a burnt-out tent on the edge of the camp. He is immediately suspicious but for some reason the authorities seem reluctant to become involved.

More strange things begin to happen and Bob's suspicions increase. And if the authorities won't look into them, Bob decides he must.

And the question is: when is a murder not a murder?

ISBN:978-1-9170011-00-6

£12.99


## The Hotel Hokusai

T. Y. Garner

It is 1893: When a young woman is found drowned in Yokohama Harbour under suspicious circumstances, downtrodden Korean eel salesboy Han compels the eccentric Glaswegian artist Archie Nith to help him investigate.

Written from the perspectives of both Han and Nith, The Hotel Hokusai follows their journey as it snakes from Yokohama's harbour to its red-light district, stopping along the way to meet two of the famous Glasgow Boys and pay respects to the Dragon King.

ISBN: 978-1-901514-70-4

£9.99

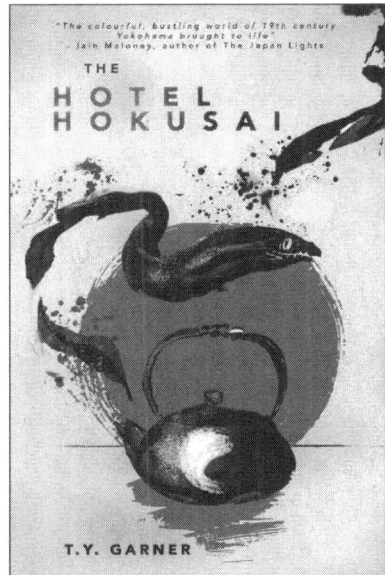

## Sheila Garvie: Mastermind or Victim

Alan Nicol

*Sheila Garvie: Mastermind or Victim* is a novel faithfully based on a sensational real case that took place in Kincardineshire in 1968 and the salacious details of which, with naked parties, sex orgies, drugs and alcohol, fast cars, violence and aristocracy, gripped the whole of Scotland.

A gunshot ends the life of Maxwell Robert Garvie on a May night in 1968. Three people are accused of the crime: his wife, his wife's lover and a young man whom Max had never met.

The narrative seeks to uncover, as far as it can, the truth regarding Sheila's involvement in her husband's death. Including flashbacks and new theories, the book suggests that appearances can be deceiving and reveals the shortcomings of a system uncaring about abuse victims.

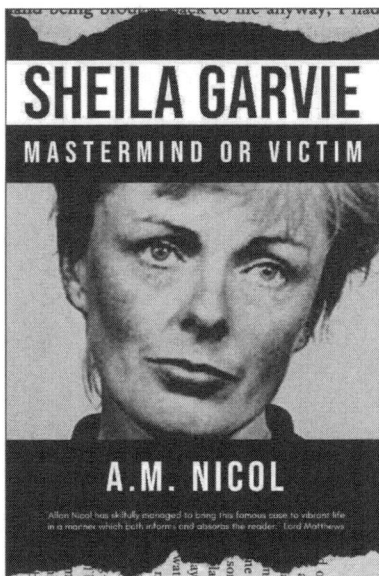

**SHEILA GARVIE**

**MASTERMIND OR VICTIM**

**A.M. NICOL**

Alan Nicol has skilfully managed to bring this famous case to vibrant life in a manner which both informs and absorbs the reader. Lord Matthews

ISBN: 978-1-901514-69-8

£9.99

## The Lanarkshire Police Chronicles

George Barnsley

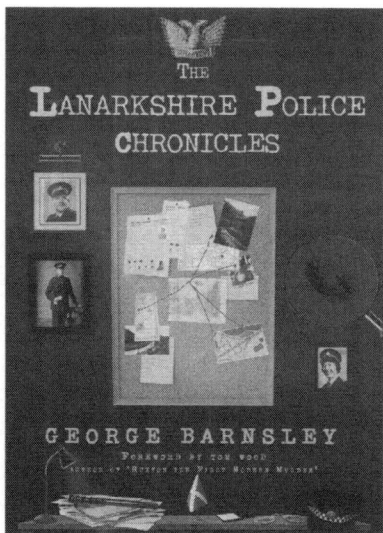

The author has extensively researched police reports from the last 150years and has collated this material into a book that is full of human interest stories.

The book is split into nine unique sections covering topics as diverse as Wartime, Community, Food and Drink, Breach of the Peace, Theft, Assault, Murder, In Memoriam, and at the heart of the book, full and moving accounts of the two Lanarkshire Policemen, Ross Hunt & George Taylor, who made the ultimate sacrifice while serving their community.

The author has drawn on his own extensive experience to provide ongoing commentary putting these incidents in some context of the development of the police service over many years, ensuring contemporary resonance as well as great historical interest.

ISBN: 978-1-901514-92-6

£12.99